Y0-BDW-577

Jewish Historiography and Iconography in Early and Medieval Christianity

Compendia Rerum Iudaicarum ad Novum Testamentum

SECTION III

JEWISH TRADITIONS IN EARLY CHRISTIAN LITERATURE

Volume 1

PAUL AND THE JEWISH LAW:
HALAKHA IN THE LETTERS OF THE APOSTLE TO THE GENTILES
Peter J. Tomson

Volume 2

JEWISH HISTORIOGRAPHY AND ICONOGRAPHY
IN EARLY AND MEDIEVAL CHRISTIANITY
Heinz Schreckenberg – Kurt Schubert
Translations from the German: Paul A. Cathey
Executive Editor: Peter J. Tomson

Published under the Auspices of the
Foundation Compendia Rerum Iudaicarum ad Novum Testamentum
Amsterdam

Heinz Schreckenberg and Kurt Schubert

Jewish Historiography and Iconography in Early and Medieval Christianity

I. Josephus in Early Christian Literature
and Medieval Christian Art

II. Jewish Pictorial Traditions
in Early Christian Art

With an Introduction
by David Flusser

1992
Van Gorcum, Assen/Maastricht
Fortress Press, Minneapolis

CIP-DATA KONINKLIJKE BIBLIOTHEEK, DEN HAAG

Schreckenberg, Heinz

Jewish Historiography and Iconography in Early and Medieval Christianity: I. Josephus in Early Christian literature and Medieval Christian Art, II. Jewish Pictorial Traditions in Early Christian Art / Heinz Schreckenberg and Kurt Schubert; with an Introd. by David Flusser; [transl. from the German: Paul A. Cathey]. - Assen [etc.]: Van Gorcum; Minneapolis: Fortress Press. - (Compendia Rerum Iudaicarum ad Novum Testamentum. Section 3, Jewish Traditions in Early Christian Literature; vol. 2)
With bibliogr., index.
NUGI 632/633
Subject headings: jewish historiography/jewish iconography/christian art.

ISBN 90 232 2653 4 bound

Library of Congress Cataloguing-in-Publication data available.

ISBN 0-8006-2519-6 (Fortress Press)

Fortress Press code 1-2519

Printed in the Netherlands by Van Gorcum, Assen

General Table of Contents

Editors' Preface

It is with a sense of gratitude that the editors see the present volume to the press. In a global climate which may sometimes seem to disencourage open-minded education and research in the humanities, these two studies of cultural interaction between two different religious communities represent a serene possibility of hope for understanding and peace. We are grateful to Heinz Schreckenberg and Kurt Schubert for their immediate readiness to share some of their learning and contribute it to our project. We also wish to express our great indebtedness to the Foundation for its confidence and courage in carrying on the project against the odds of economy, human limitations and scholarly inhibitions.

In the second place, our aim of providing a comprehensive picture of ancient Judaism in its relation to early Christianity here receives a rewarding and almost literal implementation. The 'pictures' in this book show aspects of both religious traditions which are little known and deserve much further study. Comparative study of art and literature has often remained the domain of art historians, while it could disclose additional resources for scholars of history and literature.

As we announced in the preceding volume, the present section does not follow a rigid programme. It is made up of monographical studies appearing as possibilities present themselves on the part of authors, editors and publishers. The present volume unites two studies which are rather different in subject material and method. The fact that they both are too small for separate publication, as well as their common interest in early and medieval Christian art, supported, moreover, by the use of illustrations, made us decide to combine them.

Our plans for the near future include studies on the use early Christians made of the writings of Philo, of Jewish apocalyptic traditions, of wisdom traditions and of esoteric traditions. These materials have all been more or less intensively studied in critical Christian scholarship. More difficult to integrate, it appears, is comparative study of traditions typically sedimented in rabbinic literature. We do not intend to let this deter us, however. In addition to the volume on halakha in Paul, we are planning further publications on the use made in early Christian literature of midrash, halakha and aggada. In the end, we hope, the reader who consults our series will be offered a fair representation, even if partial and refracted over separate volumes, of the range of Jewish, Christian and related sources and their possible historical contexts and interrelationships around the beginning of the common era.

Y. Aschkenasy, T. Baarda, W.J. Burgers, D. Flusser, P.W. van der Horst, Th.C. de Kruyf, S. Safrai, P.J. Tomson, B.H. Young

Acknowledgements

The following translations have been used, if necessary adapted to the context of citation: the Revised Standard Version for the Bible; H. Danby's translation of the Mishna; the translation of the Babylonian Talmud edited by I. Epstein (Soncino); the Loeb Classical Library translations of Josephus; for Apocrypha and Pseudepigrapha, the translations in Charlesworth, *OTP*; and the translation of Targum Neophyti by A. Díez Macho.

The editors are indebted to the following institutions for permission to reproduce pictures under their jurisdiction: Bibliothèque Nationale, Paris (Ashburnham Pentateuch); Österreichische Nationalbibliothek (Vienna Genesis); Pontificia commissione di archeologia sacra (Via Latina Catacomb); Princeton University Press (Dura Europos Synagogue).

Grateful recognition is extended by Heinz Schreckenberg to David Flusser, Rainer Kampling and Peter Tomson for their critical reading of the manuscript and their good advice, and by the editors to Paul Cathey, in addition to his painstaking translations, for his perceptive editorial suggestions.

General Introduction

David Flusser

I deem it an honor to be able to offer a few comments on the two following essays. We have here two fairly different monographic studies. Heinz Schreckenberg treats the literary reception and pictorial representation of one particular author, Josephus, and his historical works, while Kurt Schubert concerns himself with the interweaving of traditions in Jewish art drawn from biblical themes, traditions that were anonymously passed on and sometimes mechanically adopted. The common thread between the two, clearly documented in the extensive illustrations, is the influence of Jewish themes in ancient and early medieval Christian art. Thus the decision of the editors to include both studies under the same heading, within the broader framework of this section of the Compendia: 'Jewish Traditions in Early Christian Literature'.

In this introduction I will limit myself to a few observations and additional remarks. Concerning Josephus, I will mention his difficult, yet, considering the history of its influence, instructive passage on Jesus, as well as his reception among medieval Jews. Regarding the Jewish picture models treated in Schubert's essay I will elucidate the methodology and use that opportunity to offer for consideration additional material on Jewish motifs in Christian art.

As already mentioned, Schreckenberg's subject is more limited. It deals exhaustively with the points of contact between the Jewish material and the Christian world as well as with the Christian illustrations. If I were to comment on the Josephus-oriented pictures, I would only remark that it is also perhaps necessary to collect the Christian illustrations and other works of art which relate to Jewish literature and history of the Second Temple period in general. This would include not only the heroine Judith, but especially Christian art inspired by First and Second Maccabees. In my own experience it is not always easy to determine whether the source of a medieval illustration was Josephus or the Maccabean corpus. An investigation broadened to this extent would certainly repay the effort.

To Schreckenberg's treatment of Josephus himself and his influence in Christian literature there is little to add. Here I touch on the so-called

Testimonium Flavianum, Josephus' alleged account about Jesus. Of course the impact of this text on the larger course of Christian intellectual history has been considerable. The text as it occurs in Josephus (*Ant.* 18:63-64) and as attested in Eusebius is clearly a Christian adaptation. Perhaps we need not doubt however that the form found in Agaphius, a tenth century Arab Christian historian, is that originally penned by Josephus.[1] To be sure, this important new discovery changes little of the *Testimonium's* later history, for subsequently the text was known in Christendom only in its familiar form. But for understanding Josephus himself the Agaphius form is important.

The study of ancient Judaism has always required recourse to Josephus. From the apologetic *Dialogue* of Minucius Felix (33:5) at the beginning of the third century, to Schiller's *Räubern* (act 1, scene 2) we hear, 'read Josephus!' In Schiller a parody follows on the contemporary pre-zionistic, non-Jewish longing for a renewal of Jewish independence in Palestine. For the Church fathers on the other hand, the primary purpose for reading Josephus is to show the destruction of the Temple as a part of Christian salvation history. In an essay that has been too little noticed Hans Lewy has shown how Josephus has been used to justify the special legal status of Jews in the Middle Ages.[2] Thus, it can be seen how important a role Josephus has played for Christendom's *Tendenzen*. To complete the picture even more, one could investigate the Byzantine chronographers, at least those belonging to the period covered by Schreckenberg's essay, such as the *Chronographia* of Malalas (c. 491-578), or the *Chronicon Paschale* (631-641). To what extent did they directly or indirectly use Josephus?

Finally, I would like to call attention to the larger context of Josephus' influence on the older Christian literature. This is part of the larger question, 'What did early and medieval Christians know of ancient Jewish history and how did they regard it?' But this is actually recommending additional study, and indicating how fertile Schreckenberg's investigations are.

Heinz Schreckenberg's essay deals with how Josephus was viewed by Christians. He maintains, in part correctly, that no Jewish reception of Josephus actually occurred – a fate shared, by the way, with all ancient Jewish literature originally written in Greek or preserved only in Greek. It is little known that during the High Middle Ages this literature, including Josephus, was once again 'brought home', to the extent that it was known by the Jews in translation.[3] For more than a thousand years Josephus' writings themselves have been known in a widely disseminated classical

[1] See Pines, *Arabic Version*. See also Flusser, 'Bericht'; Bienert, 'Zeugnis'.
[2] Lewy, 'Josephus'.
[3] See following footnote.

Hebrew version, the so-called *Yosef ben Gurion* (Josephus Gorionides).[4] This work was not only known by Jews, but often used as well. It also has a direct connection with our subject because 'Josephus Gorionides' has awakened a great deal of interest among Christian. But before I introduce Josephus in his Hebrew garb I think a few remarks are necessary concerning the widespread notion that the Jews lost the will to write their own history following the destruction of the Temple in 70. A few general observations must suffice.

In order to clarify, at leasty partially, the alleged absence of Jewish historiography, we must remember that the need is felt for a work of history covering the present and recent past when 'history', in the strict sense of the word, has actually happened. The history of a particular people generally means their political history in which real 'dramatis personae' or major issues have been involved. However, when this is absent there is little fertile ground for the emergence of a historical work. Thus, no Jewish historical work has been preserved covering the time between the post-exilic restoration and the glorious Maccabean uprising and thus also, Jewish historiography ends after the destruction of the Temple. What we find is a considerably developed Jewish chronography, beginning with *Seder Olam* (second century C.E.)[5] and extending through the Middle Ages. There were also Hebrew accounts of the persecutions of the Jews and their deliverance.[6] The programs of the First Crusade enriched Jewish historiography with martyr accounts, and ongoing Jewish suffering also supplied material for this type of Hebrew historiography in later periods.

Strictly speaking, the book *Yosippon* is not Jewish historiography because it does not treat the recent past and present, but rather describes the Second Temple period up to the fall of Masada based on the Apocrypha of the Vulgate – particularly First and Second Maccabees – and the Latin translation of Josephus. It is to be numbred among the medieval Hebrew translations or revisions of Jewish literary monuments from the Second Temple period. *Yosippon* is a medieval Hebrew classic authored by a Jew from southern Italy in 953.

It is readily understandable that the Hebrew *Yosippon* was the primary source of information about ancient Jewish history for Jews. A few decades after its appearance, the Hebrew Josephus was translated into Arabic, thus becoming available to Arabs, who, like Jews, would hardly have read Josephus in the Greek original or Latin translation. Moreover, the author-

[4] See my Hebrew edition, *The Josippon*; ib vol. 2, 148-53 for Yosippon and the origins of Christianity. See also Flusser, 'Der lateinische Josephus', 127-31 for the Latin translation of Josephus; id, 'Josippon, a Medieval Hebrew Version'.

[5] Strack-Stemberger, *Einleitung*, 297f. The later Jewish chronographical literature was published by Neubauer, *Chronicles*. See also the essay on 'Seder Olam' in *Compendia* II/3b, by Chaim Milikowsky (forthcoming).

[6] Some of this Hebrew literature has been published by Malachi, *Studies*.

ity of the Hebrew version increased significantly in that the original author's name was soon forgotten and Josephus himself was mistakenly credited with authorship. This incorrect attribution is attested already in the eleventh century and remained undisputed until the new learning of the Humanists. Finally, Josephus himself speaks as author in a twelfth century revision of the work. He speaks in the first person and alleges that the Hebrew *Yosippon* was written for his own people, whereas the Greek version was intended for the Romans.

As mentioned above, the pseudepigraphic ascription (at first implied and later explicit) of the medieval *Yosippon* to Josephus increased the authority of the book in the eyes of both Jews and non-Jews. The general view was that *Yosippon* contained evidence for ancient Jewish history written by a famous eye-witness. Among non-Jews, primarily the Christians, there was a strong curiosity to know what *Yosippon* contained concerning Jesus and the beginnings of Christianity.[7] Indeed, the original *Yosippon* contained an account of the ministry of John the Baptist, just as the Greek Josephus. But one searches in vain for a parallel to the *Testimonium Flavianum* in the Hebrew version. In some later manuscripts of the book an unflattering narrative has been interpolated concerning Jesus and the beginnings of Christianity. This dwindled to a brief note in the later stages of development. This note is also found in the two manuscripts of the pseudepigraphic version from the first half of the twelfth century mentioned above. In the printed versions the note has disappeared once again, apparently out of concern over Christian censorship, or as a result of its intervention. As we learn from a twelfth century source,[8] the interpolated account of Jesus was found in a few *Yosippon* manuscripts in England; in others it was absent. We owe this information to the diligence of Robert of Criclade, prior of a monastery in Oxford, who searched for the Testimonium Flavianum in Josephus manuscripts. We see then that the Hebrew version was also included in Christian curiosity concerning Josephus.

Kurt Schubert's contribution treats Jewish influence in Christian illustrations – an important, but difficult topic. It would have been easier to write about post-biblical Jewish influence in the Christian fine arts, but this was not the author's goal. Rather, Schubert is concerned with proving that an ancient Jewish painting tradition formed the topsoil that nourished early Christian fine art. Although not the first to attempt this difficult task, he is certainly one of the most eminent scholars researching this area. The difficulty of the hypothesis is not eased by the common misapprehension that the Old Testament proscription of images was much more absolute in

[7] See footnote 4.

[8] Mentioned by Gerald of Wales, *Giraldi Cambrensis opera* 8, 64f; cf my edition of Yosippon vol. 2, 59.

the Judaism of the Greco-Roman world than it actually was. This misconception can easily be eliminated by examining the extant art of ancient synagogues, particularly the famous frescoes of the synagogue at Dura Europos, and by studying rabbinic decisions that made a certain Jewish fine art possible. Schubert is among those who contributed to the wealth of instructive material on this subject. A more serious objection is perhaps that with all the significant material proofs for the existence of a figurative art in ancient synagogues, it is not easy to prove unequivocally that certain motifs in early Christian art derive from Jewish exemplars. In order to support the case for Jewish exemplars more solidly, Schubert has employed a very instructive method that has proved itself in the field of art history: iconography.

During the Middle Ages illustrations were more dependent on their exemplars than in other periods. This came about, among other reasons, because in this period copyists were more concerned with accurately reproducing their exemplars in order to deviate as little as possible from the objective truth which they allegedly contained. This remarkable fact is demonstrated by the cases where either the exemplar or its relatives are extant. Other cases are 'documented', as it were, where a given medieval illustrated codex is a copy of an ancient illustrated manuscript. With other medieval illustrations the facts compel one to assume an earlier exemplar for the illustrations. Of course, the illustrations were not slavishly copied in most cases during this period. The degree of divergence varied from case to case depending on the creativity of the illustrator and the extent to which he understood the content of his exemplar. It is often easy to determine how and where the new illustration has diverged from its predecessor. Obviously an original motif could thus be distorted or reinterpreted, but much can be learned from such mistakes, as seen in the case where Jewish exemplars are presumed. For the distortion or suppression of an original motif rarely occurs without leaving unintended traces on the new picture. Even when no pictorial evidence is at hand, one can often draw conclusions concerning the exemplar from the dissonance in the available picture.

What we have said concerning Christian fine art in general is also valid of course for its older witnesses. And regarding Old Testament themes one cannot but ask anew whether Christian pictures depend on Jewish illustrators, particularly where the Christian picture betrays the influence not only of the biblical texts, but of extra-biblical Jewish legends as well. This last point seems to me decisive for the hypothesis that Jewish exemplars served for Christian representations of Old Testament themes, and as we have seen, this conclusion is not refuted by appealing to the biblical proscription of images. Schubert has chosen the proper methodology for establishing Jewish exemplars as the basis for the Christian illustrations of the Old Testament. He has not taken the easy path, which might easily have proved treacherous. For example, where one must assume an older exemplar when a motif has been reinterpreted, one may not always conclude Jewish influence since the reconstructed older illustrations may also have been Christian. To be certain that the exemplar is Jewish it must also be determined that the suppressed or reinterpreted motif is a pictorial representation of a Rabbinic narrative. All these conditions *together* must be fulfilled in order to establish scientifically that ancient Jewish illustrations served as the basis for early Christian fine art. Schubert has adopted the one proper method and thus his essay is a clear contribution to this crucial area of study.

As we have said, the purely iconographic method chosen by Schubert seems to be the single proper way to yield more or less certain results regarding Jewish fine art as the model for Christian painting. However, when we attempt to establish a general non-biblical Jewish influence on Christian fine art the purely iconographic method will not suffice. Nonetheless, a comprehensive study of the non-biblical Jewish material in all of Christian art would repay the effort; this would perhaps also be an indirect contribution to the study of early Jewish art. The non-biblical material could derive from ancient Jewish literature (Josephus, the Apocrypha and Pseudepigrapha), or the Rabbinic tradition. Ancient Jewish literature was not unknown to Christian readers – Schreckenberg has enlightened us in this volume concerning the dissemination of Josephus among Christians. Moreover, the Church fathers and later medieval Christian authors also transmitted Jewish motifs and legends. It must not be forgotten that an intellectual exchange existed in the Middle Ages between Jews and their non-Jewish neighbors and that the Christian intelligentsia was interested in Hebrew biblical commentaries. And Schubert's important contribution has shown us that Jewish works of art supplied nourishment for Christian art. With new technological possibilities it would not be impossible today to record all biblically related motifs in non-Jewish European art.

But even this is only a part of the problem. The question concerning ancient Jewish heritage in non-Jewish culture also includes, e.g., belles-lettres and music. Although we cannot dwell on this immense complex in its entirety, one aspect should be singled out since it is unquestionably part of art history. When we examine the Koran and early Islamic literature as well as Christian sources and fine arts we see that Jewish Rabbinic motifs and legends, adopted by both Islam and Christianity, overwhelmingly stem from the later Rabbinic period, i.e., not earlier than mid-third century CE. Many of the Rabbinic motifs and stories adopted by Christianity and Islam first occur in the latest ancient and the early medieval sources. This is also true for those Christian pictures for which Schubert presumes Jewish pictorial exemplars, as well as for the non-biblical motifs in the famous frescoes of the Dura Europos synagogue. This little known fact is difficult to explain.

We have already mentioned that Jewish motifs in Christian fine art could have been mediated not only by Jewish illustrations, but also by contact between Christians and Judaism. Often it is difficult to decide whether a given Jewish motif in Christian art derives from a pictorial exemplar, or from oral or written sources. A few examples of this type will suffice.

We begin with Michelangelo's famous horned Moses.[9] The origin of these horns is found in Exod 34:29-35, 'When Moses came down from Mount Sinai, with the two tables of the testimony in his hand as he came down from the mountain, Moses did not know that the skin of his face shone because he had been talking with God. And when Aaron and all the people of Israel saw Moses, behold, the skin of his face shone, and they were afraid to come near him.' This text is correctly understood in the early Jewish *Antiquitates Biblicae* 12:1 as, 'And Moses came down. And when he had been bathed with invisible light, he went down to the place where the light of the sun and the moon are [sic]; and the light of his face surpassed the splendor of the sun and the moon, and *he did not even know* this.'[10] Other ancient Jewish witnesses, including the Septuagint, interpret this text in similar fasion.

The word in the verse translated as 'shone' is formed from the Hebrew root קרן. In The Bible it occurs as a verb only in our text – elsewhere the root is used as a noun (קֶרֶן). The noun means 'horn' in the Bible with the exception of Hab 3:4, where, similarly to Exod 34:29-35, it is translated as 'rays flashing'. But here as well the Septuagint and thus also Jerome speak of 'horns'. For this and other reasons it is not surprising that the proselyte Aquila (Akylas, second century) translated the text into Greek as the 'horned face' of Moses. Based on Akylas Jerome produced the famous 'cornuta facies' of Moses (Exod 34:29-35) in his Vulgate. Jerome adopted Akylas' translation in the certainty that the horned countenance of Moses was already present in the Hebrew Bible.[11]

As can be seen from Jerome's exposition, he understood Moses' horns metaphorically. Much more difficult is the situation in Rabbinic literature. It would certainly be wrong to banish the horned Moses entirely from Judaism – already the Greek translation of Akylas forbids this. In many Rabbinic texts it is hardly possible to determine whether they are describing horns or light rays. Of course the difficulty is also linguistically conditioned since קרן means both 'horn' and 'ray'.[12] Some Rabbinic texts combine the concepts, providing Moses with 'horn rays'.

[9] See Ruth Mellinkoff's superb monograph, *The Horned Moses*. The author was unable to evaluate fully the Jewish sources, in part because some of these were unavailable at the time of writing.

[10] Trans. D.J. Harrington in Charlesworth, *OTP* 2, 319 (Italics, Harrington). See also Dietzfelbinger's edition, p33. The best edition, with French translation and commentary, is in *Sources chrétiennes* (Paris 1976) vol 1, 126f; vol 2, 114.

[11] See Mellinkoff, *The Horned Moses*, 77-79 and 168f, fn 5-9. For the metaphorical understanding of Moses' horns see also Jerome, *Adversus Pelagianos dialogi*, 1:29.

[12] Rashi's commentary to Exod 34:29 is instructive here: 'Light also breaks through in the manner of a horn.' According to Mellinkoff Rashi's view influenced medieval Christian illustrators in that they provided Moses with horn rays.

Rabbinic legends customarily speak of Moses' 'horns of glory', or 'beams of glory' (קרני הוד). The origin of this typical usage is as follows: Exod 34:29-35, speaks of the horned (or radiating) countenance of Moses. According to Num 27:20 Moses appoints Joshua as his successor by investing him with some of his majesty (הוד). The Ephraimite, Joshua, belonged to the tribe of Joseph and one of the blessings Moses pronounces on the tribe of Joseph is, 'His firstling bull has majesty (הדר),[13] and his horns are the horns of a wild ox' (Deut 33:17). Rabbinic tradition generally interprets (properly so) these words as referring to Joshua, a descendant of Joseph. Thus, the horns of the wild ox attributed to Joshua are connected to the 'horned' countenance of Moses (Exod 34). We have also seen that Moses bestows his 'majesty' (הוד) on his successor Joshua (Num 27:20). The Hebrew words for 'majesty', הוד (Num 27:20) and הדר (Deut 33:17), are synonymous. The majesty of Moses and Joshua became identical and thus Moses' 'horns of majesty' originated. Such a seemingly complicated thought process was not unusual in this period. The ambiguity of the 'horned' or 'radiating' countenance of Moses is already discernible in the Septuagint and the Greek translation by Akylas. Because of the casuistic connection between Moses' 'horned' countenance and the horns mentioned in the Joseph blessing, the horned aspect of Moses became indispensable to all Jewish homilies and legends even though his 'radiating' countenance rarely disappears completely.

The horns of Moses could be understood so concretely by Jews that in two early synagogue prayers celebrating the Feast of Weeks (remembrance of Moses receiving the Tora) the horns served him as weapons. Both compositions employ a variant on the legend of the strife between Moses and the angels over who should possess the Tora.[14] One of these, probably dating from the sixth century, is Aramaic.[15] Here God speaks to Moses, 'I have set horns of majesty (קרני הוד) on your head, that you may ram an angel when he draws near.' In a still older poem[16] Moses ascended to Heaven's gate to receive the Tora where 'horns of majesty' (קרני הוד)[17] were placed on his head that he might ram the angels (with them)'. According to both poems this never became necessary. The notion of Moses' horns as a potential weapon at the giving of the Tora is unknown outside these two poems.

It is not very probable that the Christian portrayals of the horned Moses depend on a Jewish exemplar since they are unattested until the twelfth century. Nor is it certain that the Latin Bible translation alone is responsib-

[13] הדר is synonymous with הוד.
[14] See Ginzberg, *Legends* 3, 109-14; 6, 45-48.
[15] See text in J. Heinemann, *Studies*, 150f. All the old Hebrew poems of the same type are soon to be published by Joseph Yahalom in the Israel Academy of Sciences and Humanities.
[16] Published in Fleischer's essay, *Antiquity*, 401.
[17] See above, fn 13.

le. Perhaps the horned Moses could also have become known in Christian art by other means, e.g., the Jewish literary tradition. Concerning Moses' halo in Byzantine illustrations the situation may be different, but to understand the possible Jewish pre-history we must range somewhat far afield. In the Essene Community Rule (1QS 4:7-8) it is said concerning the lot of the blessed that 'everlasting joy in eternal life' and 'a crown of glory with raiment of splendor (כליל כבוד עם מדת הדר)[18] in eternal light' are ordained for them. Here then we have a garment of light worn by the blessed with their 'crown of glory'. This can only mean a magnificent diadem or wreath, yet, as we will see, the Essenes almost certainly believed that the blessed would be adorned with halos. Whether this Qumran text is connected with the history of halos in Christianity is a question best left to the specialists in Christian beliefs and Christian art.

A Jewish liturgical text confirms that the 'crown of glory' in the Qumran text means halo. This is a poetic section in the worship service for Sabbath morning.[19] In a strophe on the giving of the Tora to Moses it is said, 'you set a crown of glory (כליל תפארת) on [Moses'] head when he stood before you on Mount Sinai, and he descended with the stone tablets in his hand.' Here Exod 34:29-35 is used poetically: Moses descended from Mount Sinai with the tablets in his hand without knowing that his countenance was radiating. It is certain then that the 'crown of glory' refers to the rays radiating from his face. Thus the radiating countenance of Moses formed a crown of rays, or a halo. Regarding the blessed dead of the Essenes, it is now clear that their glowing crown was a halo since, among other things, the Hebrew expressions for 'crown of glory' are practically identical in the Essene text and the synagogue prayer.[20]

The halo surrounding Moses' head in the old synagogue prayer is important not only in itself, but also as an interesting occurrence for the possible influence of ancient Jewish art on Christian illustrations. It has been observed[21] that in four of the five Byzantine manuscripts of the twelfth and thirteenth centuries containing the first eight books of the Bible (the so-called Octateuch), Moses is depicted with a halo as he receives the tablets of the Law.[22] Exactly as in the same scene of the synagogue prayer, this is a pictorial representation of the radiating countenance of Moses. There seems to be a connection here between the Byzantine illustrations and Jewish pictorial representations of Moses with the stone tablets and halo. It should also be considered whether Moses' halo in the Jewish

[18] See especially Leany, *Rule*, 144.

[19] On this poetic piece see Fleischer, *Eretz-Israel Prayer*, 51f.

[20] In the Essene text, כליל כבוד; in the synagogue prayer, כליל תפארת.

[21] See Mellinkoff, *Horned Moses*, 5f.

[22] Moses' halo in San Vitale in Ravenna means little since he is depicted opposite Jeremiah who also has a halo.

liturgical piece is not a result of influence from a Jewish pictorial representation.

I conclude with a few words concerning the new section of the Compendia of which this book is the second volume. Our purpose is to investigate Jewish traditions in early Christian literature. This task demands an objective and non-apologetic treatment. Neither the tension between the two religions nor the fertile reinterpretation of Jewish content within Christendom may be forgotten. In my view enough progress has been made today that we may forego giving special attention in this endeavor to the important Christian-Jewish dialogue. Our task in this section is to illuminate both civilizations with help from the Jewish heritage. If thereby the essence of European culture, both past and present, becomes more understandable the new section will also have fulfilled an educational purpose.

I

Heinz Schreckenberg

Josephus in Early Christian Literature and Medieval Christian Art

Detailed Table of Contents

CHAPTER THREE: *Josephus in Early Christian Texts*

CHAPTER FOUR: *Josephus in Medieval Christian Art*

Chapter One

Introduction

Josephus in Christian Tradition

With the exception of the Bible no other ancient text is as important for the history of Judaism and Christianity as the works of Josephus. Were we dependent upon the Jewish tradition alone, however, which ignored not only Josephus, but Philo and the Septuagint as well, there would be neither a Hellenistic-Jewish literature, nor could we supply the term 'Hellenistic Judaism' with any content. As a significant Jewish historian, oddly enough, Josephus had neither contemporaries nor successors, although the social and religious existence of the numerous Jewish communities in Mesopotamia and the Mediterranean continued almost unimpaired into the period of late antiquity.[1] One reason for this is that the material and spiritual affinity of Josephus' works to the Christian world-view created a maelstrom that drew the books of the Jewish historian almost completely into the Christian sphere, thus making him a stranger among the members of his own faith.[2]

This is of course insufficient to explain that peculiar fact of Jewish literary history, that its first and, as some think, most important historian,[3] the spiritual ancestor of Heinrich GRAETZ and Simon DUBNOW, remained for centuries almost forgotten by his own people. One must also consider that after 70 the Jewish religious environment and educational climate changed, and a gradual withdrawal occurred from the universal languages of Greek and Latin into the securely enclosed environs of the Hebrew language.

[1] See Schreckenberg, 'Wirkungsgeschichte', 1210f. For the medieval 're-judaization' of Josephus' Christian-transmitted work, see above x-xii.
[2] See Schreckenberg, *Untersuchungen*, 48-53: 'Josephus in der hebräischen Tradition', (cf *REJ* 23 [1891] 318) and Goodenough, *Symbols* 1, p9: 'It is only through Christians that Philo, Josephus, Jewish Apocrypha have survived'. Some details concerning Yohanan ben Zakkai in Rabbinic literature may derive from Josephus or a source close to him, as shown by Schäfer, 'Jochanan b. Zakkai', 83-97. Cohen, 'Parallel Historical Tradition', 7-14 also identified isolated dependencies on Josephus in Rabbinic literature. This must be further explored, but so far the connections between Rabbinic literature and Josephus remain vague and never attain the clarity of Patristic citations and Josephus manuscripts. Meanwhile comparative studies such as Goldenberg, *Halakhah*, contribute to our knowledge of the problem.
[3] Thus Zeitlin considers Josephus the most important writer of Jewish history; cf his 'Survey'. Here, scholarly opinion justifiably is rather divided.

Here begins a development which led to Jews in the Early and High Middle Ages knowing, besides their native Hebrew, usually only the local vernacular – e.g., one of the early forms of the Romance languages or Middle High German. The receptivity to Greek and Latin education, literature, and philosophy, which, e.g., Luke and Josephus still have in common, declined in late antiquity making way for the purely inner-Jewish development of the Talmud and Midrashim. For many centuries then Jewish scholars wrote mostly in Hebrew or Aramaic. As late as the High Middle Ages important texts by Jewish authors were known in the Christian sphere only via Latin translations. Apparently the alienation between Jews and Christians, which had been increasing since antiquity, and the ever fewer possibilities for communication were reciprocally conditioned. A different situation developed in the Islamic sphere, with the blossoming of Jewish-Arabic culture in the tenth-twelfth century. Even more reminiscent of the Golden Age of Hellenistic-Jewish literature is the receptivity for non-Jewish culture evinced by modern Jewish authors since Moses MENDELSSOHN. The eclipse from Jewish tradition of Greek Jewish literature including Josephus is all the more remarkable.

Josephus' thematic and intellectual affinity with many books of the Old and New Testaments, particularly Luke-Acts, has as such long been well-known. Since Eusebius' *Church History* Christian theologians have read Josephus as a historical commentary to the New Testament or an exegetical handbook to the Old. For it was already apparent at first glance that the texts of the Jewish author (*War*, *Antiquities*, *Life*, *Against Apion*) often filled in gaps left by New Testament authors and in general reported a great deal of background information that provided a somewhat complete picture, otherwise unavailable, of the New Testament era. However, the importance of the reception and influence of Josephus for the development of early Christian views of history and its own identity is still little known.[4] One of the aims of this study is to increase somewhat our still inadequate knowledge in this area.

Stages in the History of Research

Several significant details in the history of research can serve as stepping stones on the path of the Josephus tradition through Christian history from the modern period backwards to the early Christian period. At the same time they reveal *a posteriori*, so to speak, important lines of development

[4] More on this topic in Schreckenberg, *Tradition*; id, *Untersuchungen*; id, 'Wirkungsgeschichte'. Josephus is mentioned in passing by Bolgar, *Classical Influences* 1, p165: 'Orosius and Sallust supply the twin keys to medieval historiography: "claves scientiae". Suetonius probably comes next of the ancient historians, followed by "the Latin Josephus"; Livy tags along far in the rear.' Josephus' importance is badly underestimated here. Incorrectly, Artz, *Mind of the Middle Ages* has not mentioned him at all.

that begin with the reception of Josephus by early Christianity. The way then leads from the end of the road back to its beginning.

Theologians of the nineteenth century speak of Josephus' works as 'a kind of Fifth Gospel'.[5] Many named the writings of the Jewish historian 'the Little Bible'.[6] The edition of the Greek text by RICHTER (1826-27) appeared as *Pars I* of the *Bibliotheca Sacra Patrum Ecclesiae Graecorum*, which formally documents the Christian claim to Josephus as a kind of Church father. Accordingly, the publication of the complete Latin Josephus was planned for the *Corpus Scriptorum Ecclesiasticorum Latinorum*, although only *Pars VI, De Judaeorum vestutate sive contra Apionem* (ed BOYSEN) appeared. Here the Jewish historian has become a *scriptor ecclesiasticus*. Therefore it is not surprising when, for centuries, in Anglo-American Protestantism he was counted with the Bible as 'permitted reading' on Sundays.[7] In any case, in the more recent scholarly tradition he is considered as *pecus aurei velleris*, i.e., as an author who has no conception of the great value of his reports for succeeding generations.

It is therefore readily understandable that, very early on, New Testament scholarship made use of the Josephan accounts for exegesis. The annotated edition of the New Testament text, *Η ΚΑΙΝΗ ΔΙΑΘΗΚΗ* (Amsterdam 1751-52) by WETSTEIN, pointed the way here. With its many parallels drawn from Josephus and Philo, among others, it became a kind of forerunner to the *Corpus Hellenisticum* or *Corpus Judaeo-Hellenisticum*.[8] Thereafter, a remarkable stage in the history of research is represented in the *Scholia hellenistica in Novum Testamentum Philone et Josepho patribus apostolicis ... deprompta* by GRINFIELD. Here, beginning with Matthew and proceeding by chapters, linguistic and subject parallels to the New Testament are collected. The view – regarded today as erroneous – that Josephus belonged to the early Jewish-Christian sect, the Ebionites, and was moreover a bishop in Jerusalem, was part of the scholarly discussion of the eighteenth century.[9]

The traditional affinity between the Bible and Josephus is also reflected in the printing of collections of parallels (concordances) and portions of text from Josephus in many editions of the Bible since the early sixteenth century, especially since the beginning of the Reformation period. One example is the *Biblia cum concordantiis veteris et novi testamenti et sacrorum canonum ... additae sunt concordantie ex viginti libris Josephi de antiquitatibus et de bello iudaico excerpte*, Lugduni 1518. In the Latin

[5] Keim, *Aus dem Urchristentum* 1, 1.
[6] Berggren, *Bibel und Josephus*, XII.
[7] Zafren, 'Printed Rarities', 144.
[8] See Windisch, 'Zum Corpus Hellenisticum', 124f; Delling, 'Zum Corpus Hellenisticum', 1-15.
[9] By the influential scholar and translator of Josephus, W. Whiston; cf Schreckenberg, *Bibliographie*, 38, 43.

translation of the Bible by the Reformation humanist, Sebastian CASTELLIO (Basel 1556; first published 1551), there appears in columns 1197-1282 a *Historiae continuatio ex Josepho* covering the period from Esdras to Christ, indeed, as the title page makes clear, as *Supplementum historiae biblicae*. More than any other single event the destruction of Jerusalem according to Josephus' account in the War was printed as an appendix in many Bibles and prayer books. At the same time the custom developed of reading sections from this impressive account in the worship service on the tenth Sunday after Trinity.[10]

Finally, it must be noted that the number of Josephus manuscripts in medieval libraries, cathedral-schools, and universities must have been large. The Latin translation in particular was not merely an *instrumentum laboris* in almost all cloister libraries, but was a firm part of the reading plan in the prescribed course of studies for Benedictine monks during Lent.[11] So far then, our preliminary look at some of the significant stages in the history of Christian literary use of Josephus. The lines of effect and consequence which bind these stages with one another all have their points of departure in early Christian literature. Some factors of this effect and consequence can already be foreseen.

Habent sua fata libelli

Even before beginning our investigation of the reception of Josephus into the Christian writings of the first five centuries, we are presented with a startling picture: with Josephus, a chasm yawns between the desired and the actual effect of his work, far wider than in any other ancient writer. The historian could neither foresee nor influence, let alone prevent the course that the Christian interpretation of his works would take. In order to understand the details of this extraordinary and unique development, we will have to investigate the literary and intellectual characteristics of Josephus as well as of his recipients. In addition, the intellectual framework, the 'ambient', in which the reception takes place, must be described, as well as certain literary characteristics of the New Testament (particularly Luke-Acts) which have this ambient in common with Josephus, or, at the very least, attest to an intellectual proximity. In other words, new insights into

[10] See Aring, *Christen und Juden*, 248. In 'Wirkungsgeschichte', 1298-1306, I have tried to show that, as a logical result, Josephus' *War* has been pressed into service in the Christian mission to the Jews from the early Christian period almost to the present time. A representative example would be: *Die Zerstörung der Stadt Jerusalem nach dem jüdischen Geschichtsschreiber und Augenzeugen Josephus*, published by the Berliner Gesellschaft zur Beförderung des Christenthums unter den Juden (Berlin Society for the Encouragement of Christianity among the Jews), Berlin 1863.

[11] Wilmart, 'Le couvent', 93, 113; cf Mundo, 'Bibliotheca', 67. For the extant medieval manuscripts of Josephus, see Manitius, *Handschriften*, 207-13: 'Josephus'.

the significance of Josephus for early Christianity will be gained not by examining him and his early Christian recipients separately, but by viewing the field of interaction that was generated, and the motives and interests at work in it. Thus we must ask how Eusebius and others read the Lucan writings in the light of the historical experience mediated to them by the works of Josephus. Why do they make such vehement use of this Jewish author at all? What transformation does the tradition undergo in its annexation?

Ancient literary theory already recognized that a sizeable discrepancy could arise between the intended and actual effects of texts. Thus the well-known verse 1286 (only part of which is usually cited) from the didactic poem *De litteris, syllabis et metris* by Terentius Maurus (end of the second century):[12] *pro captu lectoris habent sua fata libelli*, i.e., books have their own destiny in accordance with the intellectual capacity, abilities, and possibilities of their readers; more precisely: the consequences effected by books are dependent upon their readers' ability and desire to understand; and probably as well: at bottom, the interpretive will of the readership determines how a book is received, i.e., how it is used and what effects it produces. In this sense, many early Christian theologians appear to read their views and interpretations into Josephus' text, indeed, not without concrete methodological examples. For the Stoics and later Platonists exegeted Homer in basically the same fashion, drawing their own philosophical perspectives from the *Iliad* and the *Odyssey*.

Josephus and Early Christian Identity

Our subject, 'Josephus in Early Christian Literature', is interwoven with the development of early Christianity and its ideas. Thus we will see how Christian theology in the second-fourth centuries developed a type of historical thinking, which on the one hand was influenced by the intellectual climate of its time, and on the other – and here Josephus occupies an important place – also exerted its influence on it. Thus we notice first of all that with the preliminary highpoint of early Christian use of Josephus in the fourth and fifth centuries begins the gradual deterioration of Jewish rights in the Roman Empire. For until then the Jewish religion – in contrast to long suppressed Christianity – enjoyed the status of *religio licita*, i.e., one of the officially permitted religions of the Roman Empire. In any case, the social status of the Jews and their religious freedom remained essentially intact for centuries after 70 CE.[13]

It is now generally well-known to what extent Christian authors of the

[12] Keil, *Grammatici Latini* 6, p363.

[13] Schreckenberg, 'Wirkungsgeschichte', 1210f; and already Conzelmann, *Heiden-Juden-Christen*, 30f.

second-fifth centuries used Josephus in their apologetic efforts. It seems that this Jewish chief witness for the 'Christian truth' contributed decisively to buttressing historically Christian self-understanding and ultimately proving Christianity to be the superior religion and 'true Israel'.[14] Many details require further investigation, above all the various stages in the development of thought that lead from the first halting attempts at finding its identity, to the apologetic conflicts, all the way to the church-historical concerns of a Christianity by now confident of victory and interested in its own past.

Originally an inner-Jewish group, a sort of messianic Jewish sect that lived in the expectation of the immediate coming of the kingdom of God,[15] early Christianity will have wrestled from the beginning with identity problems, indeed, almost inevitably, will have experienced a certain anxiety in this regard. It had not yet attained that self-confidence which could only grow out of an apologetically established recording of church history. Identity could be achieved at first only by separation, chiefly from other (still inner-Jewish) groups, and thereafter from the various religions of late antiquity and the flood of syncretism. The historical thinking of early Christianity, becoming active in the second century, plainly helped decisively in the young group's search for an identity on its way to becoming a church *sui generis*.[16] A significant stage in this development is the conception arising in the second and third centuries of Christianity as the 'third genus' which replaces Judaism, perservering in its errors, as well as paganism.[17] After the separation from Judaism and a first phase of finding its identity, the Church had to secure and expand, both historically and apologetically, the hard-won beachhead. Only the writing of history, the discovering of coherent purpose within history, could effectively end the identity problems and other uncertainties that accompanied the gradual uncoupling from Judaism.

One important circumstance made this much easier: after Josephus there was no more writing of history among the Jews. There was no Jewish historiographer who could have opposed to Eusebius' *Church History* an

[14] Cf already Schreckenberg, 'Wirkungsgeschichte', for certain details of this development.

[15] This is pursued with good arguments most recently by Rowland, *Christian Origins*. Among other things Rowland shows that Paul, rather than hellenizing a more or less matured Christian doctrine, transferred from Pharisaism to another inner-Jewish group, the disciples of the Messiah, Jesus of Nazareth. For early Christianity as a Jewish sect, cf also Lichtenberger, 'Paulus und Josephus in Rom'. Also, it is often too little noticed that the Christian congregations developed out of Jewish communities of the Mediterranean area, in which development Gentile *sebomenoi* probably played a certain role. Judaizing non-Jews within ancient Jewish congregations could most easily become the core of a Gentile Christian community. Cf Lampe, *Stadtrömische Christen*, 26ff, and in general Kasting, *Anfänge*, 11-27.

[16] A general discussion of these questions is given by Sanders, *Self-Definition* 1, p1ff: 'The Problem of Self-Definition: From Sect to Church'.

[17] Examples in Schreckenberg, *Texte* 1, p210, 238; cf Stanton, 'Aspects', 377-392.

equivalent history of the Jewish people from the second-fourth centuries, and with the same self-confidence. Thus, it remained for Christian theologians to paint salvation history with no other colors than those of their own historical experience, and to deliver this to posterity. Only after the expectation of the imminent Parousia and the concomitant telescoping of time had subsided by the second century at the latest, was there room for a thorough-going historical and church-historical interest. Coming to terms with the world for a longer period than at first supposed, perhaps even permanently, seemed unavoidable; it became necessary to assess the Christian past and to accomodate it into history and salvation history.

In this situation the discovery of Josephus' works by Christian circles of the second-fourth centuries must have seemed like a gift from Heaven.[18] They offered rich material, in particular for the a posteriori representation of the Jewish catastrophe of 70 as the triumph of Christianity. A feeling of inferiority with a corresponding need for self-justification over against a venerable Judaism controlled the Christian-Jewish relationship even in the fourth and fifth centuries. Christianity was long regarded as a sect or offshoot of the much older (and therefore more respected) Judaism, which before 70 and deep into late antiquity enjoyed the relatively undisturbed existence of a *religio licita*, a sanctioned religion, in the Roman empire. Early Christianity was only able to overcome its disadvantaged status gradually in the course of the fourth century.[19]

Roughly contemporary with the beginning of the use and influence of Josephus in Christianity was a growing insight that Jesus himself was not only the messianic savior but also a historical personality. Historical, even critical, argumentation suggested itself, indeed became imperative, if early Christianity was to be taken seriously by educated non-Christians in the cultural world of the Roman Empire. With the progressive development of the Church from an inner-Jewish group[20] to a Christianity that opened outwards, wanting to be recognized in the circle of Hellenistic culture, indeed to become a world religion, awoke also the desire to satisfy philosophical demands. In Hellenistic Judaism there were already strong tendencies to understand biblical monotheism as philosophical monotheism. Both Philo and Josephus placed Moses on a par with the great Hellenic philosophers and understood his law-giving as philosophy.[21] This was the spadework for the later efforts of the early Church at proving Christianity also to be true philosophy. Josephus in particular was extremely useful to Christianity for such purposes. As a theologizing historiographer who made

[18] Cf Bardy, 'Souvenir'.
[19] For the relatively tolerant legislation toward Jews in the late imperial period see Schreckenberg, *Texte* 1, p368-72 (cf index s.v. Codex Theodosianus), as well as Linder, *Jews*.
[20] See now also Nickelsburg, 'Revealed Wisdom', 73-91.
[21] Amir, 'Begegnung', 2-19.

his plea for the Jewish religion by hellenizing it and presenting it as a philosophy, he provided material and thought which could, with minimal changes, become elements of Christian argumentation.

Early Christian Literary Themes in Medieval Art

Christian art of the early and high middle ages appears to have drawn its themes to a large degree from early Christian literature.[22] Many subjects turned up in Christian painting only after they had been discussed for centuries in Christian literature, proving themselves as central and fertile themes which ultimately were to find their way from the confines of theological discussion to the larger audiences for art. Since pictorial themes as a rule have acquired great popularity during their literary prehistory, their selection and disposition during the Middle Ages allows us to draw important conclusions regarding their evaluation in early Christianity. For the medieval pictures collect, reflect, and focus many themes from the Patristic period in the broadest sense, and so allow us to recognize from which texts the strongest influences were felt, and which material received the widest hearing. In other words, an investigation of the iconographic reception and influence of Josephus the 'Church father' is a proper way to understand the motives and interests that accompanied and encouraged Christian appropriation of the Jewish historian.

The time frame of early Christianity is therefore only formally exceeded in our study since the iconographic reception of Josephus, which did not even begin until the Early Middle Ages, has primarily patristic positions as content. We have therefore a unique opportunity to relate the formation of the tradition in the sphere of art to the same process in literature, and thus allow the Christian Josephus tradition, as it were, to interpret itself. This may allow deeper insight than hitherto possible.

Our investigation of the literary texts concerns the time from the first and second to the fifth centuries, whereas 'medieval Christian art' comprehends a greater time period – approximately 700-1500. This will require us to cull the sources somewhat, e.g., by leaving out many illustrations in the Bible paraphrases of the Antiquities, which, as a rule, yield little content, particularly for Christian-Jewish apologetic, since they also appear in the same or similar form as countless miniatures in Bible manuscripts, and thus are by no means typical for Josephus. Deutsch, in his *Iconographie*, has already provided good access to some of this material. We will attempt here to go beyond Deutsch with the pictures typical for Josephus, and also to make new, relevant pictures available for discussion.

[22] Schreckenberg, *Texte* 2, p447-629; cf Schreckenberg, 'Adversus-Judaeos-Thematik', 127, for the time-delayed portrayal of Patristic themes in medieval Christian art; see also Schreckenberg, 'Judenbild', 37.

Chapter Two will proceed by investigating the literary and intellectual preliminaries to the early Christian reception of Josephus. For this it will be necessary to cast an eye first on the literary features of Josephus himself, and then on texts that show affinity with him, above all Luke-Acts. We conclude the chapter by outlining the literary and intellectual ground common to Luke and Josephus, which is an important factor in the latter's influence. In Chapter Three we will examine the relevant early Christian texts chronologically, with a view toward the role that Josephus plays in them. The aim of Chapter Four is to present, in each case chronologically, first, all the medieval depictions known to us that portray Josephus (i.e., so-called author's portraits or fantasy portraits); second, miniatures that present him as one of the *dramatis personae* in his own history; third, pictures of historiographical highpoints in his work that have special significance for the Christian view of history, such as the siege and destruction of Jerusalem in 70; and fourth, such miniatures in the Josephan manuscripts as serve to interpret and assess the Christian-Jewish relationship.

Chapter Two

Preliminaries to the Early Christian Reception of Josephus

Josephus as Hellenistic Jewish Author

LIFE AND WORK

In various respects Josephus' influence on early Christianity is determined by his literary singularity. We must first of all therefore examine his literary characteristics. *Yosef ben Mattityahu, ha-kohen*, known as Flavius Josephus, was born as son of a noble priestly family between September 13, 37 and March 16, 38, and died probably c. 100 in Rome. His *Jewish War*, written in the years 75-79,[23] describes the events of the years 66 till 70 (or 74) together with the pre-history of the war. The *Antiquities of the Jews* was published c. 93-94, with the *Life*, an autobiography, by way of an appendix. Here Josephus relates the history of the Jews up to his own time, making liberal use of a Greek Bible translation not entirely identical with our Septuagint. Besides this he probably only made sporadic use of the Hebrew text or an Aramaic targum, though Josephus' use of the Bible has still not been fully expounded.[24] In the composition of the *Antiquities*, however, he made comprehensive use of the world history, *Historiai*, by Nicolaus of Damascus (died after 4 CE), the court historian of Herod the great, and further, of Strabo (c. 63-64 BCE – 23 CE). The methodological model for the *Antiquities* were the twenty books, *ΡΩΜΑΙΚΗ ΑΡΧΑΙΟΛΟΓΙΑ*, by Dionysius of Halicarnassus, a historian who lived and taught rhetoric in Rome from 30 – 8 BCE. This rhetorical historiography, garnished with many fictitious speeches, seeks to educate Greeks in an entertaining manner about Roman history, heroes, and institutions. Likewise Josephus, intending to inform the Graeco-Roman world about the history and religion of the Jews and to offer an apology for them in the face of much misunderstanding and hostility, uses the Hellenistic literary style to make his book pleasing and attractive for the educated reader. In his *Life*, Josephus presents chiefly a justification of his activity as general of the Jewish rebels

[23] Published perhaps during the reign of Titus (June 79 – Sept. 81), who alone vouchsafed the 'imprimatur' (*Life*, 363); it is thought that the seventh book in its extant form first appeared under Domitian, 81-96, perhaps even later; but this is uncertain; cf Schwartz, 'Composition'.
[24] For a survey see Feldman, 'Use, Authority'.

in Galilee. *Against Apion* is an apology for the Jewish faith against non-Jewish authors – an apology in which historiographical principles are expressed in the context of debate with the Greek historians. The work, however, is not named *apologia* by Josephus himself at 2:147, as concluded by Cohen;[25] for here, Josephus means not the literary genus, but *apologia* generically as a defensive argument, in which the quality of the Tora becomes a defensive weapon. As Vespasian's prisoner of war, Josephus prophesied the general's future elevation to the throne of Caesar (*War* 3:399-408), and after having been released from captivity in 69, was given the family name of the *gens Flavia*, as was customary with freedmen, his Jewish name, Joseph, becoming the *praenomen*, Josephus. He was now called Josephus Flavius, although, as we shall see, in the early Christian literature he is also named Flavius Josephus. Later, in Rome, he received Roman citizenship from Vespasian and was allowed to live in his former private residence (*Life*, 423). He had perhaps also represented himself to Titus and Vespasian as a man of royal lineage (cf. *Life*, 2: βασιλικὸν γένος), whom it might be desirable to have on one's side, or perhaps to use for political purposes as circumstances dictated. He had already proved his usefulness for the Flavian dynasty, and the War, which he had written in the seventies as a kind of court historiographer, promised to spread the fame of the Emperor's house even farther.

Josephus was a 'traditional Pharisee, who did not adjust himself to the new rabbinic orientation after 70'.[26] His role as court historian, which is only valid, if at all, for the War, did not lead, according to all that we know, to an abandonment of his religious identity. On the contrary, he remained a believing Jew, and promoted sympathy and understanding for the Jewish people and their religion, for whom he hoped to secure a proper place within the Roman Empire. He does this by weighty citation of numerous pro-Jewish decrees from Roman authorities, chiefly in the fourteenth book of the *Antiquities*, by praising the exemplary quality of the Jewish religious laws (e.g., *Ant.* 1:15; *Ag. Ap.* 2:291-296), and, not least of all, by maintaining that obedience to the (Jewish) laws, i.e., pious observance of the Law, will bring εὐδαιμονία (prosperity, true happiness) to men,[27] an argument that cannot have failed to impress his readers with their wide interest in the popular philosophies. Whether Josephus is to be regarded as the greatest of Jewish historians, whether he is, as Herodotus for the Greeks, the *pater*

[25] Cohen, 'History and Historiography', 1.

[26] Thoma, 'Volk-Gottes-Verständnis', 112; he believes Josephus to have been a Pharisee of the Shammaite school. But Josephus lacks the zealotic thinking characteristic of the Shammaites, and supports the Hillelite understanding of divorce (I am grateful to P.J. Tomson for this observation).

[27] For example, *Ant.* 1:14-15, 20. Numerous other instances can be found in Rengstorf, *Concordance*, s.v. εὐδαιμονία and εὐδαίμων.

historiae of his people – there is sufficient warrant for regarding him as the most significant predecessor of Heinrich GRAETZ (1817-1891).

CHARACTERISTICS AS AN AUTHOR

The otherwise unremarkable fact that Josephus writes his works in Greek must be mentioned at the outset as part of his literary character. For thereby, albeit unintentionally, he fulfills an essential prerequisite for his influence on early Christianity. Had he written in his native Aramaic or Hebrew, it is probable that his books would never have been preserved, or that their influence would have had a completely different history. As a child of the educated upper class of Jerusalem, he had probably already learned some Greek and Latin, enough so that he was able to travel to Rome in 64 on a difficult mission to seek the release of (Zealotic-minded?) Jewish priests who had been sent there in bonds, presumably under suspicion of anti-Roman activities (*Life* 13-16).

He writes a classical prose that can be defined as an atticistic reaction to the *Koine*,[28] and he is master of the *ars narrandi* of his time.[29] For example, he often arranges his material in a 'dramatic episode style', or the style of Greek tragedy; also, in accordance with the literary and rhetorical technique of *dinosis*, he exaggerates not a little, and readily simplifies the facts in complicated cases or strengthens the plausibility of motivations to action; and occasionally the relations between man and woman are portrayed as a romantic love story.[30] In short, strong influences from the narrative technique of the novel and novella, and the customary treatment of material in ancient rhetoric, intrude into the writing of history. This is also true especially for Josephus' handling of biblical material. Thus it has been seen that Josephus' concern in the reworking of 3 Ezra in *Ant.* 11:1-158 was 'to spare his Hellenistic readers the most glaring contradictions, inconsistencies, repetitions and trivialities of 3 Ezra'.[31] One particularly noticeable influence from Hellenistic literary conventions is that he often sketches an unrealistic, highly imaginative portrait of the *dramatis personae*, in order to make them appear more impressive and bring them closer to the reader. Moses then, becomes a wise, charismatic leader of Israel, and Abraham appears almost as a Greek philosopher. Women as well, such as Rebecca, are idealized in the Hellenistic style to become exemplary representatives of the Jewish people, apparently in order to personalize the Jewish religion and history and thereby make it seem more pleasing to interested non-Jews. Everything is carefully chosen for the taste of the contemporary reading

[28] Pelletier, *Flavius Josèphe, adaptateur*.
[29] Villalba i Varneda, *Method*, 64-241; Basser, 'Josephus'; Feldman, 'Use, Authority', 476-81.
[30] Feldman ib 501-3.
[31] Pohlmann, *Studien*, 113.

public, the educated middle and upper class.[32]

Another such concession to contemporary taste is the urbane comment to such miraculous claims as the extreme longevity of Noah and the patriarchs (*Ant.* 1:108), 'But on these matters let everyone decide according to his fancy', while giving a rational explanation by referring, *inter alia*, to the diet of that time as being more conducive to longevity (*Ant.* 1:106). Characteristically, he is even able to combine reason and theology as, for example, *Ant.* 5:226, νὺξ γὰρ ἦν καὶ ὁ θεὸς τοῦτο ἤθελεν, 'for it was night and God willed it so', or *Ant.* 4:322 κατὰ βούλησιν ... θεοῦ καὶ φύσεως νόμῳ, 'in accordance with the will of God and by a law of nature'. Here also the urbane courtesy shows through that seeks to spare the readers any 'unreasonable' demands made by the intrusion of the supernatural. With no rationalistic reservations or limitations, however, he allows world-historical events (such as the destruction of Jerusalem and the rule of Rome) to be prophesied already in the Bible (e.g., *Ant.* 10:79, 276; cf. *War* 6:312-313). This is one of the numerous bridges that connect Josephus with the New Testament, which understood the salvation event bound up with Jesus of Nazareth as the fulfillment of biblical prophecy.

As we have seen, the Jewish historian has the literary characteristic of dramatically ordering various – in part, disparate – plot elements and effectually bringing them to an end, as in a play.[33] Characteristically then, he often combines this with the moralizing lessons that doing evil will lead men to ruin, or bring with it the deserved punishment of God (e.g., *War* 7:271, 453; *Ant.* 18:9). This could encourage, indeed, was bound to encourage, moralizing interpretations of Jewish history in early Christianity.[34] Perhaps the widespread *Bible moralisée* and other such richly illustrated lay bibles of the High Middle Ages still stand in this tradition of a moralizing assessment of Jewish history. This seems not improbable when one considers the wide distribution of just the Latin version of Josephus in medieval cloisters. In certain respects Josephus' *Antiquities* already represents a type of lay Bible, a simplified, revised Bible, arranged especially for the tastes of non-Jews into a readable, pleasing compendium of Jewish history and literature. Basically, this is the procedure followed by many medieval illustrated Bibles, though here as a rule the didactic aim is attained by pictures in the form of miniatures.

[32] See Bailey, 'Portrayal', 168f; cf Daniel, *Apologetics*. Cohen, *Josephus*, 90 and Attridge, 'Josephus', 206 speak correctly of Josephus' 'rhetorical historiography'. Josephus' numerous echoes of Homer were also certainly intended to impress his educated readership, as Kopidakes, 'Josêpos homerizôn', correctly supposes.

[33] See e.g. Basser, 'Josephus', for *Ant.* 1:37-52, the Fall of Adam and Eve.

[34] Schreckenberg, 'Wirkungsgeschichte', 1198ff: 'Moralisierende Geschichtsdeutungen'; Attridge, 'Josephus', 224.

CREDIBILITY

The question of Josephus' historical dependability and credibility is bound up with his literary characteristics. Scholars have answered this question differently. Josephus is probably most trustworthy wherever he reports geographical and topographical items, matter, and content of the Jewish religion and historical facts. He is rightly seen as least trustworthy with regard to the evaluation of individuals and groups, and their activities, i.e., where he himself had been actively involved.[35] He writes his *War* with tendentious partisanship, *cum ira et studio* so to speak, but once this is taken into account, his work is nonetheless a historical source of unique rank. Despite his subjective judgements, the *War* remains a significant historiographical accomplishment; for 'there is no real historiography without interest and evaluation, without penetrating questions concerned with deeper connections, causes and effects, without reflection on chance and destiny ... guilt and fate'.[36]

To be sure many smaller and greater imprecisions are disturbing, for example, the claim that even the smallest village in Galilee had 15,000 residents (*War* 3:43).[37] In *Ag. Ap.* 1:42 it is pompously affirmed that all Jews remain faithful to their laws and, when necessary, die cheerfully for them, while *War* 7:52 reports that in this situation only part of the Jews chose death. In *Ant.* 3:276 Josephus reports in a free explanation of Lev. 11:7 (cf. mKet 2:9) that priests are not allowed to marry prisoners of war, inter alia, (since every captive woman was assumed to have been sexually violated, and as such forbidden to a priest).[38] As a priest, on the other hand, he admits, to having married a captive woman (*Life* 414; his claim in this connection that she was a 'virgin' only proves that he was aware of his lapse in behavior).

He claims, on the one hand, to translate only the Hebrew Bible, 'neither adding nor omitting anything' (*Ant.* 1:17; 10:218; cf. 1:5; 4:196-197; *Ag. Ap.* 1:54). But on the other hand, he uses extensively for his depiction only a Greek Bible translation, adds or omits weighty issues (e.g., the offensive worship of the golden calf in Ex. 32), and, as he himself admits (Ant. 1:17; 4:196-197), arranges the biblical material according to his own viewpoints. The formula 'neither adding nor omitting anything' is nonetheless perhaps of limited credibility when one assumes that he wants his report of the Jewish religious traditions to be true in content (i.e., without deviation

[35] The course of the *War*, 66-70 is critically examined by Rhoads, *Revolutionaries*; Harter, *Causes*; Price, *Jerusalem*.

[36] Hengel, *Geschichtsschreibung*, 49 (ET, 52); useful information on many questions in Josephus research is provided above all by Rajak, *Josephus*; Attridge, 'Josephus'; Schwartz, *Josephus*; Mayer, 'Josephus Flavius'. Hölscher, 'Josephus', is dated but still useful.

[37] Cf Byatt, 'Josephus'.

[38] On this see Daube, 'Three Legal Notes', 191-4.

from the *halakha*), in contrast to the loose, irresponsible behavior of the Greek authors with regard to their own Greek tradition (*Ag. Ap.* 1:44-46). Josephus' partly incorrect claims regarding his faithful rendering of the biblical tradition are probably particularly intended for the ears of his Jewish compatriots, in order to forestall any doubt on the correctness of his historiographical portrayal of the Jewish religion and history. Indeed, he had sold copies of his War (*Ag. Ap.* 1:51) and probably other works as well to 'a large number' of Jews, and is concerned in all his works for veracity from the Jewish standpoint.

OBJECTIVES AND INTENDED AUDIENCE

Josephus' decision to write in Greek was also a choice for the rules and stylistic customs already present in the Greek literary tradition. As an author, certainly, he represents 'several personae (Pharisee, prophet, priest, historian)'.[39] One might add to this that he is also an apologist and theologian, or better, a historian with a theological (or historico-theological) claim. It would be a mistake however to understand his works as theological tractates. Indeed he wants to sketch for his – chiefly non-Jewish – readers a favorable, theologically correct picture of Judaism, wherein, while not openly proselyting, he still portrays a convincing religion of considerable respect, great antiquity, and great merit which is unjustly attacked by its opponents. This pro-Jewish element is the tie that binds the 'several personae', as well as being the achievement least disputed by his Jewish and non-Jewish critics: the imparting of knowledge about Jewish religion and history.

Josephus sold his *War* to 'a large number' of non-Jewish participants in the War of 66-70, as well as 'a large number' of Greek-educated Jews (*Ag. Ap.* 1:51). From further remarks about his goals as an author and his intended audience (e.g., *War* 1:16; *Ant.* 1:5, 9, 15; 4:196), it can be seen that he writes for readers of the educated Graeco-Roman upper class (or middle class).[40] He knew of course that Jewish readers could also benefit greatly from his work. For his writings imparted not only comprehensive instruction in the history of his people, past and present, but they also strengthened the consciousness of religious identity among his compatriots, since they were then able to see themselves as members of a venerable, convincing, indeed peerless, community of faith. Incidentally, early Christian apologetic literature was similarly structured. It represented its own views over against non-Christians or Christian heretics, but, at the same time, served internally to form Christian thinking and strengthen Christian

[39] Bomstad, *Governing Ideas*, correctly points this out.
[40] Momigliano, *Juden*, 73 remarks accurately, 'he must also reckon, to a great extent, with Greek speaking Jewish readers – probably much more than he admits'.

identity and faith.[41] We must conclude therefore that Josephus writes basically for the entire Graeco-Roman world, including the Jews. The potential readers (ἐντυγχάνοντες, *Ant.* 1:15, 129; 3:81; 4:196, 197; 8:26, 56, 132; 9:242; 12:59; 15:379; *Life* 345, 367; *Ag. Ap.* 1:1; 2:136, 147) are in any case not restricted to a particular group; that means, *inter alia*, that the Jews are neither excluded nor specially intended as addressees.[42] On the contrary *Ant.* 1:5, for example, speaks of 'all Greeks' (i.e., including educated Romans who understand Greek), while *Ant.* 1:9 speaks again of 'Greeks' (in the sense of non-Jews). Only in *Ant.* 4:197 does Josephus address expressly his Jewish readers.

Perhaps *Ant.* 16:174 describes most precisely Josephus' intended public: his historical work 'is chiefly meant to reach the Greeks (i.e., those who know Greek, the educated Graeco-Roman world)', therefore also, if secondarily, the Jews.

The question presents itself here concerning Josephus' own self-consciousness regarding the dichotomy Ἕλληνες-βάρβαροι, (Greeks-barbarians; cf. Paul in Rom 1:14) and Ἰουδαῖοι-Ἕλληνες, (Jews-Greeks; often in the New Testament, e.g., Rom 1:16; 2:9-10; 3:9; 10:12). He does not use the antithesis Ιουδαῖοι-Ἕλληνες, but speaks regularly of Ἕλληνες-βάρβαροι (*War* 5:117; 6:199; *Ant.* 1:107; 4:12; 8:284; 11:299; 16:176; 18:20; *Ag. Ap.* 1:58), where Ἕλληνες generally refers to the educated middle and upper classes (i.e., those who know Greek) of the *Imperium Romanum*, and βάρβαροι refers to all other inhabitants of the ancient world, including, it seems, the Jews. This is obviously the case, for example, in *Ant.* 14:187; 15:136; *Ag. Ap.* 1:116, 201 (however, in *Ag. Ap.* 2:282, βάρβαρος refers to non-Jews with the exception of the Greeks!). Thus one can truly describe Josephus as an 'oriental writer'.[43] However, he would probably have rejected for himself the possible equation Ἰουδαῖοι = βάρβαροι. He is a Jew and acknowledges it. Through his knowledge of Greek and Greek literary traditions however he certainly understands himself to be a Hellenist as well. A literary-sociological comparison of the self-understanding of Josephus and the New Testament writers would be most useful, beginning with the above mentioned dichotomies.

In the case of the very pro-Roman *War*, the Jews would seem to be the least likely candidates for the intended audience. Yet, as we have seen, Josephus says that he sold even this work to many Jews. The Aramaic original, intended above all for the Jews of Mesopotamia, cannot entirely

[41] Cf Schreckenberg, *Texte* 1, p16.

[42] Troiani, 'Lettori', incorrectly appears to limit Josephus' intended circle of readers to Greek-educated Diaspora Jews; Bilde, *Josephus*, 102 overlooks the intended Jewish audience.

[43] Cohen, 'History and Historiography', 9. It seems therefore only consistent that Christian miniatures in medieval Josephus manuscripts provide him with an oriental Jewish hat (see below).

many of the rudiments of the author's aims directed at a Jewish audience must have been retained in the Greek version. Even HATA assumes that the rewriting of the new Greek version of War consists of the addition of numerous digressions (geographical excurses, military details, speeches, etc.), thus, that the Aramaic first edition was only greatly expanded, while the basic text did not undergo any serious changes. Consequently there is no need to assume an audience only of 'Romans and Greeks', while ignoring the Jews as potential readers. Indeed, all Josephus' works were *also* intended for internal Jewish instruction.

Josephus' effect on non-Jewish readers was presumably also a factor in his reception by early Christianity. He was perhaps first made known to Christians via educated pagan readers. In any case, those pagans who read with interest Josephus' praises of the Jewish conception of God, must have also appeared, from Christian perspective, to be receptive to the Christian faith. As late as the third century there were still many pagans who were attracted by Jewish-Christian monotheism and Jewish-Christian ethics, and wavered undecided over which of the two religions they would attach themselves to.[45] Small wonder then that the Christian mission found fertile soil in the pagan readers of Josephus. After all, the New Testament message was intended, as were the works of Josephus, for 'Jews and Greeks' (i.e., pagans who knew Greek, including the Romans).[46] And, just as the New Testament authors, Josephus makes no concessions in essentials to the pagan religions. Both write in Greek, for only thus can the desired effect be achieved. The result is a unique possibility for comparative study of the process of hellenization which in certain respects runs parallel in the New Testament and in Josephus. Consideration of the sociological aspects of

[44] Hata, 'Greek Version' interprets the 'translating' of *War* 1:3 as 'a rewriting of the first version': 'In making the Greek version Josephus rewrote the first version *drastically* [emphasis, Hata] so that it might become more interesting and informative for his new audience – Romans and Greeks' (p108). But 'Ἑλλάδι γλώσσῃ μεταβαλεῖν means a Greek translation, and much of the content of the Greek version of *War* seems to be intended, at least partially, to make Jews reflect on the vanity of anti-Roman political messianism. Doubtless the Aramaic original intended to present to the Jews of Mesopotamia a positive view of Rome in the years 66-70, and to dampen possible thoughts of revolution. But the pacifistically inclined Diaspora Jews of the Mediterranean were reaffirmed by the Greek version as well. Therefore we cannot agree with Hata's limiting of the audience to 'Romans and Greeks'.

[45] Schreckenberg, *Texte* 1, p242-7.

[46] For example Acts 14:1; 18:4-5; Rom 1:16; 2:9f; 3:9; 10:12; 1 Cor 1:24; 10:32; 12:13; Gal 3:28. For the New Testament formula 'Jews-Greeks' cf Schreckenberg, *Texte* 1, 146-8; according to Rajak, "Archaeology", 477, 'a reconciliation of the two nations (sc. Jews and Greeks) is, as we know, his ultimate aim'. If this is correct – and there are good reasons for thinking so – it would point to a certain affinity between Josephus and the New Testament. That Josephus only partly achieved his goal of a reconciliation between the Jews and the political realities of the Roman empire is quite another matter, since the gradual abatement of Jewish nationalism did not begin until the failure of the revolts during the reign of Trajan (115-117) and Hadrian (132-135). Cf Bein, *Judenfrage* 1, p21.

literature could be helpful here.

Josephus is an apologist for Judaism above all in the *Antiquities* and *Against Apion*. Throughout, he not only defends the Jewish religion but also describes it as a religion of venerable age (in antiquity, a very weighty argument); a religion satisfying even the most demanding expectations; a teaching attractive even to non-Jews; a religion whose wise laws bring happiness to mankind;[47] indeed, a religion far superior to pagan polytheism. This is one of the factors in Josephus' popularity among early Christian authors; for here they found ample stimulation and ammunition for their anti-pagan apologetic.[48]

HELLENISTIC POPULAR PHILOSOPHY AND JEWISH THEOLOGY

Josephus' importance as instructor of early Christianity extends still further. Not the apologist alone, but the historian who indulges in excurses into philosophy as well, made an impression. Origen, Eusebius and other theologians thought and argued extensively in concepts drawn from Greek philosophy. For them, an author was welcome whose appreciation of Moses as the wise lawgiver was couched in the language of philosophy, and who portrayed such important figures of Jewish history as Moses and Abraham almost as Plato's philosopher kings and Stoic wise men.[49] To be sure, the comparison of Pharisaism to Stoicism is lame (*Life* 12), and the Pharisee Josephus is not a Stoic.[50] However, he was certainly educated in philosophy and well versed in the popular philosophy of his day. He was thus able to make proficient use of Greek philosophical terminology in acquainting his public (for the most part conversant with this thought world) with the Jewish religion as a form of true philosophy. In Josephus' time Stoicism, rather than late Platonism, was still the intellectual homeland of most educated people.

The question presents itself, of course, whether and how significant

[47] This spoke to the widespread felt need in antiquity for εὐδαιμονία, above all among educated groups, a need which popular philosophy and the mystery religions each tried to satisfy in their own way.

[48] As Josephus from the Greeks, so the Church fathers learned from Josephus. In this connection cf Schäublin, 'Josephus'.

[49] Feldman, 'Hellenizations', 150; incorrectly, Conzelmann, *Heiden-Juden-Christen*, 189: 'One cannot really speak of Josephus' knowledge of Greek philosophy'.

[50] Otherwise, Mayer, 'Josephus Flavius', 259: 'Josephus war Stoiker'. Similarly, already Norden, *Agnostos Theos*, 12, 19 considers Josephus' conception of God to be influenced by Stoicism. More accurately, Weiss, 'Pharisäismus und Hellenismus', 432 speaks of Josephus' 'Sympathie für die Stoa' and a certain affinity in substance. Martin, 'Josephus' Use', correctly traces *heimarmene* in Josephus to the influence from Hellenistic astrology – which however in turn is strongly influenced by Platonic and Stoic ideas with regard to conceptions of fate. The lack of comprehensive studies means that Josephus' relation to the philosophy of his day can be only vaguely described. Studies such as those by Flusser, *Judaism*, 610-6 are helpful.

content of the Jewish religion was obscured or distorted by being clothed in Greek terminology. Here opinions vary. Some see Josephus portraying Judaism not merely as true philosophy, but as a universal offer of salvation, a kind of world religion.[51] Others maintain that in order to stress philosophical definitions and to portray the Jewish patriarchs as Stoic wise men, he diminishes the importance of God or relinquishes the claim to election, presenting Judaism merely as one among many respected religions.[52] This arises out of a traditional view in Josephus research according to which the Jewish author was a characterless, would-be Roman and an assimilated cosmopolite. It is perhaps correct that he never regretted the loss of his homeland, Jerusalem and Judaea. He shows neither the pain of separation, nor homesickness, nor longing for Zion. It seems that only the practice of Tora is important to him, indeed that Tora itself becomes his intellectual habitat. Much later Heinrich HEINE speaks in this sense of the 'portative fatherland' of the Jews.[53]

To answer our question then, it is clear that Josephus nowhere diminishes the overarching importance of belief in the One God and the Tora. To be sure, he makes free use of popular philosophical conceptions such as *pronoia* (foreknowledge, divine providence), *tyche* (fortune, providence, fate) and *heimarmene* (destiny, fate, providence). But for him these are merely modes of operation of the One God, interpretation aids drawn from the popular philosophy of his day which was particularly influenced by Stoicism, but also shaped by other sources. Although he uses these concepts he never allows them to replace God or even to stand beside him. The case is rather that without God, nothing on earth happens, not even the change of earthly dominion, a major theme of the War.[54] However, Josephus does play down the revelatory character of the Tora, and says little about the election of Israel, the exclusive covenant of God with his people, and their messianic hopes. His main emphasis by far is to show the superiority of the Jewish religion by reason, e.g., by its world-wide acceptance and

[51] Cf Conzelmann, *Heiden-Juden-Christen*, 199 referring e.g. to *Ant*. 6:343; 18:128. For Josephus' interpretation of Judaism as 'true philosophy' see e.g. Weiss, 'Pharisäismus', 427f.

[52] Daniel, *Apologetics* argues in this direction.

[53] Van Unnik, in Conzelmann, *Heiden-Juden-Christen*, 190 remarks appropriately: 'Nowhere in Josephus does one sense that he is conscious of a difference between Judaism at home and Judaism abroad, given of course the possibility of living according to the Law.' Cf Dexinger, 'Messianisches Szenarium', 250: 'Although Judaism was uprooted from its geographical homeland, through the Bible it remained faithful to its spiritual homeland.' According to *Life* 422, Josephus received from Titus, in return for his lands at Jerusalem where Roman occupation troops had made their camp, 'a parcel of land in the plain' (i.e. probably the coastal plain). Presumably he directed the administration of this property from Rome, thus failing to develop a new sense of home.

[54] E.g. *War* 2:140: οὐ γὰρ δίχα θεοῦ περιγενέσθαι τινί τὸ ἄρχειν, 'since no ruler attains his office save by the will of God'; cf the strong affinity to Rom 13:1, οὐ γὰρ ἔστιν ἐξουσία εἰ μὴ ὑπὸ θεοῦ, αἱ δὲ οὖσαι ὑπὸ θεοῦ τεταγμέναι εἰσίν, 'for there is no authority except from God, and those that exist have been instituted by God'.

its philosophical quality. Thus, it seems, he hopes to make a greater impression among his readers.

With regard to his appreciation of the Tora, Josephus differs from Philo in one very important point. To be sure, he also overemphasizes the philosophical, thus giving it a Hellenistic gloss completely foreign to the biblical Tora. But he shows no tendency to understand the laws allegorically, thereby relativizing their relevance. Their literal demand is sternly retained, not reduced to an almost philosophically understood existence.[55] Only the high-priestly vestments and the architecture of the Temple does he interpret allegorically *(Ant.* 3:181-186).

Josephus and the Judaism of his Day

A PHARISEE, FAITHFUL TO THE LAW

Josephus' influence on early Christianity is by no means fully accounted for by his authorial characteristics, but is also due to his position in the Jewish cultural spectrum of his time. For all the friendliness toward Rome, which shows above all in his *War*, he is obviously true to his standpoint as a Pharisee Jew.[56] There is indeed no reason at all to doubt his statement that he attached himself (as an initiate) to Pharisaism as a young man (*Life* 12). According to CONZELMANN, 'for the Jews [Josephus] is an apostate'.[57] However, the texts which he cites (*Life* 423-424, 429; *War* 7:447-448) provide no support for this, but show rather that the historian, as numerous other prominent Jews (all of them apostates?), was slandered by revolutionary insurgents. It is well known that at the beginning of the war many Jerusalem Jews were pacifistically inclined without therefore being suspected of apostasy. Thus Josephus' report in his *War* suggests the presumption,

[55] See Heinemann, 'Allegoristik', 138: 'Aber er (Josephus) denkt weder daran, den Berichten der Tora, mögen sie den Griechen glaubhaft erscheinen oder nicht (Ant. III 81), durch Allegorisierung eine Scheinwirklichkeit zuzuschreiben, noch zeigt er die geringste Neigung zur Verflüchtigung der Gebote.' See also Heinemann, 'Josephus' Method', 180-203. Heinisch, *Einfluß*, 28 (*Ant.* 1:24, where ἀλληγορεῖν, 'to allegorize' is briefly mentioned), 181 (*Ant.* 1:73), 215 (*Ant.* 2:228), 238 (*Ant.* 3:178) is also helpful here.

[56] Even Schalit, 'Erhebung', 327, otherwise rather unfavorable in his judgement of Josephus' character, admits: 'Josephus war gläubiger pharisäischer Jude'. For Delling, 'Josephus' also the Jewish historian is 'letzten Endes toratreuer Pharisäer'. So also Josephus is primarily defended against the charge of apostasy by Windisch, *Orakel*, 65-69; Michel, 'Prophetentum'; and Smith, 'Palestinian Judaism', 67f. On the other hand Michel, 'Rettung', 974 qualifies: '...ihn schlechthin "pharisäisch" zu nennen, hat seine Bedenken'; and e.g. Weber, *Josephus*, 23 (cf 25, 77, 128) calls him a 'Römling und Apostat'. Mason, 'Josephus a Pharisee?' is not convincing in his interpretation of *Life* 10-12, for Josephus makes a definite decision for Pharisaism which, along with Sadducaism, he had come to know while still in his father's house and its environs. It was only Essenism that he had to study *in situ*, with Bannus in the wilderness.

[57] Conzelmann, *Heiden-Juden-Christen*, 31.

'that almost everybody in the court of Gamliel II had either fled Jerusalem during the early stages of the war, or had been absent from the first and stayed away'.[58] There are also good reasons for comparing Josephus and his behavior with Yohanan ben Zakkai, who, according to the legendary Talmud account (bGit 56a-b), went over to the Romans and greeted Vespasian as (future) ruler.[59] One is also reminded of Jeremiah, to whom Josephus compares himself (*War* 5:391-393).[60] The attempt by SHUTT to defend the Jewish historian completely misfires.[61] He presents him as a 'liberal Jew', who, e.g., with τὸ ϑεῖον means 'the Deity', without necessarily referring to the God of Israel. But this is a misunderstanding; for just as with ϑεός and ὁ ϑεός, in Josephus τὸ ϑεῖον is consistently to be understood universally. In Josephus' view it is self-evident that the God of Israel is also the universal God. With his terminology he is merely considering his philosophically educated readers who understood τὸ ϑεῖον and ὁ ϑεός without difficulty in the context of Greek, above all Stoic, henotheistic and monotheistic views. This is also true in the sphere of ethics. Here also Jewish religious conceptions far outweigh the Hellenistic elements in Josephus' thinking.[62] Moreover, that he has not relinquished the concept 'people of God', but rather thinks universally wherever apparent syncretistic ideas encroach, is clear alone from his self-coined word ϑεοκρατία (theocracy; *Ag. Ap.* 2:165). For here, God is first and foremost the God of Israel, but then also the God of all the world at large, the God of the pre-Socratics, of Plato, and of the Stoics, as can be seen in the larger context (*Ag. Ap.* 2:157-171; cf. the universalistic tendency in *Ag. Ap.* 2:284). This universalism is one of the bridges that connect Josephus with the New Testament.

The very fact that Josephus acknowledges himself a believing, pious Jew became an important factor for his reception in early Christianity. An apostate, or dissident, an unstable or doubting Jew could never have made so favorable a pro-Christian witness from the enemy camp as Josephus actually became.

DISTANCE FROM THE SYNAGOGUE TRADITIONS AFTER 70

Josephus' value for the Christian authors of the second-fifth centuries was probably enhanced by the fact that he himself did not participate in the new rabbinic orientation that took place after 70 and thus did not publish in his native language – the Aramaic original of the *War* can be regarded as an

[58] Neusner, *A Life*, 166.
[59] Cf Michel, 'Prophetentum'.
[60] See Windisch, *Orakel*, 65ff: 'one may as well call Jeremiah apostate as Josephus'.
[61] Shutt, 'Concept'.
[62] Already convincingly demonstrated by Hoffmann, *Ethik*; correctly also, Bilde, *Josephus*, 201: 'The hellenistic designations for God do not represent any major changes in the Jewish concept.'

exception. In accordance with this distancing from rabbinic Judaism, Josephus, strangely enough, reports nothing worth mentioning about the institution of the synagogue and its importance for the survival of Judaism after 70, although it was the synagogues of the Diaspora where the liturgy and the traditions of Jewish religious communities developed, traditions which contributed to the unbroken continuity with which Judaism overcame the loss of the Temple. The synagogue service, the forms of reading, translating and commenting on the Bible which developed in and with it, as well as Jewish customs surrounding the synagogue and the care for religious education of children and adults – none of this holds any interest for Josephus. He mentions briefly only that Moses had introduced the custom of Tora study on the Sabbath (*Ag. Ap.* 2:175; cf. *Ant.* 16:43).[63] A rabbinically oriented author, more involved in the Tora tradition and thereby less interested in contemporary non-Jewish Hellenistic literature, would, as such, have been far less useful to early Christianity.

TENDENTIOUS DEPICTION OF MESSIANIC MOVEMENTS

To the tendentious distortions of the War belongs the hostile depiction of the Zealots, indeed, of all the various groups of rebels against Rome in the period before 70, a long-recognized phenomenon.[64] With obvious intent, Josephus refuses to recognize the apocalyptic and messianic groups of his day which, as opposed to the Jewish historian, bound up their messianic expectations with an anti-Roman militancy. Josephus' θεοκρατία (*Ag. Ap.* 2:165) requires no independence from Rome, but rather faithfulness to Tora by the Jewish people, no political Messiah, but the piety and righteousness of its citizens. Thus he considers the various rebel groups as bandits and seditionists who despise God's commandments and do not truly act in the interest of the people.

At any rate, he differentiated for the most part between militant and more peaceful groups of the populace and considered the ἅλωσις (capture) as a disciplinary punishment of God, as a great suffering, in which a way to (messianic?) salvation is possible were God to be reconciled through contrition and penitence (*War* 5:19-20).[65] Early Christian theologians took from such statements material appropriate for their purpose, and, feeling

[63] Momigliano, *Juden*, 70 remarks correctly: 'Er (Josephus) läßt kein Verständnis der Institution erkennen, die die Juden sogar zusammengehalten hatte, bevor der Tempel verschwunden war: die Synagoge.' Bilde's criticism (*Josephus*, 166) of Momigliano goes too far.

[64] Among the new studies on this topic, the following deserve special attention: Bomstad, *Governing Ideas*; Kallander, *Defense*; Guevara, *La resistencia*, 140ff, 156ff, 162ff; Michel, 'Rettung', 968; Schreckenberg, 'Wirkungsgeschichte' 1112f, 1159; most recently, Hengel, *Zealots*; and Schwier, *Tempel*.

[65] The sentence δύναιο δ' ἂν γενέσθαι πάλιν ἀμείνων, εἴγε ποτὲ τὸν πορθήσαντα θεὸν ἐξιλάσῃ (Yet might there be hopes for an amelioration of thy lot, if ever thou wouldst

themselves supported by Josephus, interpreted the ἅλωσις as the destroying wrath of God, which also included the entire Jewish Diaspora. In the course of the Christian Josephus tradition, the differentiations that Josephus himself had made disappeared, the rebel groups were identified with the Jewish people *per se*, and the fall of Jerusalem with the fall of Israel. This generalization, which in rudimentary form is already present in the *War*, is consistently continued and extended. Josephus' anti-Zealotism therefore is an important precondition for his influence in Christianity. From the Christian standpoint, the victory of the Romans over the insurgent groups could, in a certain sense, appear almost as a victory of Christianity over Judaism, or at least the preliminary to this victory. Indeed, the legendary Christian Josephus traditions especially, as for example in the *Vindicta Salvatoris* legends, made the Roman rulers the avengers of Jesus Christ, who undergo baptism and march into the Holy Land to punish the Jews for their crimes against the Saviour.[66] Here the equation Romans = Christians is realized, and the legendary has superimposed itself over the historical.

Since Josephus disparages the political messianism of his compatriots, or treats it at most as a marginal phenomenon, it is small wonder that in the *Antiquities* neither the Land promises nor the theology of the Land appear; for a political revolution related to the land of Israel was irreconcilable with Judaism's peaceful existence under Roman rule, which he hoped for. For Josephus it is not the land of Israel that stands at the center of Jewish life, but the geographically unfixed observance of the Law which brings about salvation and blessing (and eventually redemption?).[67] These are the very convictions that strengthen his influence on early Christianity; for the express expectation of a Jewish Messiah would have rendered him far less interesting from the Christian viewpoint. There was, so to speak, a vacuum which invited supplementation with the fictional witness to Christ (*Ant.* 18:63-64). Jewish history as represented by Josephus became in the Christian assessment a sort of *praeparatio evangelica*, a preparation for the New Testament message and a preliminary stage of the new Christian religion. In addition, in his canon of the Bible (*Ag. Ap.* 1:38-42) Josephus distances himself from Apocalyptic – another vacuum, to be filled in by Christian eschatology.

propitiate that God who devastated thee!) is somewhat unclear, but the interpretation of γενέσθαι ἀμείνων as a messianic (or pre-messianic?) salvific healing is perhaps not far-fetched. See Nikiprowetzky, 'La mort', 487. However, it must be seen that God's favor toward men, his *eudaimonia* and salvation, result primarily from practicing Tora.

[66] Examples of such legends can be found in Schreckenberg, *Untersuchungen*, 53ff, and *Texte* 1, p463-5.

[67] Cf Amaru, 'Land Theology', 201-29.

JOSEPHUS' OWN MESSIANIC PRETENSIONS?

We come now to a particularly difficult question in our study: did Josephus himself entertain certain messianic ambitions? It is first necessary to view briefly the 'messianic scenario' of the post-Herodian period before 70, and above all the persons, groups and movements mentioned by Josephus that can more or less be characterized as 'messianic':[68]

1. Judas son of Ezekias (*Ant.* 17:271-272; *War* 2:56).
2. Simon of Peraea (*Ant.* 17:273-276; *War* 2:57-59).
3. A movement similar to the group led by Simon of Peraea (*Ant.* 17:277; *War* 2:59).
4. Athronges (*Ant.* 17:278-285; *War* 2:60-65).
5. Judas of Galilee (*Ant.* 18:4-9, 23-25; *War* 2:117-118).
6. Theudas (*Ant.* 20:97-98).
7. The Egyptian false prophet (*Ant.* 20:169-172; *War* 2:261-263).
8. The 'impostor' (γόης; *Ant.* 20:188).
9. The religious enthusiasts who led their followers into the wilderness (*Ant.* 20:167-168; *War* 2:258-260).
10. Manaemos (Menahem), son of Judas of Galilee (*War* 2:433-440, 442-449; *Life* 21, 46).
11. Simon bar Giora (*War* 4:514-544, 556ff, 763ff and elsewhere).
12. John of Gischala (*War* 4:389ff and elsewhere).
13. The Samaritan Messiah (*Ant.* 18:85-87).
14. Jonathan the Weaver (*War* 7:437-450; *Life* 424-425). His activities took place in the period ca. 71-73, after the fall of Jerusalem in 70, but by their nature are connected to the period 66-70.
15. Rome-hating 'impostors' (γόητες; *War* 2:264-265).
16. A false prophet in Jerusalem who prophesied God's salvation even after the burning of the Temple (*War* 6:285).

The agitation which became concrete in these various messianic movements covering a broad spectrum of the populace, or as the case may be, (national) messianism per se, was regarded with caution not only by the Rabbis but also by Philo.[69] To apocalyptic enthusiasm, Philo opposes an

[68] We refer here above all to the dependable information in Dexinger, 'Messianisches Szenarium'.

[69] Dexinger, 'Messianisches Szenarium', 250ff, 266ff. Philo, who like Josephus was influenced by Hellenistic thinking, also attempted 'to portray the Old Testament religion so that it could meet the demands of Graeco-Roman thinking. This tendency must certainly have determined his attitude towards messianism' (p250). Obviously any noticeable echo of the messianic movements between the death of Herod the Great and the fall of the Second Temple is absent in Rabbinic literature. Like Josephus, the Pharisee circles of the first century distanced themselves from it. 'Moreover, the structure of these [messianic] ideas may have been such that, after 70, no one wished to speak of them' (ib 266). With regard to the Rabbis of late antiquity, it is well known that messianic expectation takes a place of minor importance as compared with observance of the Law.

expectation of the messianic age that hopes to reach its goal by means of rationality, insight, and (rational, philosophical) conviction. Just as in Josephus the founding of a ϑεοκρατία had no need of a (national-revolutionary) Messiah, but rather pious fulfillment of the Law based on insight, so it is also true, '...that Philo needs no Messiah in his philosophical thinking: it is not a mysterious figure, but moral rationality that can usher in the Ideal Age. On the other hand he is confronted by the messianic traditions of his day. Thus he must opt for reinterpretation. Israel's role is hallmarked by the task of persuading, not by ushering in the Ideal Age with a military victory. For his educated readers, such an idea would have been at best embarrassing.'[70]

The limitations of this study make it impossible to address *in extenso* the activities of the persons and groups listed above. However, even a cursory glance at the cited passages shows that Josephus exhibited many similarities of behavior with other contemporary popular leaders while serving as general of the revolutionaries in Galilee, and consequently cannot be summarily excluded from such an investigation. These popular leaders represented, each in his own way, the diffuse religious moods of their time. Some chose the means of political and military action as a way of forcing God, so to speak, to intervene and thus bring about his kingdom (ϑεοκρατία), i.e., they sought 'to create an eschatological situation',[71] an environment in which God could manifest himself. In my judgement, Josephus himself was not entirely free of messianic pretensions. It has been correctly observed that he thought 'that he was divinely authorised to play a leading political and military role'.[72] He not only puts great value on his descendancy from a most noble priestly family (*Life* 2), but, more importantly, emphasizes his royal heritage (*Life* 2; *Ant.* 16:187). He not only portrays himself as the 'ideal general',[73] but in certain respects also as a 'second Moses' and 'an ideal figure like the Philonic Moses: priest, prophet, and legislator'.[74] It is consistent with this that the Galileans greet him as 'benefactor and saviour' (εὐεργέτης καὶ σωτήρ, *Life* 244, 259). Josephus speaks not only of his almost unlimited power in Galilee (τότε μέγα δυναμένου, *Life* 347), he not only describes himself (indirectly) as the most important leader of the Jews in the war against Rome (*War* 3:143-144, 340), but he also reports (flattered?!) that a powerful rival had accused him of desiring to enter Jerusalem in triumph as despot (*War* 2:626), i.e., a kind of messianic entrance, as indeed another insurgent leader, Simon bar Giora, actually did, being greeted as 'saviour and protector' (*War* 4:575). Also

[70] Dexinger, 'Messianisches Szenarium', 252. There is not the least suggestion by Dexinger that Josephus himself may have considered himself a messianic candidate. For ϑεοκρατία see also Amir, '*Theokratia*'.

[71] Parente, 'Account'.

[72] Attridge, 'Josephus', 191.

[73] Cohen, *Josephus*, 91, 93f.

[74] ib, 92f.

consistent with our assumption of certain messianic pretensions in Josephus are his efforts as 'warlord' to revive within his environs righteousness and sinlessness, i.e., to bring about a kind of messianic peace and well-being by virtuous living (*War* 2:581): the army is to abstain from their 'customary misdeeds, from theft, robbery and plunder, and defraud no more their neighbor for the sake of vile profit'. This ethical paranetic clearly exceeds the demands of military discipline, and brings to mind the principles of early Christian ethics as they were reported by Pliny:

> [They] bound themselves by a solemn oath, not to any wicked deeds, but never to commit any fraud, theft or adultery, never to falsify their word, nor deny a trust when they should be called upon to deliver it up.[75]

If our assumption that Josephus himself was not entirely free of messianic ambitions is correct, we must ask why he addresses this only indirectly and in somewhat veiled references. The answer is that of the various leaders of messianic movements known to us through the Jewish historian, none of them make this claim expressly! Even Jesus of Nazareth, according to the oldest strata of the New Testament (Mark, Q), nowhere presented himself as Messiah, apparently because it was generally understood in first century Judaism that no one could name himself as the Messiah, but had to wait for the call from God. Thus Jesus' (forced, and finally, unavoidable) answer to the question of his messiahship is itself the cause of his death.[76]

Josephus described at some distance of time the period before 70. He reported with obvious disapproval the messianic movements of his day which, in his judgement, were incapable of bringing about a lasting situation of peace and well-being, and from whom God justifiably withheld his divine call. On the other hand, allusively at least, he lets his readers know – *sapienti sat* – that he considered himself suitable to lead his people in a time of crisis on the right road to salvation. Indeed, he even believes himself to have been the recipient of God's revealed will concerning the Jewish people, and to have been entrusted by God with foretelling the future (*War* 3:351-354).

To present himself as Messiah was impossible; on the other hand, to show himself in retrospect to be a failed Messiah candidate was likewise impossible. However, as author he could still attempt to formulate a kind of doctrine of salvation, a philosophically based theocracy in which the messianic peace became reality for Jews and Greeks reconciled in faith in the one God. In Josephus' view this state of affairs was not eschatological, nor bound up with the imminent end of the world, nor was it to be brought about by a powerful Messiah figure shaking off the Roman yoke. The lasting eschatological peace could only be realized through philosophically

[75] *Epist*. 10:96, ed Melmoth 2, p402. For the aspect of adultery cf *Life* 80: γυναῖκα μὲν πᾶσαν ἀνύβριστον ἐφύλαξα, 'yet I preserved every woman's honor'.
[76] Mark 14:62-64; cf O'Neill, 'Silence'.

based insight into the salvation and redemption bringing power of the Tora, and not through (the ephemeral) war against Rome. Here also, *mutatis mutandis*, a strong affinity to early Christian ideas appears.

It must be admitted that Josephus' role as 'warlord' in Galilee, his self-understanding, is not clearly defined. It seems that, finding himself in a competitive situation with other (latent or openly messianic) groups and movements, he shared, at least partially, their motives and interests, and in his depiction of the events much later, perhaps out of vanity, lets it be known what possibilities had been open to him in his day. Apparently he believed, at the very least, that he could operate in the approach leading to messianic salvation, and be active here in preparing the way.

The very vehemence with which he polemizes against various actors in the messianic scenario could be an indication that – up until his capture in Jotapata – he himself was a part of this scenario as one of its candidates. In central convictions as well, there are more things in common than Josephus' reports reveal at first glance. For example, for him, just as for Judas the Galilean (*War* 2:118; *Ant.* 18:23), only God is to be recognized as ruler and king; his conception of θεοκρατία alone shows this (*Ag. Ap.* 2:165). Moreover, it would be methodologically false to use the messianism of Jesus of Nazareth, transcendentally transformed through a long Christian tradition, to judge the closely-related messianic movements of that time. The spectrum of the messianic scene was probably more extensive and differentiated than it at first appears. Perhaps one must grant Josephus a place in it as well.

Josephus and Rome

As historian, Josephus is convinced of Rome's invincibility and thus, that any resistance to the God-willed world dominion of the Romans is futile. And perhaps he sees as well the advantages of the *pax romana* since Octavian's victory, a world-wide peace the blessings of which not only Rome itself but all peoples enjoyed.[77] As political realist and rational

[77] Cf Wengst, *Pax Romana*, who accurately describes the attitudes of the various New Testament texts towards Rome, in particular the relative sympathy of the Lucan writings, but whose overall picture of the Roman 'power structure' is probably too negatively drawn. Doubtless it was a 'Gewaltfrieden' (p171), but the majority of Mediterranean inhabitants do not seem to have viewed it so critically. Wengst's picture derives partly from his unbalanced selection of sources and partly from his own rather emotional standpoint. Nevertheless the texts cited by Wengst, especially those of the New Testament, do not regard the *pax romana* as an ultimate state of well-being, but as something temporary. Cassidy, *Society* shows that Luke neither accepts Rome's dominion theologically nor defends Christianity against it. Fully conscious of the incompatibility of Christian principles with those of Roman rule, Luke seeks a *modus vivendi*. Thus an important goal of his work is 'to provide his fellow Christians with guidance for their exercise of Christian discipleship within the context of Roman rule' (p158). If this is correct – and the argument seems sound – there are clear affinities with the literary goals of Josephus here.

historiographer, like Thucydides, he recognizes above all the positive elements in the historically given situation: under the certain protection of Roman rule, the Jews can practice their religion and teach it to their children unmolested. This by no means indicates unqualified acceptance of Roman power, and he had no intention of conceding the everlastingness of the Roman Empire.[78]

By naming his work on the events of 66-70, *Jewish War* ('Ιουδαϊκὸς πόλεμος; *Ant.* 1:203; 18:11; *Life* 413; cf. *Ant.* 20:258; *Life* 27, 412), Josephus uses a formula evoking the Roman perspective, as, for example, Julius Caesar in his *Bellum gallicum*. His appearance on the scene as a prophet is also in Roman interests; for in *War* 6:312-313 (cf. *War* 3:361, 399-408) it is Vespasian who fulfills the prophecy about the world ruler from Judaea (Num 24:17-19, or Dan 7:13-14; 12:1; Gen 49:10).[79] In a certain sense he actually did see himself standing in the prophetic tradition of Jeremiah (cf. *War* 5:391ff), or perhaps as a new Daniel, but in any case – not least of all because of his priestly office – as a legitimate prophet (*War* 3:351ff). Moreover, Josephus the Pharisee seems to have believed himself possessed of a prophetic gift peculiar to the Pharisees.[80] Jeremiah (*Ant.* 10:79) and Daniel (*Ant.* 10:276 to Dan 9:24ff) having prophesied the future dominion of the Romans, Josephus, with similar activities (*War* 3:399-408), found himself in the best of company.

At all events it is clear that Josephus attaches no messianic qualities at all to Vespasian. He did indeed secure Vespasian's favor by means of the prophecy; without the latter's pardon either execution or life imprisonment awaited him after the triumphal procession, for thus Rome customarily dealt with captured insurgents. And it is true that he refers biblical texts which could be interpreted messianically (among these perhaps Dan 2:34 as well) to Vespasian as new ruler, but this is not a 'kind of Roman messianism', nor, for Josephus, does Vespasian appear even within the framework of 'pre-messianic events'.[81] Neither does Yohanan ben Zakkai imply messianic reverence when he addresses Vespasian as 'king' (bGit 56a-b). To be sure it was somewhat bold for Josephus to interpret biblical texts with messianic components (such as Num 24:17-19) not in a religious-messianic sense, but with profane, political-historical, and non-Jewish reference. In

[78] Oepke, *Gottesvolk*, 130.

[79] Dexinger, 'Messianisches Szenarium', 255ff mentions in this connection Dan 2:34 as well. But which text Josephus actually meant remains uncertain.

[80] For the question of succession to Daniel see also Momigliano, *Juden*, 75: 'Man kann sich schwerlich des Eindrucks erwehren, daß Flavius Josephus in irgendeiner Schicht seines Bewußtseins sich mit Daniel gleichsetzte.' See also Cohen, 'Josephus, Jeremiah, and Polybius', who correctly notes clear affinities between Josephus and Jeremiah; and cf Cohen, *Josephus*, 232: 'He viewed himself as a Jeremiah redivivus (cf B.J. 5:391-393) who announced God's will.'

[81] *Contra* Dexinger, 'Messianisches Szenarium', 255ff.

any event here too he retained his reserve against everything that resembled political messianism.

Moreover, Josephus' friendliness towards Rome is limited in another way: he nowhere praises the lot of Roman subjects and never Roman religion or culture. On the other hand he values the legal protection which the consul Lentulus, Julius Caesar, the Triumvirate, Augustus and others granted the Jews by decree.[82] There are two reasons that Josephus cites this legal protection, in certain respects the forerunner of the medieval letters of safe conduct for Jews issued by the Frankish rulers, so extensively. On the one hand he thereby documents anti-Jewish activity, from whichever quarter it proceeds, as violating the traditions of Roman law. That is, he safeguards, legally so to speak, the living space of the Jewish people within the Roman Empire against potential enemies. On the other hand he provided his fellow Jews, to whom as we have seen the *Antiquities* was also addressed, with confidence that they could live unmolested and legally protected within the Roman Empire, enabled them to appeal to this protection if necessary and actually created the basis of trust for internally accepting the status quo after 70.

At the bottom of such intentions certainly is Josephus' deeply motivated, overall view with regard to a prosperous future for the Jewish people, not merely the shallow, tactical effort, after the pro-Roman *Jewish War*, to regain his compatriots' favor with the pro-Jewish *Antiquities*.[83]

Josephus' proximity to the imperial family repeats itself to some extent in the situation of the Church father, Eusebius. Both are in their own way favorable towards Rome. Whereas Josephus was, in certain respects, court historian, Eusebius could, with some justification, because of his political and spiritual proximity to Constantine, be considered the emperor's court or state bishop. Among other things Josephus in his books identifies with the interests of Judaism and its need for a secured existence within the Roman Empire, just as Eusebius in his way acts for early Christianity. It may have been this which made the bishop feel related to the Jewish historian, whose works he consults most extensively. But unlike Josephus, who recognizes the Roman power as divinely ordained and affirms its practical use, Eusebius is comparatively unreserved in seeking an alliance with the political power in order to realize the idea of a Christian empire

[82] *Ant.* 14:190-212, 213-216, 217-222, 223-227, 241-246, 256-258, 259-261, 262-264, 306-323; 16:160-173; cf 14:186-189, 265-267; 16:174-178. See Saulnier, 'Lois romaines'.

[83] Thus the negative judgment of Josephus by Laqueur, *Historiker*. Cf Weber's comment (above n56). Also, it is already questionable whether one can call the *War* mere 'pro-Roman propaganda', and broadly attribute a 'pro-Jewish tendency' to the *Antiquities* (Thoma, 'Weltanschauung', 51f); for in the *War* it is not 'all things Roman' as such that are elevated, but Titus and Vespasian. The *Antiquities* too is less a propaganda tract than an impressive Jewish confession of faith, of adherence to the traditions and values of Jewish religion and history. If it made an impression on non-Jews, so much the better. But this does not make the *Antiquities* a 'Tendenzschrift'.

that anticipates the Heavenly kingdom. But Josephus' θεοκρατία is basically non-political and in any case constitutionally undefined (*Ag. Ap.* 2:165). It needs no emperor, but rather a priestly aristocracy to guide the people.[84] As one of its members, he feels justified in his role of admonisher and teacher of Israel.

Josephus and Jesus Nazarenus

HIS SILENCE ON CHRISTIANITY

That Josephus, although contemporary with the evangelists, mentions Jesus of Nazareth and Christianity only rarely (*Ant.* 18:63-64; 18:116-119; 20:200 – see below p58), has always been considered as less than satisfactory from the Christian point of view. For it was obvious that his acquaintance with the Jesus movement was better than the minimal echo in his work betrays. It may be conceded that to a writer living in Rome at the time this movement must have appeared as another of those apocalyptic-messianic Jewish groups present before 70. These also he mentions for the most part only briefly, and in the context of the relevant accounts lets the readers know indirectly that there are more γόητες, ἀπατεῶνες (deceivers), πλάνοι (seducers), and pseudo-prophets than he actually names (*Ant.* 17:217; 20:167-168; cf. *War* 2:258-260).

However, Josephus must have seen that the Jesus movement, in contrast to other less important undertakings, continued to flourish even after 70. By that time it increasingly laid aside its inner-Jewish character and became a group *sui generis*, whose congregations developed alongside the Jewish Diaspora communities and gradually began to compete with them.

Why then is Josephus for the most part silent concerning a movement already fairly significant during his lifetime? As an opponent of the anti-Roman political messianism of his time, he probably did not want to see Judaism compromised by this group. For in the eyes of educated Greeks and Romans the Jesus movement appeared for a long time yet as a messianic-apocalyptic Jewish (or strongly judaizing) sect, and the aversion of Rome to such sects, in particular to Christianity, cannot have been unknown to him. As a conscientious historiographer he was obliged in any case to report at least briefly and somewhat objectively about the groups before 70. They were already a part of past history, but, in that respect also, no longer virulent in the eighties and nineties. With Christianity the situation was different. For most of its contemporaries this developing group still had no clear identity, still no recognizable profile that would have distinguished it from Judaism. Extensive literary combat against such a group

[84] Cf also Weiler, *Theocracy*, 3-23: 'The concept of theocracy: its origin and meaning in Josephus'; Tosato, 'La teocrazia'.

would, unnecessarily in his view, have placed too high a value on it.

Our interpretation is not contradicted by the extensive account of John the Baptist (*Ant.* 18:116-119), but confirmed by it: Josephus saw John still as a genuinely Jewish figure, whose activities by no means transgressed or compromised the framework of Judaism. Perhaps he even saw in John affinities to the hermit Bannus with whom he had lived for three years as a youth (*Life* 11-12).

In short: an extensive and objective description of the beliefs and goals of early Christianity could easily have disturbed his apologetically well-rounded, grand picture of the Jewish religion and thereby have made it less attractive to Greeks and Romans. What remains therefore is only the briefest possible, relatively unpolemical, reference, doing no injury to Judaism's claim to truth and making no concessions to the new, still developing movement.

This suggestion allows us to avoid the numerous hypothetical attempts to find the missing, comprehensive criticism of Christianity in Josephus. We begin with FORNARO:[85] Moses (*Ant.* 4:326) is enveloped in a cloud and disappears in a valley. With the biblical account of his death Moses wanted to prevent the Israelites from believing in his ascension and reception into Heaven by God. Thus Josephus formulates his report, argues Fornaro, in order to criticise the Christian belief in the empty tomb and the ascension of Jesus of Nazareth. However, Josephus' tendency to explain the miraculous rationalistically to his enlightened Hellenistic readers is more likely at work here. Similarly, and just as unconvincing, is the attempt[86] to prove that he is combatting Christian views in his depiction of the Flood, the Abrahamic and Sinaitic covenants, and other themes, by, for example, reducing or even eliminating the biblical-theological importance of the covenant bonds which the Christians made theological use of for their own purposes. Such hypotheses are too weakly founded. Their plausibility disappears if the (indeed remarkable) silence by Josephus on the subject of Christianity can be explained in other ways. At any rate it is not possible to smuggle through the back door, so to speak, extensive, though hidden, positions on Christianity. Even a rebus fails of its purpose if it is too strongly encoded.

THE TESTIMONIUM FLAVIANUM

Josephus' *Antiquities* contains an account of Jesus of Nazareth (*Ant.* 18:63-64), which under the name *Testimonium Flavianum* has received an enormous amount of attention from both Church fathers and modern scholars. As it stands, the passage can hardly be authentic in its entirety.

[85] Fornaro, 'Il Christianesimo'.

[86] Paul, 'Anitiquities'; see further Schreckenberg, 'Flavius Josephus und die lukanischen Schriften'; and Feldman's appropriate criticism of Paul, 'Josephus' Portrait', 56.

Most scholars correctly consider the brief reference to James, 'the brother of the supposed Christ' (*Ant.* 20:200) and the more elaborate account of 'John the so-called Baptist' (*Ant.* 18:116-119) as genuine. Josephus probably did not consider John part of earliest Christianity and therefore discussed him more extensively. *Ant.* 18:63-64 on the other hand, which bluntly states about Jesus, 'He was the Christ', is generally regarded as a Christian interpolation. Nonetheless, it could very well contain a genuine nucleus, consisting of a passing reference made in the context of the Pilate account in the neutral, aloof style of *Ant.* 20:200. Presumably Josephus briefly related Pilate's execution of a messianic pretender in connection with his historical report about the Roman governor.[87]

The tradition-historical problems associated with the *Testimonium Flavianum* will be dealt with in the sections on Origen and Eusebius (below p58, 65). Here we will briefly examine the text itself. Already the very first word is unparalleled in Josephus in this form,[88] the historical present γίνεται as meaning: 'there lived at that time...' Likewise unparalleled is (ἔργων) ποιητής (doer; this contra VERMES, 'The Jesus Notice'), and other material which we cannot here examine further. Furthermore, the hypothesis (*argumentum*, προγραφή) to the eighteenth book of the *Antiquities*[89] does not mention the Jesus text. Such information on the content, intended to give the reader an overview of the book, was customarily placed separately at the beginning of the individual books by the booksellers or even by the authors themselves; at all events it originated already in antiquity. For the most part such 'hypotheses' provide no more than an approximation of the contents, but the likelihood that *Ant.* 18:63-64 is spurious is strengthened by this fact. That Photius fails to mention the *Testimonium* in his broad range of excerpts from Josephus also strengthens this impression. In fact its absence from this single manuscript is weightier than its presence in the remaining codices.[90] An even more serious objection to genuineness is that the phrases οὐκ ἐπαύσαντο (they did not cease) and εἰς ἔτι τε νῦν ...

[87] Less likely is the association first suggested by Mensinga, 'Eigenthümlichkeit', between *Ant.* 18:63-64 and the Mundus-Paulina episode in 18:65ff, the supposed cohabitation of a woman with a god, understood as a travesty on Jesus' divine conception. Most recently see Baras, 'Testimonium Flavianum'. Worthwhile are Nodet, 'Jesus' and Birdsall, 'Enigma', who considers the entire passage the work of a clever falsifier. As against this Attridge, 'Josephus', 216 concludes, 'It seems likely that the passage is at basis genuine, although it has probably been altered in some details, by Christian transmitters of the text.' Laqueur's thesis (*Historiker*) that Josephus added the *Testimonium* to please Christians and thereby ingratiate himself among them may be regarded as a curiosity.

[88] See Rengstorf, *Concordance*, s.v.; Eisler, *Iêsous basileus* 2, p772f, has misjudged this.

[89] Niese, *Flavii Josephi opera* 4, p138f; cf Niese 4, LVII and Plümacher, 'Neues Testament', 112f.

[90] Schreckenberg, *Tradition*, 120-2. See also Grant, *Eusebius*, 100: '...The passage was certainly absent from the text of Josephus which Photius carefully excerpted at Constantinople in the ninth century'. Two recent examples from the boundless literature on the *Testimonium*: Poetscher, 'Josephus Flavius'; and Meier, 'Jesus'.

οὐκ ἐπέλιπε τὸ φῦλον (and the tribe ... has still to this day not disappeared) date things in the relatively remote past, while Josephus speaks of the only slightly more recent war (66-70) as in the present; similarly *Ag. Ap.* 1:46: τοῦ γενομένου νῦν (!) ἡμῖν πολέμου, 'of the war we are now experiencing'. If a war already thirty years past at the time of the composition of *Against Apion* can be spoken of as in the present, an event only slightly older can hardly be regarded as in the distant past. On the other hand the formulation 'still to this day' fits perfectly the time frame for a forger active long after Josephus. The same is true of Christian exegesis of the prophets – Isaiah, among others – (τῶν θείων προφητῶν ... εἰρηκότων, 'the divine[ly inspired] prophets having spoken ...') which since the second and third centuries has been used for anti-Jewish apologetic purposes.

A CATALYSIS FOR CHRISTIAN INTERPRETATION

At all events the reports on John the Baptist and James in *Ant.* 18:116-119 and 20:200, and perhaps the genuine kernel of the *Testimonium* in *Ant.* 18:63-64, were sufficient to generate a process of Christian interpretation. Moreover, the accounts in Josephus which offered numerous details concerning persons and events of New Testament history had a powerful motivating effect in this process. The attraction was made even stronger by Josephus' asseveration (only too readily believed) that he intended to report everything historiographically 'precise' and 'true' (e.g., *War* 1:2, 6, 9, 16; *Ant.* 14:3). Another potentially effective factor was his promise to report biblical history without emending it (i.e., without adding or omitting anything, e.g., *Ant.* 1:17; 10:218; 20:260-261; *Ag. Ap.* 1:42). This does not mean that he translated his sources, chiefly the Bible (from Hebrew), word for word and then reported them literally, but that he worked within the given framework of Jewish tradition as God-given, without arbitrarily altering it. If this is correct, the same respect stands behind his words as is shown by the Preacher in Eccl 3:14: 'I know that whatever God does endures for ever; nothing can be added to it, nor anything taken from it'. The claim to historiographical veracity by Josephus, who, although a Jew, gives an account of Jesus of Nazareth, contributed to his later Christian traditionists regularly describing him with the epitheton ornans, 'truth-loving'.[91]

Of the many Josephus accounts touching New Testament history, those that suggested a direct bridge to a Christian perspective on the same events have special importance. Thus the affinity between the sale of surviving Jewish prisoners-of-war into slavery (*War* 3:540; 6:414-419; cf. *War* 6:384:

[91] Schreckenberg, 'Wirkungsgeschichte', 1164ff. In this connection Bilde correctly interprets the '"translation" of the Bible' in the *Antiquities* as intended 'to render the essential contents of the text' (*Josephus*, 97).

'sold for a trifling sum'), and Luke 21:24, 'they will be led captive among all nations', was recognized early on. We will return to this later.

The conspicuous attraction of the Jewish author Josephus for early Christianity rests in the uniqueness both of his person and work. His receptivity as a Jew to Greek education, historiography and literature, his apologetic goals and the specific contents of his works all heightened his affinity to the New Testament and accumulated a power of attraction which waited only for the initial spark. It came as soon as Christians began to read Josephus in the light of the gospels, or the gospels in the light of Josephus.

The New Testament and Josephus

LITERARY FEATURES OF THE NEW TESTAMENT TEXTS

One essential prerequisite to the early Christian reception of Josephus was provided not by Josephus himself, but by the literary characteristics of New Testament authors – primarily Luke – that promoted interaction with Josephus. In order to describe this interaction adequately it is first necessary to glance at the literary characteristics of the New Testament texts: Matthew and Luke use Mark's gospel as their base of information. The Jesus sayings present in Matthew and Luke, but absent in Mark, are ascribed to the reconstructed source commonly called Q. The Gospel of John was written down c. 95, Luke c. 80-90, and Matthew c. 70-80. Mark's gospel and Q were certainly extant before 70. The latest New Testament writing, 2 Peter, was composed c. 135, and the earliest, 1 Thessalonians by the Apostle Paul, c. 50.

The so-called New Testament canon was not compiled until the end of the second century, and the reception of Josephus by early Christianity begins already in this period. In accordance with this development, Justin Martyr in the second century still refers to the three synoptic gospels, which were read along with the Old Testament prophets in the worship service, as the Apostles' biographical 'memoirs' (ἀπομνημονεύματα) of Jesus (e.g., *Dial.* 103:8; cf. *Apol.* 1:66; *Dial.* 100:4). Almost until the end of the second century, it was the Septuagint and later the pre-Vulgate (*Itala*), and not the New Testament texts, which Christians regarded as Scripture. Not until the need for a defense against Gnosticism in the second half of the second century did it become necessary to gather the various New Testament texts into a single corpus. Only then did these texts acquire the character of Holy Scriptures which, as a 'New Testament', were set over against what now became the 'Old Testament'. For the first time a theological exegesis of the Bible began to develop which searched the Old Testament for texts pointing to Jesus of Nazareth, and, far beyond the precedent set by the New Testament, everywhere sought a correlation between promise (OT) and fulfilment (NT).

The development of early Christianity begins already in the period when the New Testament texts were written, i.e., above all in the second half of the first century. In certain respects however the New Testament disputations with the Jews still reflect inner-Jewish processes, long before the 'self-definition' of the Jesus group had matured. Not until the expectation of the imminent Eschaton in an apocalyptic second coming of Jesus had faded away did the nascent Church perceive the importance, indeed the absolute necessity, of coming to terms with history, and of securing and defending its own ground within it. This could only be accomplished by establishing its own literature and historiography. Moreover, there was already early on an interest within Christianity in its own 'primitive history'.

The two-volume work 'Luke-Acts' – probably not separated into discrete parts until the course of the canon formation – shows how Luke attempted to meet this historical desideratum. He is in fact the first, and until Eusebius the only, Christian historian, or as we might say, theological historiographer, who combines in his two 'historical monographs' kerygma and historical report. His church history is at the same time a kind of world history, at the center of which stands Jesus of Nazareth. That he, probably the only Gentile Christian among the four Evangelists, also represents Jesus as having an extraordinary interest in the events of 70 (destruction of Jerusalem),[92] cannot be merely fortuitous.

LUKE AND JOSEPHUS COMPARED

A *syncrisis* of the works of these contemporaries reveals their characteristics and differences more precisely. If Luke has written a 'Hellenistic-Roman interpretation of the unfolding of God's providence', wherein he adapts the 'Roman ideology of fate',[93] the case is similar with Josephus and his theologizing historical report in the *War*. At all events Luke is so characterized today that many of his features more or less apply to Josephus as well.[94] Thus Luke's historical work is liberally embellished with speeches of the *dramatis personae* that have been freely drafted by the author himself; his style is Hellenistic-classical, which implies that he is bent on a broad influence in the world of the Greek-speaking, educated reader; he puts great value on showing that Christianity is taken seriously even by contemporary philosophers; in any case he intended that his work 'be able to hold its own in the eyes of the Hellenistically educated reader'; he wanted 'to attempt writing literature in a Hellenistic sense, in the sense of that

[92] Giblin, *Destruction*.

[93] Schulz, 'Vorsehung'; ib 112: 'Das christliche Schicksal als zielstrebiges, geordnetes Ganze anzusagen, als gleichsam vorsehungsgeschichtliche Entelechie, ist klassisch römisches Erbe, das Lukas kerygmatisiert hat.'

[94] For the following see Plümacher, *Hellenistischer Schriftsteller*, 10, 25, 98, 137; id, 'Griechischer Historiker', 239, 241, 244; cf id, 'Neues Testament'. Compare p17f above.

world where his work was to have its effect'; he was convicted that 'in the history of Christianity and its leading figures, he was describing a supremely important matter; and above all he was concerned with connecting the Christian church and its heroes with Hellenistic *paideia* and with world history and its great figures'. Thus the Christian primitive community is characterized 'as a kind of philosophical "idealpolis"', as, in similar fashion, biblical heroes are reshapen into creators of culture having secular significance by Josephus and other Hellenistic-Jewish authors. Indeed, Christianity has world-wide and world-historical importance.

Luke and Josephus construct the proems to their works with similarly far-reaching pretensions and both employ the device of the dedication (Lk. 1:3; Acts 1:1; Josephus, *Ant.* 1:8; *Life* 430; *Ag. Ap.* 1:1; 2:1, 256). Both interweave letters into their depiction (Acts 15:23-29; 23:26-30; *Ant.* 12:226-227; 13:166-170), and are careful to provide frequently a dramatic arrangement of episodes, the so-called 'dramatic episode style', and a kind of 'tragic-pathetic' historiography.[95]

A few significant Lucan characteristics create a certain distance to Josephus. Luke is positive towards Rome, as are most New Testament writers, in a pragmatic sense without being truly sympathetic. But he avoids connecting the fate of early Christianity with Rome, as does Josephus, although not without reservations, with Judaism. Luke sees a leading representative of early Christianity as an accepted interlocutor with Greek philosophers in Athens (Acts 17:18ff), and thus probably desires to demonstrate Christianity as respectable, noteworthy and equal to the demands of philosophy, but he does not develop these beginnings to nearly the extent of Josephus' historico-philosophical and historico-theological concepts. Not until the mid-second century, when the necessity arose, does Christianity become more philosophical in order to define and secure its identity further in confrontation with late Platonism and Gnosticism.[96]

Luke stands closer to Josephus in the question of mission. Here both are reserved. To be sure, Luke is not opposed to non-Christians reading his work, indeed he aims at influence among the educated public, but he writes chiefly for Christians. Josephus, while reckoning with readers among his own compatriots, as we have seen, writes chiefly for Greeks and Romans. The strong apologetic elements which permeate his work confirm that he is primarily considering non-Jewish readers. However, he avoids obtrusive proselytizing. As for Luke, it must also be remembered that not until after the relatively late formation of the canon was the New Testament also available as a corpus to non-Christian readers, and therefore that a wide influence in the non-Christian sphere would have been difficult. Josephus, while avoiding open proselytizing throughout, allows himself to express his

[95] Plümacher, Griechischer Historiker', 255ff.
[96] Cf Armstrong, 'Self-Definition'.

pride occasionally in the wide reception that the Jewish religious customs and the Jewish lifestyle have enjoyed in the entire ancient world:

> The masses have long since shown a keen desire to adopt our religious observances; and there is not one city, Greek or barbarian, nor a single nation, to which our custom of abstaining from work on the seventh day has not spread, and where the fasts and the lighting of lamps and many of our prohibitions in the matter of food are not observed. Moreover, they attempt to imitate our unanimity, our liberal charities, our devoted labour in the crafts, our endurance under persecution on behalf of our laws. The greatest miracle of all is that our Law holds out no seductive bait of sensual pleasure, but has exercised this influence through its own inherent merits; and, as God permeates the universe, so the Law has found its way among all mankind (*Ag. Ap.* 2:282-284).

With naive pride Josephus also reports what the Greek geographer Strabo – somewhat hyperbolically – says in his account of the Cyrenian Jews in 85 BCE:

> There were four classes in the state of Cyrene; the first consisted of citizens, the second of farmers, the third of resident aliens (metics), and the fourth of Jews. This people has already made its way into every city, and it is not easy to find any place in the habitable world which has not received this nation and in which it has not made its power felt (καὶ τόπον οὐκ ἔστι ῥαδίως εὑρεῖν τῆς οἰκουμένης, ὃς οὐ παραδέδεκται τοῦτο τὸ φῦλον, μηδ' ἐπικρατεῖται ὑπ' αὐτοῦ; *Ant.* 14:115-116).[97]

Despite the absence of pertinent sources, it can be concluded that even from the earliest transmission of Josephan texts by Christians a very particular form of reception was possible: non-Jewish readers, impressed by Josephus' apology for ethical monotheism, could become more receptive to the religious convictions of early Christianity. We know that many Gentiles long held Christianity to be a variant of Judaism, or considered both to be so similar that they wavered in the decision about which of the two religions to accept.[98]

[97] The ET by Marcus, ἐπικρατεῖται ('to be dominated', 'to be ruled') is incorrect. Strabo is exaggerating polemically, and there is no need to weaken the sense of the word. Marcus' alternative translation in the footnote, 'which has not been occupied by it' or 'in which it has not become dominant' would be better. Roos, 'Lesefrüchte', 236f, interprets ἐπικρατεῖν in *Ant.* 14:115 as 'to take possession of something' and believes it to be a *terminus technicus* from civil law, but this is unconvincing.

[98] We refer once again to the evidence of the poet of late antiquity, Commodian; see also Schreckenberg, *Texte* 1, p242-7.

AFFINITY AND MUTUALITY

Certain points of contact between Josephus and the New Testament were already indicated, cursorily, while addressing other questions. We will now address the affinities themselves, for it is the internal and formal relationship of the two text groups which forms the most important factor for the influence and efficacy of Josephus.

We have seen that Josephus and the New Testament writers were contemporaries and therefore potentially open to the same *Zeitgeist*. They regarded the same Bible as Holy Scripture, albeit with the difference that for the early Christians, even moreso than for Josephus, the Septuagint gained in importance while the Hebrew Bible receded into the background. Josephus believed, with Paul and the Evangelists, that the biblical prophets foresaw the future (or more precisely, the present of the first century in which Josephus, Paul, and the Evangelists lived).[99] In the New Testament the evidence is so trivial that we need not trouble to list examples; in Josephus, *War* 3:352; 4:386-387, and *Ant.* 12:322 should be mentioned. Josephus, like Paul, is a Jew by birth and was educated in Jerusalem.[100] A comparative investigation of the synoptic gospels, particularly Luke, with Josephus reveals that Luke and Josephus arrange and edit their material and/or their sources according to similar viewpoints.[101]

Most widely known are the numerous thematic affinities regarding persons and events of New Testament history.[102] The correspondences and agreements often go further, in part extending over complex situations,[103] which is a subject too little known at present, and represents a broad,

[99] See above p20, the prophecy of the destruction of Jerusalem and Roman rule; cf Momigliano, *Juden*, 75f. For further evidence in Josephus see Rengstorf, *Concordance*, s.v. προφητεία, προφητεύειν (prophecy, prophesy). Cf also Attridge, 'Josephus', 223.

[100] Lichtenberger, 'Paulus'.

[101] Downing, 'Redaction Criticism', 29: 'Luke's Gospel ... the stated intentions and widely agreed "tendencies" are often identical with those in Josephus.' I agree completely; cf ib 46f: 'His stated aims and many of his more obvious tendencies are closely paralleled in Luke among the synoptists'. Cf Feldman, 'Use, Authority', 476ff.

[102] I have dealt with this extensively in 'Flavius Josephus und die lukanischen Schriften'. More particularly Schenk, 'Gefangenschaft' usefully compares the accounts of John the Baptist in Josephus (*Ant.* 18:116-119) and the gospels.

[103] An example is provided by Grimm in *TLZ* 107 (1982) 277: 'Die enge Zusammengehörigkeit von Stadt, Tempel(dienst) und Volk in den lukanischen Schriften finden wir etwa im Bellum Judaicum des Josephus auf breiter Ebene.' This observation evinces the need for more extensive and thorough investigations, such as Baumbach, 'Sadduzäerverständnis' who notes that both Josephus and the New Testament play down the actual importance of the Sadducees in favour of the Pharisees. Rivkin, 'Defining', also sees definite agreements in the assessment of the Pharisees: 'The hitherto discordant sources are now seen to be in agreement. Josephus, Paul, the Gospels, and the Tannaitic literature are in accord that the Pharisees were the scholar class of the twofold law.' It is doubtful whether Giet, "Guerre des Juifs", and 'Les épisodes', is correct in concluding from 'coincidences' of passages of Revelation with the account of imperial history in the *War* that its author knew Josephus, but this needs further study.

almost untapped, area of research. The area of linguistic relationship between Josephus and the New Testament is for the most part *terra incognita*. A comparative investigation here of individual words, word meanings and entire semantic fields, could lead to new insights even into complex situations. Methodologically, SCHÜRER had already shown the way.[104] SCHLATTER made a further stride in the right direction but his work here was little noticed.[105] KITTEL's *Theological Dictionary of the New Testament*, which throughout compared the linguistic usage in Josephus, produced a rich yield.[106] There remains however an extraordinary amount yet to do in this area, indeed, regarding the linguistic comparative investigations, no more than the first beginnings have been made. That being so, it is difficult to understand why almost no relevant works have appeared in the last two decades.[107]

It is increasingly recognized that Josephus and Luke not only make similar use of Hellenistic literary technique, but, in part, also choose similar content and pursue similar lines of thinking. This is so, e.g., regarding Josephus' attitude towards his non-Jewish audience, and Luke's toward his non-Christian audience.[108] It is evident here that the assimilation on Josephus' part goes somewhat further than that in Luke. In any case, the hellenization of Christianity and Judaism can be investigated by comparative analysis of the situation in Josephus and in the New Testament texts. Both Luke and Josephus write a classicistic prose; they link selected interesting episodes together ('dramatic episode style'), as opposed to a continuous, coherent chronicle; they aptly distribute fictional, well-drafted speeches and letters throughout their account, sometimes with pointillistic

[104] Schürer, *Archiereis*, 593ff.

[105] Schlatter, *Johannes*, 385-93, lists words common to John and Josephus and words in John not found in Josephus; id, *Matthäus*, end, indexes words in Matthew not found in Josephus; id, *Lukas*, 562-658: 'Die sprachliche Verwandtschaft des Lukas mit Josefus, aufgezeigt an der Apostelgeschichte'; 659-708: 'Das Lukas mit Josefus Gemeinsame'; 708-10: 'Die lukanischen Worte, die bei Josefus fehlen'. Just as useful but virtually ignored was Schlatter's *Wie sprach Josephus?* Cf id, *Der Glaube*, 582-5: 'Die Parallelen zu den neutestamentlichen Worten bei Josefus'.

[106] Kittel, *TDNT*; lists of comparisons with usage in Josephus contained in *TDNT* can be found in Schreckenberg, *Bibliographie*, 220f (and *Supplementband*, 76).

[107] Bjerkelund, 'Parakalô', 98-104 should be mentioned in connection with the usage of παρακαλεῖν (to send for help; to urge, exhort, beseech) in Josephus as compared with the παρακαλῶ texts in Paul. Stimulating in method but not in results is Zeitlin, 'Galileans?', which compares the word 'Galilean' in Josephus and the New Testament (especially Luke 13:1-2; Acts 5:37); for this see also Foresti, 'Gesù'.

[108] See Downing, 'Common Ground'. Although Judaism, already in the pre-Christian period, was not particulary interested in proselytism, it held a certain attraction for non-Jews. The reasons have been correctly described by Roper, *Factors*: above all, 'contact with the outside world, resulting from the Dispersion', 'the development of high morale', '*Exclusivity* – the belief that the religion has "light" denied to others', '*Identity* – an understanding by the religion that it is "special"', '*Exteriority* – an eagerness to share the light with outside world'. This points to strong structural affinities with early Christianity.

effect; and they reduce the historical continuum to paradigmatic events. Josephus as well as Luke (as, to a lesser extent, the other evangelists) basically seek to provide grippingly narrated histories, that, to be sure, are also intended to carry a weighty message. Just as Luke is a kind of theological historian – or more precisely, theologian *and* historian – Josephus is a theologizing historian, i.e., in certain respects, historian *and* theologian. Luke's message is the proclamation of the Messiah, Jesus of Nazareth; Josephus' goal is above all to mediate to the world an apologetic, theologically founded, favorable picture of Judaism, and to prove the Jewish religion to be ethically unimpeachable, rationally well-grounded, and sufficient to satisfy the demands of philosophy. By means of his historiography, Luke is attempting to secure a place in history for a still young and struggling Christianity; Josephus writes to recommend the established and venerable religion of Judaism – endangered and under attack from many sides – as worthy of the highest estimation.

The strong affinity of Luke to Josephus is also seen in that 'of all the non-Jewish writers of antiquity, Luke has by far the best knowledge of Judaism, its liturgy in the Temple and the synagogues, its customs and its parties, and on the whole he reports them in an accurate and indeed positive way'.[109] For his part, Josephus is the author who reports (to be sure, always apologetically and positively) most extensively *in judaicis*. Luke shows a certain interest in, almost an inner connection with, the Jewish background to the New Testament events, and certainly shows no plain anti-Judaism. Strictly speaking, there was even a basis for a certain solidarity; for 'in his time the Christians were evidently still themselves the victims of Gentile hostility to the Jews'.[110]

Luke and Josephus have one thing further in common: neither found a true successor. 'Christian historiography – if we disregard the chronicling of bishop lists by Julius Africanus and others ... – did not begin again until Eusebius of Caesarea',[111] and Josephus' conception of a world history of Judaism was first taken up again by Heinrich GRAETZ in the nineteenth century. The vacuum in both cases is perhaps to be explained by the uniqueness of Luke's and Josephus' work: each created a unique, astonishing, indeed classical, source work, that was not destined to be soon equalled or surpassed. Neither targeted only Christians (Luke), or Jews (Josephus), but each wrote – Josephus more so, Luke less – for a Gentile audience, consisting of the demanding, educated middle and upper classes of their time, in which they could hope to find a certain receptivity to the content of their writings. To be sure, the writings of each served the teaching and edification needs of his fellows in the faith (this is stronger in Luke, but also throughout in Josephus); for, 'of course, those elements

[109] Hengel, *Geschichtsschreibung*, 59 (ET, 64).
[110] ib (ET, 64f).
[111] Plümacher, 'Griechischer Historiker', 263.

which make Judaism attractive to outsiders are precisely those which also strengthen its hold on insiders, and it is impossible to tell whether the literature was written in order to attract gentiles to Judaism or to encourage Jews to stay within the fold'.[112] This is also valid, *mutatis mutandis*, for Christian literature. At all events, the interest in things Jewish and Christian, in particular ethical monotheism as an alternative to polytheism, which by many was seen as crude or even laughable, was a factor with which both Luke and Josephus could reckon.[113]

Josephus' relatively friendly attitude towards Rome resembles the pragmatic desire to avoid confrontation of the early Christian writers. The parallels extend right into the details of the payment of taxes (*War* 5:405; Luke 20:22ff). It is even apparent that both Josephus and Luke were influenced by 'Hellenistic-Roman' (in part, Stoic) ideas of Providence. This has been amply demonstrated by Schulz.[114] From Josephus' chapter on 'portents' (*War* 6:290-309), omens concerning the destruction of Jerusalem, we may correctly conclude, 'that the fate of Jerusalem was understood at this time in apocalyptic and 'messianic' categories', and that this fact 'is of great importance for evaluating the destruction in the synoptic apocalypses'.[115] Apocalyptic-eschatological ideas were rife among Jews and Christians in the first century, and Josephus, as the New Testament, mentions Theudas (*Ant.* 20:97-98; Acts 5:36) and other 'sign prophets' who wanted to proclaim and hasten eschatological salvation by working wonders.[116]

For the subsequent influence of both the Lucan and the Josephan writings, it is not unimportant that both attempt to direct the eye of their readers to the broader horizon of world history. Already in the second half of the first century, early Christianity advanced a universal claim, above all in the figure of Luke who as a Gentile Christian seemed predestined for this role. Similarly, Josephus speaks to the great domain of the Graeco-Roman world, and significantly, from the city which would soon become the spiritual center of Christianity: Rome. Josephus, himself something of a cosmopolite, wanted to provide the *oikoumene* with authentic, reliable information concerning the War of 66-70, in his eyes an earth-shaking event, and not content to stop there, to mediate the image of a highly-respected, often misunderstood religion, which even after 70 still had the right to an honorable place in the Roman empire. Luke as well, more than the other evangelists, had a message for the world.

[112] Cohen, *Maccabees*, 57.
[113] Cf Amir, 'Korrekturen'; and Lichtenberger, 'Paulus'.
[114] Schulz, 'Vorsehung', 104ff. See especially the connection with the words *fatum*, prophecy, fate, destiny; ἀνάγκη, force, constraint, necessity, compulsion; πρόνοια, εἱμαρμένη, τύχη.
[115] Berger, 'Prodigien', 1431.
[116] See Schreckenberg, 'Flavius Josephus und die lukanischen Schriften', 195-8. Barnett, 'Sign Prophets', sees an inner connection between the pseudo-prophets described by Josephus and the activity of Jesus of Nazareth, but his interpretation is unconvincing; cf Kallander, *Defense*.

Indeed Josephus became known early on in the extensive Jewish Diaspora, as is attested at least for North Africa (*War* 7:448). The copies that he had sold to 'many' of his compatriots (*Ag. Ap.* 1:51) provided further publicity. This accorded with the clear tendency in his works to strengthen the Diaspora with a self-confident presentation of the Jewish religion, which encouraged Jews as well. Doubtless this helped prepare the ground for the world-wide missionary zeal of early Christianity, for the nearly omnipresent Jewish Diaspora proved itself to be fertile ground for the growth of the Church – small wonder, given the spiritual affinities of Luke and Josephus.

Chapter Three

Josephus in Early Christian Texts

First and Second Centuries

THE LUCAN WRITINGS

The numerous correspondences between the Lucan writings, written in the years 80-90, and the Josephan, composed in Rome from the mid-seventies to the late nineties, have long produced theories of Luke's dependence on Josephus, and vice versa. Since the beginnings of early Christianity reach back into the period shortly before the New Testament texts were composed, this problem cannot be ignored here.[117] At the present time definite conclusions are still not possible and the discussion remains open. It seems probable that Luke and Josephus wrote independently of one another; for each could certainly have had access to sources and information, which he then employed according to his own perspectives. A characteristic conglomerate of details, which in part agree, in part reflect great similarity, but also in part, appear dissimilar and to stem from different provenances, accords with this analysis. Presumably the two authors use neither the same

[117] I mention some of the most important stages in the history of research on this problem. Krenkel, *Josephus*, 337 attempted to prove 'daß Lucas sämtliche Werke des jüdischen Geschichtsschreibers nicht nur genau gekannt hat, sondern auch den Ertrag seiner Beschäftigung mit denselben für sein Evangelium und die Apostelgeschichte ausgiebig verwertet hat.' Belser, 'Lukas' believed, by contrast, that Josephus knew both of Luke's works and took them into account in his own works. Soltau, 'Petrusanekdoten', considered it possible that Jesus' ascension (Acts 1:9-11) was directly borrowed from *Ant.* 4:320-326 (disappearance of Moses). Koch, *Abfassungszeit*, 35f maintained that Luke was not dependent on Josephus. Hérenger, 'Flavius Josèphe' argued that the Evangelists drew their material largely from Josephus' works. The same theme, with no new perspectives, is discussed by McNeile, *Introduction*, 35-37. Knopf, *Einführung*, 144-55 attempts once again to prove that Acts is dependent on Josephus, with arguments already employed by Krenkel and others. Against this Williams, *Commentary*, 19-22 answers the question 'Did Luke use Josephus' Antiquities?' in the negative. Parente, 'L'episodio' assumes an influence on Acts 21:38 from the relevant accounts in *War* 2:261-263 and *Ant.* 20:160-166. Finally, Nodet, 'Jésus' claims to find connections between *Ant.* 18 and Luke: Luke's depiction, he alleges, is a reply to Josephus' polemical intentions in the context of his accounts of Jesus and John the Baptist; cf Schreckenberg, *Tradition*, 69, and id, 'Flavius Josephus und die lukanischen Schriften', 316f. The discussion will probably continue. An answer to the open questions could be facilitated by a comprehensive comparison of linguistic usage between Luke and Josephus with the help of Rengstorf, *Concordance*.

sources nor each other. It is probable, 'that in historical matters, Luke and Josephus are equally reliable witnesses who cannot be played off against each other. In fact, the historical reports of Josephus and the Lucan writings supplement and illuminate each other much more than they contradict each other'.[118]

CLEMENT OF ROME

Less probable, but not to be completely dismissed, is the possibility of Josephus' influence on Clement's *Epistle to the Corinthians* (*SC* 167). 'Terminological agreement' has been noted in numerous places.[119] Josephus and Clement lived in Rome during the same period, and to some extent probably moved within the same intellectual milieu, so that affinities in their texts should not be surprising. That they knew each other, however, remains a speculation. Similarly, NODET has recently conjectured that Tacitus (died c. 120) was acquainted with Josephus via early Christianity.[120] Using the Flood as his example, GOSSMANN has shown that there are grounds for literary dependency between Josephus and Ovid.[121] Although their basis is narrow, such suppositions are legitimate. In any case there were good public libraries and a lively trade in books in first century Rome, and thus numerous private libraries. If, for example, Tacitus already knew Josephus' works, for which there is some probability, then this was also possible for Christians of the period. In the case of Clement's epistle, more certainty could be achieved by making a linguistic comparison using RENGSTORF'S *Concordance*.

PSEUDO-JUSTIN

In his list of authors writing about Moses and his great importance, Pseudo-Justin (Justin died c. 165; Pseudo-Justin is probably a fourth century production) mentions Josephus and Philo in chapters 9, 10 and 13 of *Cohortatio ad Graecos* (*PG* 6, p257, 261, 268), as 'exceedingly wise' (σοφώτατοι) and well-known (δόκιμοι) Jewish historiographers. How well Pseudo-Justin actually knew Josephus' works is unclear. Despite certain affinities between the *Cohortatio* and *Against Apion* no influence or dependency has hitherto been proved.[122]

[118] Schreckenberg, 'Flavius Josephus und die lukanischen Schriften', 206f.

[119] Van Unnik, *Flavius Josephus*, 57. Clem. 4:12 and *Ant.* 4:11ff e.g. speak of *stasis* and *stasiasai*, 'sedition'.

[120] Nodet, 'Jésus'; cf Bruce, 'Tacitus'; Schreckenberg, *Tradition*, 69.

[121] Goßmann, 'Möglichkeit' concludes that either Josephus depended on Ovid, or both used a common source.

[122] Schreckenberg, *Tradition*, 70; Hardwick, *Josephus*, 6, 52-56, 156, 167f, 176; cf Schreckenberg, *Texte* 1, p200. The age of such pseudepigraphical writings is generally uncertain, and the question of genuineness often undecided. In what follows we list texts of this type chronologically as though they were genuine, as is customary in questions of literary history.

THEOPHILUS OF ANTIOCH

The use of Josephus for anti-pagan polemic is first seen clearly and prominently in Theophilus of Antioch's (c. 180) *Ad Autolycum*, where the strong influence of *Against Apion* makes itself felt.[123] To be sure, he knows Josephus as author of the *War*, but what interests him are the proofs offered in *Against Apion* that the Jewish biblical tradition (and therein the Christian faith as well!) is older and more trustworthy than the Greek literary and philosophical traditions. Theophilus is the first Christian author whom we know employed Josephus for anti-pagan apologetic purposes. Two aspects here are striking: First, Christians understand themselves not only to have replaced the Jews as the people of God, but also self-evidently regard the Jewish tradition as their own. 'Theophilus did not deem it necessary to provide a link between the biblical tradition of the Jews and the Church. That Christianity was the heir to Jewish antiquity is assumed.'[124] A second aspect, just as striking, is that Josephus' *War*, with its impressive account of Jerusalem's fall in 70, is for Theophilus (if he knew this work at all) still undiscovered as a quarry for apologetic arguments. In any case, this work now gradually becomes known in Christian circles and its influence begins to spread. By its 'influence' (*Wirkungsgeschichte*) we mean the tangible literarily influence of Josephus; for it is probable that educated Christians had read his works since the end of the first century, even if one does not share the opinion of those who already include Luke in this connection.

MELITO OF SARDIS

Melito of Sardis (died c. 190), in his *Easter Homily* (*SC* 123), interprets the Feast of the Passover typologically, and there briefly recapitulates the history of man since Adam in order to prove the world's need for salvation. In his description of the dominion of sin as Adam's legacy and the corruption of Israel leading to her destruction, he has occasion to mention a case of cannibalism, in which a mother, laying hands on her own flesh and blood, consumed her child (*SC* 123, p88). With a probability bordering on certainty, this is a reference to the *teknophagia* (devouring of children) of Maria in besieged, starving Jerusalem (*War* 6:201-213, presumably influenced by Lam 4:10).[125] Melito could assume that his allusion to Josephus would be understood, which speaks for a certain knowledge of the Jewish historian in Christian circles. To be sure, it is uncertain whether Melito knew the *War* in

[123] *SC* 20 (book 3); Schreckenberg, *Tradition*, 70; Hardwick, *Josephus*, 9-19, 157f, 168.
[124] Hardwick, *Josephus*, 19.
[125] Schreckenberg, *Untersuchungen*, 13-14; id, 'Wirkungsgeschichte', 1123; Hardwick, *Josephus*, 20-25, 157, 172; that Josephus and Philo were known in the latter half of the second century, even if not widely, can no longer be doubted. Cf also Harnack, *Geschichte* 1/2, p858: 'Both [Philo and Josephus] were read by Christians already in the second century'.

its entirety, or perhaps only alludes to this passage indirectly via another source, or even through hearsay. In any case, for Melito as, *mutatis mutandis*, for Josephus, this *teknophagia* is the gruesome highpoint of a dreadful development; in Melito's view, it can only be healed through Jesus Christ's salvific act. It is important to stress that Melito still does not suppose a causal nexus between Jesus' death and the dreadful end of Jerusalem as described by Josephus. But an initial, preparatory step is taken in that direction, a step that marks the trail for what later becomes a very broad road.

Second and Third Centuries

IRENAEUS

Irenaeus of Lyon (died c. 202) mentions in passing the Ethiopian campaign of Moses and the help he received from an Ethiopian princess whom he later married; he makes use of *Ant.* 2:238-253 (Frag. 33; *PG* 7, col 1245). Whether Irenaeus had read all of Josephus' works himself or only the *Antiquities*, is uncertain. It is possible that he knows the text via an intermediary source. In another passage he says that, after the seeds of early Christianity had been sown from Jerusalem outwards throughout the whole earth, the city had to fall because it had become worthless, not able to bear fruit (*SC* 100, p416-8). Either he did not yet know Josephus' *War*, or he saw no need to cite it – more precisely: he had not yet perceived its value for anti-Jewish apologetic that early Christian theologians found in it subsequently.[126]

MINUCIUS FELIX

In Minucius Felix' apologetic dialogue *Octavius* (*CSEL* 2, p1-71), which can perhaps be dated to c. 210, the Gentile partner in the dialogue emphasizes the superiority of the Roman divinities, and calls to witness the fact that the Jews' reverence for God was unable to protect them from a dreadful fate. The Christian answers:

> Read their [the Jews'] writings [the Bible], or, apart from the older literature, read the works of [the Jew] Flavius Josephus, or, if you prefer Roman authors, consult the work of Antonius Julianus on the Jews; then you will know that their own unworthiness is to blame for their fate, and that all their misfortunes were prophesied to come upon them if they persisted in their superstition. Thus, you will understand, they forsook God rather than being forsaken by him, and

[126] For Irenaeus see Schreckenberg, *Tradition*, 71; id, *Texte* 1, p205-8; id, 'Wirkungsgeschichte', 1123; Hardwick, *Josephus*, 34-36, 156, 162.

> were not, as you have so unscrupulously expressed it, carried with their God into captivity, but were, as traitors, delivered by God up to their fate. (*Octavius* 33:4-5)[127]

The punishment of the Jews is not explained as deriving from crimes against Jesus. He is nowhere mentioned, nor indeed, are any of the central Christian teachings. Nor is the anti-Zealotism of the *War* yet really employed as an anti-Jewish apologetic, and Josephus is not yet called upon expressly as a witness against his own people. Nevertheless, a further step in this direction is taken, and the beginnings of the later Christian 'punishment theology' become recognizable. Here also the manner in which Josephus is mentioned allows no certainty about whether Minucius Felix had read the *War* himself. It is good testimony, however, that educated Romans knew Josephus, and that his historical work was to some extent respected.

CLEMENT OF ALEXANDRIA

Clement of Alexandria (died c. 215) knows 'the Jew Flavius Josephus' (*Strom.* 1:147,2; *GCS* 52, p91: Φλαύιος Ἰώσηπος ὁ Ἰουδαῖος) and perhaps details of the destruction of Jerusalem as well; for in the same place he refers to *War* 6:440 and its context, and moreover mentions Josephus' Ἰουδαικαὶ ἱστορίαι, i.e., the *Antiquities*. The references to the Jewish historian occur in connection with his exposition of the great antiquity of the Jewish people, and his view that Greek philosophy is dependent upon the philosopher Moses.[128]

TERTULLIAN

Tertullian (died probably after 220) uses Josephus here and there without naming him, but at one point in his *Apologeticum* (19:6; *CSEL* 69, p51), with reference to *Against Apion*, mentions 'the Jew Josephus, who, himself a native Jew, defends Jewish antiquity', i.e., the great age of the Jewish traditions: *Judaeus Josephus antiquitatum Judaicarum vernaculus vindex*. The discussion in context is again about the proof already known to us of the Jewish tradition's greater antiquity, and therefore its superiority to the Greek traditions. Since for Tertullian also early Christianity is the new and true Israel and continues the biblical tradition, he can without further ado accept Josephus' anti-pagan apologetic in *Against Apion*, and use it as an important element of Christian anti-pagan apologetic. The Jewish historian becomes *de facto* an apologist for Christianity! Thus, the ancient biblical

[127] *GLAJJ* 1, p458-61; cf 10:4, The Jews are 'forsaken and in misery'. Cf Schreckenberg, *Tradition*, 70f, 182f; id, *Texte* 1, p210; id, 'Wirkungsgeschichte', 1132; Hardwick, *Josephus*, 26-33, 156, 162ff.

[128] Schreckenberg, *Tradition*, 71; id, *Texte* 1, p211-3; id, 'Wirkungsgeschichte', 1123; Hardwick, *Josephus*, 37-45, 158, 168-170, 174.

tradition has become as a matter of course a retrogressive extension and pre-history of Christianity.[129]

HIPPOLYTUS

Hippolytus (died c. 235) provides in his *Refutatio omnium haeresium* 9:18-29 (*GCS* 26) a parallel account to Josephus' description of the Essenes (*War* 2:119-166). Comparison of these two very similar reports[130] has not yet led in the discussion to a *communis opinio* regarding the relationship of the texts to one another, i.e., to a conclusion on one of three possibilities: a) they use a common source; b) Hippolytus uses Josephus directly but revises him; or c) Hippolytus uses Josephus indirectly (via an intermediary source that has altered Josephus somewhat). BURCHARD gives weighty reasons for the second of these possibilities, according to which Hippolytus used *War* 2:119-166 directly 'in a form which differed from the extant manuscripts no more than they differ from one another'.[131]If Burchard's arguments are correct, Hippolytus strongly christianized his Josephan text and made the Essenes look like a kind of 'pre-Christians'. This accords completely however with a tendency in early Christian authors to lay claim to and annex the Jewish tradition. In this way, perhaps internal evidence can tip the scales in judging the relationship between the two texts.

JULIUS AFRICANUS

Julius Africanus (died after 240), whose chronography (the first Christian world chronicle) is only extant in some citations in Eusebius, Georgius Syncellus, and others, uses *inter alia* the twelfth book of Josephus' *Antiquities*. In the tradition of his older contemporary, Clement of Alexandria, he erects a scaffolding of 'Christian' history to Moses and the creation of the world. The Church as 'true Israel' (an expression first coined by Justin Martyr, *Dial.* 11:15) and 'new Israel' was in this way able to prove its antiquity, and thus its superiority over later Greek philosophy.[132] It may be that Julius Africanus did not write his five books, *Χρονογραφίαι*, primarily for the apologetic purpose of proving the greater antiquity of Moses and Jewish wisdom in comparison to the Greeks; but, indirectly at least, his work contributed to the traditional efforts of his time to fix the beginnings

[129] Schreckenberg, *Tradition*, 71; id, *Untersuchungen*, 26; id, *Texte* 1, p216-25; id, 'Wirkungsgeschichte', 1123, 1135, 1139, 1192, 1203; Hardwick, *Josephus*, 67-72, 163f.

[130] Schreckenberg, *Tradition*, 72f; id, *Untersuchungen*, 14; id, *Texte* 1, p227f; id, 'Wirkungsgeschichte', 1124, 1193; Baumgarten, 'Josephus'; Hardwick, *Josephus*, 73-82, 156f, 162. Besides that in *GCS* 26, the edition by Marcovich, *Hippolytus* is now available.

[131] Burchard, 'Essener', cited p38.

[132] See Schreckenberg, *Tradition*, 71; id, *Untersuchungen*, 26f; Hardwick, *Josephus*, 46-51, 158, 168f.

of Christianity as early as possible. That Josephus was useful in these endeavors is certain, even if it can no longer be determined to what extent he was used by these early Church authors.

ORIGEN

With Origen (died not later than 253) we reach the first highpoint of Josephus' adoption by early Christianity. This Church father, more so than his predecessors, considers Christianity the true philosophy, and by defending the great age and renown of Judaism, he also defends the rank of Christianity. The extent of citations, allusions, or free use of Josephus by Origen is known.[133] Some of these are relevant mostly for the emendation of the Greek text of Josephus, which does not require our attention here. What is important for us is the rich harvest of information Origen offers on the transmission history of Josephus.

First of all *Contra Celsum* 1:47 (*GCS* 1, p97) commands both a special and a general interest. Here the Church father praises Josephus for his account of John the Baptist (*Ant.* 18:116-119), but takes him to task for not believing in Jesus as Christ and failing to blame the fall of Jerusalem and the destruction of the Temple on the crime against Jesus, but rather saying, with slight distortion of the truth: 'This befell the Jews as punishment for James the Just, the brother of the so-called Christ, for they had killed this most righteous of men' (i.e., James). – Nowhere in Josephus does a text in this form appear and it appears to be contaminated from *Ant.* 20:200 and 18:116.

We note first of all that Origen's Josephus codex, which was available to him in Caesarea, or which he had seen during his visit to Rome in one of the libraries there,[134] did not contain the *Testimonium Flavianum* at least not in the inflated form known to us. Origen read here, and in a number of his other equally unclear references to the Jewish author, a text that either differed significantly from that known to us, or he used an intermediary source that, for its part, had already changed Josephus' words. Editors of

[133] Schreckenberg, *Tradition*, 73-76; id, *Untersuchungen*, 14-16; id, 'Wirkungsgeschichte', 1124, 1133f, 1204; id, 'Works of Josephus', 317f; Mizugaki, 'Origen'; Hardwick, *Josephus*, 83-92, 158-60. Greek text see *GCS* 2; 3; 10; 33; 40. For theological evaluation in the context of the Christian anti-Jewish literature cf Schreckenberg, *Texte* 1, p228 35.

[134] For the various libraries of Rome in Josephus' time see Plümacher, 'Bibliothekswesen', 413f. We know from a casual note by Josephus (*Ag. Ap.* 2:51) that he had sold copies of his *War* to 'many' Romans and Jews. So he may have his other works, so that his books would have been available in Rome's public libraries (cf Schreckenberg, *Tradition*, 174). The acquisition of such expensive works was certainly not possible for smaller Christian congregations; cf Hengel, *Geschichtsschreibung*, 13, 15 (ET, 5f, 8f). But in any case literary interest and book learning were matters for the well-to-do, educated middle and upper classes, to which the leading Christian theologians generally belonged. Moreover, we know that private libraries in Rome were already quite common in Josephus' time (Schreckenberg, *Tradition*, 175).

fragment collections of ancient texts continue to encounter the same problem today; for it is often difficult to isolate an author's *ipsissima verba* when the citation is embedded in an argumentative context. This was possibly the case with Origen's source which he may, in good faith, have taken for the genuine Josephus text.

Perhaps the cause for the deterioration of the Josephus tradition was a confusion of James with John the Baptist. In *Ant* 18:116 the destruction of Herod Antipas' army is seen as a judgement of God for his treatment of John the Baptist, which explanation could easily have been the seed crystal or catalyst for the creation of a specimen of Pseudo-Josephus. The pattern is the same in both cases: the death of an important person from the circle surrounding Jesus of Nazareth is punished collectively. This is in fact the case in Josephus (*Ant.* 18:116; 20:200), whereas the contaminated version of Origen confuses the two names (James for John), and reports a different punishment (not the destruction of Herod's army, but the destruction of Jerusalem). The *tertium comparationis* is that both are punishments of God (ϑπὸ ϑεοῦ, *Ant.* 18:116). This favored inadvertent or intentional distortions.

Regarding the *Testimonium Flavianum*, we have pointed out the possibility that originally Josephus mentioned Jesus in passing, without much polemic, as a ψευδοπροφήτης (pseudo-prophet) or ἀπατεών, even as certain others he had mentioned (*War* 2:259-263; 6:288; *Ant.* 20:167). It is just as possible that the entire passage is secondary. It is not only absent from Origen, but also from the ancient table of contents to the eighteenth book of the *Antiquities*, and apparently from the Josephus codex of the patriarch Photius.[135]

We must also note that Origen, with Josephus' help, formulates a 'punishment theology' postulate: Josephus actually *should have said* that the destruction of Jerusalem resulted from the Jews' attack against Jesus. The causal nexus postulated here appears regularly in the later Christian writers as a readily believed fact. 'Josephus should have said' becomes unconsciously 'Josephus said', and the historical report becomes, in the interest of apology, a historical hodge-podge. Origen himself has already begun this process; he emphasizes in another text, without direct connection to Josephus citations, that Jerusalem's destruction was the just retribution for the Jews' mistreatment of Jesus.[136] Perhaps he had in mind here *Ant* 18:116, ϑεοῦ ... μάλα δικαίως τινυμένου, but largely forgot that the thought process there was different and associated this aspect of God's righteous

[135] See above p3.

[136] See the texts in Schreckenberg, *Texte* 1, p233; cf also Baras, 'Testimonium Flavianum', 343 referring to *Contra Celsum* 4:22: 'Here Origen states, this time without reference to James' martyrdom, that the destruction of Jerusalem was a just retribution for the mistreatment of Jesus.' Baras also notes correctly (343): 'It seems, therefore, that Josephus served Origen not so much for explicit documentation and direct quotation as for supporting his own Christian historiosophy.'

punishment with the end of Jerusalem. To be sure, Josephus formulates the idea of God's righteous punishment, but as a set piece in an incompatible context it loses its authenticity.

Contra Celsum 2:13 (*GCS* 1, 143) is also instructive: 'Vespasian's son Titus conquered Jerusalem, as Josephus writes, on account of the Lord's brother, James the Just, but as the truth reveals (παρίστησι), on account of Jesus, the Anointed of God'. Here, in a similar way, *Ant.* 18:200 (death of James) has probably been mixed with *Ant.* 18:116-119 (God causes the destruction of Herod Antipas' army by the Arab king Aretas as retribution for the murder of John the Baptist). The *tertium comparationis* is once again the just punishment for the murder of a man of God. From Josephus' mentioning of Jesus (*Ant.* 20:200 and possibly 18:63-64) on the one hand, and Origen's criticism of his explanation for the destruction of Jerusalem on the other, the idea suggested itself (almost unavoidably) of reporting not what the Jewish historian actually said but what he should have said, and – with the help of a proof-text taken from an apparently related context – of regarding his report of the destruction as an account of God's retribution for the murder of the Saviour. Since Josephus in any case was not far from the truth (οὐ μακρὰν τῆς ἀληθείας γενόμενος, *Contra Celsum* 1:47), a slight adjustment of the facts could appear not only permissible but necessary to the Church father: 'the [higher] truth [of God's salvation] proves conclusively' (ἡ ἀλήθεια παρίστησι)! Here the subjective truth of Christian faith has become objective 'truth'.

It is hardly possible to determine with certainty which corruptions in Josephus' text are due to Origen himself and which are to be traced to an intermediary source (a distorted Josephus codex or theological 'secondary literature') that Origen may have used in good faith. If the latter were true he would be open to the charge of disseminating unchecked material that could have been verified in a Josephus manuscript. In either case our observation that the transmission was adjusted – or even falsified – for apologetic reasons is valid.

Together with such considerations, however, one must also keep Origen's work methods in mind. The possibility cannot be eliminated that, in the enthusiasm of dictating his several hundred books, Origen allowed wishful thinking to get the better of him. Instead of writing himself, Origen customarily dictated his works to as many as seven (!) stenographers in turn. The stenograph was then reproduced in book script by as many scribes (girls among them).[137] 'Between the dictation of the author and the text transmitted to us, we find therefore the ear and hand of the stenographer, and the eye and hand of the copyist, which observation, understandably, is of no little importance for the criticism of the transmitted text'[138] – of no

[137] See Eusebius, *Hist. eccl.* 6:23,2 (*GCS* 9, p568-70) for Origen's working procedures, which included 'girls specialized in calligraphy'.
[138] Bardenhewer, *Geschichte* 2, p99.

little importance, as well, one must add, for the proper assessment of the Josephus citations transmitted by Origen. Exact separation between genuine citations and secondary theological context (including glosses in the margins of a manuscript) was difficult under these circumstances.

The problem appears also in the *Commentary on Matthew*, 10:17 (*GCS* 40, p22), where, according to Origen, Josephus said it was 'because of the wrath of God' (κατὰ μῆνιν θεοῦ) over the mistreatment of James, that the Jews suffered so much and the Temple was destroyed. Here also the explicit mention of Josephus' name gave the Church father's judgement an air of authenticity that made a strong impression on Christian posterity. The Greek original of Josephus' text was by this time disseminated in numerous copies, but the individual theologian was unable to check such citations for accuracy, and probably not greatly concerned about it. Ancient texts were reproduced without control or authorization, and it was commonplace for various manuscripts of the same text to differ from one another. In addition, the verification of individual citations – in the absence of registers – would have required a great deal of time. Distortions in the transmission of a profane text were thus almost unavoidable. Whether the fictitious Josephus citation κατὰ μῆνιν θεοῦ κ.τ.λ. was taken bona fide and unverified by Origen from his source, or whether he created it himself, it has – on the basis of his authority – had its place for many centuries in the Josephus tradition. It was important that it fit into the framework of Christian-Jewish apologetic and that it possessed the air of authenticity; for κατὰ μῆνιν θεοῦ (or μῆνις τοῦ θεοῦ) appears as a formula in Josephus (*War* 6:40; *Ant.* 1:164; 2:344; 4:8; 9:104, 246). God's punishments, in particular, are explained in this way. Thus it was believed that the great pestilence under Herod the Great, in which a large part of the people died, came about κατὰ μῆνιν θεοῦ, i.e., as a punishment for the king's murder of Mariamne (*Ant.* 15:243). Every one who had read Josephus and still had this formula in mind, would have been irresistibly tempted to consider *Comm. on Matt.* 10:17 as genuinely Josephan. Here, as in other similar cases, a genuine fragment of Josephus is transposed into an incompatible context as an anti-Jewish proof-text. Apparently, a slight adjustment of the facts in the interest of a convincing establishment of a new Christian view of history seemed permissible. In any case this passage in Origen provides an instructive example for the origin of fictitious Josephus citations.

Another kind is the use of *War* 6:201-213 (the *teknophagia* of Maria) in Origen's commentary on Lamentations (*Fragmenta in Lamentationes*, no. 105, to Lam 4:10; *GCS* 3, p273). This is very probably in the same tradition that begins with Melito of Sardis, i.e., the suffering of the Jews during the siege of Jerusalem in 70 is seen as having already been prophesied in the Bible. Here also it is uncertain whether Origen uses Josephus via an intermediary source. However this does not alter the fact that he makes anti-Jewish apologetic use of the Jewish author to prove the fulfillment of the biblical prophecies of doom. Indeed, the Lamentations of Jeremiah, composed in Palestine after the destruction of Jerusalem in 587 BCE, fit the context of the events in the year 70. In the further course of early Christianity then, above all in Eusebius, Josephus also bears witness to the realization of appropriate New Testament prophecies of doom, as we will see. Moreover, the *teknophagia* here and in other Christian authors serves representatively as a most impressive example of the fearful punishments suffered by the Jews, as the Christians were persuaded, for their maltreatment of Jesus. This also becomes an important motif in the Judaica of medieval iconography, as chapter four will show.

A characteristic example of the very free treatment of Josephus is found also in *Fragmenta in Lamentationes* no. 115, on Lam 4:19 (*GCS* 3, p275), where an imprecise reference to *War* 5:546ff is made. Here, as elsewhere, the possibility must be considered that Origen has made this citation or allusion in the heat of dictation and not always with the actual text of the source before him.

We must here leave off discussing individual texts and refer to the literature mentioned above.[139] But in any case we have clearly seen that Origen is the first Christian theologian who comprehensively uses the Jewish historian for the apologetic interests of Christian theology, and this must certainly have included numerous non-extant works. Moreover, with his 'theology of history' based on Josephus, Origen is an important forerunner of Augustine, as MIZUGAKI has correctly shown.[140]

Both the manner in which Origen uses Josephus and the frequency with which he refers his readers to him bear witness to the widespread availability of Josephus manuscripts in Christian circles in the first half of the third century. This brings us to the question of editorial redaction, particulary prevalent among widely read works: Origen cites the *War* variously as ἅλωσις, *Halôsis* or περὶ ἁλώσεως (*PG* 12:1529; *GCS* 3, 273, 274). This has prompted the hypothesis, repeated by scholars ever since EISLER and THACKERAY, that the title refers to an original Greek (and therefore supposedly no longer extant) version of the *War*, i.e., the original version, which, it is argued, provided the basis for the lost first Aramaic edition of the *War*.[141] However, investigation of the history of the transmission of the text has led to another result. Josephus regularly speaks of the *War* as αἱ

[139] See above n133, and in particular the texts listed in Schreckenberg, *Tradition*, 73ff, and Mizugaki, 'Origen', 328.

[140] Mizugaki, 'Origen', 336: 'Josephus' historical account, which has an apologetic trait, is incorporated by Origen in his history of theology, which has the identical trait. Such an attempt of Origen anticipates the "theology of history" that is vastly constructed by Augustine in De civitate Dei.'

[141] Attested *War* 1:3. For the history of research see Schreckenberg, 'Neue Beiträge', 87; *Untersuchungen*, 73f; 'Wirkungsgeschichte', 1119f. Unfortunately Bilde also comments (*Josephus*, 71): 'one cannot exclude the possibility that ... it is the title which Josephus himself gave his work.'

περὶ τοῦ Ἰουδαϊκοῦ πολέμου βίβλοι, (the books on the Jewish War; *Ant.* 20:258; *Life* 27, 412) or ὁ Ἰουδαϊκὸς πόλεμος (the Jewish War; *Ant.* 1:203; 18:11; *Life* 413) or simply πόλεμος (War; *Ant.* 1:6; 18:259), so that doubtless we must accept Ἰουδαϊκὸς πόλεμος as the genuine title. The thirty books of Josephus were, just as those of other ancient authors, transcribed from scrolls into codex form during the early phases of Christian transmission, perhaps in the first half of the third century. On purely practical grounds the twenty books of the *Antiquities* were divided into four codices, and the *Life* was appended to the final pentad (Books 16-20). Later, Books 1-10 and 11-20 plus the *Life* were bound into two volumes. *Against Apion* and the *War* were each bound separately. The text critic can still easily recognize this method of codification in the diversity of the transmission situation in the four individual transmission blocks and the slight difference from pentad to pentad within the two decades. Such a division into pentads was customary and is known to us through the transmission history of numerous ancient authors.

It seems that editorial redaction took place as the scrolls were collected and codified, as is seen by the book titles used in the medieval manuscripts. This redaction combined the *War* and the *Antiquities* under the common title Ἰουδαϊκὴ Ἱστορία and gave the subtitle Ἅλωσις or Περὶ ἁλώσεως to the *War*. The *Antiquities* kept the original title Ἀρχαιολογία, 'Antiquities' (*Ant.* 20:259, 267; *Life* 430; *Ag. Ap.* 2:1, 54, 127; Ἀρχαιολογίαι appears once, in *Ag. Ap.* 2:136; cf. Ἰουδαϊκά, *Ant.* 13:72, 298; Ἰουδαϊκὴ πραγματεία, 'Jewish History'; *Ant.* 13:173).

The postposition of the Ἅλωσις betrays the hand of the Christian redactor; for the Christian theological reinterpretation of the events of 70 in the sense of an irreversible salvation-history *peripeteia* had already begun by this time. The *War*, without doubt Josephus' earliest work, was anachronistically placed behind the *Antiquities*. This had a specific purpose: 'In this way, Jewish history, as seen from a Christian point of view, ended chronologically in a catastrophe that took place as a result of the Jews' rejection of Jesus. Even NIESE adheres to this order of the works in his major critical edition (Berlin 1885-95).'[142] The Christian theological-historical perspective was responsible for this combination of Josephus' two main works into a corpus of this kind. The New Testament era, with its culmination point in the year 70, had to be placed in order after the Old Testament events narrated in the *Antiquities*; for thus the Fall of Jerusalem appeared to Christian readers as the foundering and justly deserved end of the Jewish people, consistent with, and consequent upon, salvation-history. The secondary title Ἅλωσις can be recognized as a Christian interpretation in that it abbreviates the period of the *War*, 66-70, into the summer of the year 70, in which the ἅλωσις actually occurred. In contrast to the complete

[142] Schreckenberg, 'Works of Josephus', 317.

report of Josephus, which also includes the prehistory of the *War*, the Christian title concentrates interest on the 'decisive' fact.

Thus it seems either that Origen already knew the Christian redaction of Josephus under the title Ἅλωσις, or less probably, that the redactor was influenced in his choice of title by Origen or other theologians unknown to us who used it. In any case, the words, οὐ μακρὰν τῆς ἀληθείας γενόμενος (*Contra Celsum* 1:47, see above), which appear to legitimate a slight adjustment of the facts in the interest of the 'truth', is, *mutatis mutandis*, also valid for this title. Renaming the work and changing its chronology seemed to be minimal alterations, allowed, indeed demanded, in the interest of truth. That this Christian truth found itself in opposition to historical truth was incidental.

Fourth Century

METHODIUS OF OLYMPUS

The passing reference to *War* 6:435-437 in *De resurrectione* 3:9 by Bishop Methodius of Olympus (died in 311) is of value only for the emendation of the Greek text of Josephus.[143] Methodius takes issue here with Origen's use of Josephus in one of his lost works. He provides no new insights into the reception of Josephus by early Christianity, and is mentioned here only for the sake of completeness.

PSEUDO-EUSTATHIUS

Pseudo-Eustathius (Eustathius of Antioch, died in 337) excerpts Josephus' geographical excursus on Lake Asphaltitis (*War* 4:476-485) and many passages from *Ant.* 1-2. The interest of the citations is purely text-critical and is reduced further still in that the author uses his source very freely. In other respects as well the relationship between the author and his source remains unclear.[144] No new insights are provided by Pseudo-Eustathius either, but he should be mentioned at least to attain a detailed and precise picture of the situation as a whole.

EUSEBIUS

With the writings of Eusebius of Caesarea (died c. 339-340), which had a particular significance for later theologians, the early Christian reception of Josephus receives such a strong impetus that for centuries to come he

[143] *GCS* 27, p403; cf Schreckenberg, *Tradition*, 77; *Untersuchungen*, 23f; Hardwick, *Josephus*, 93-95, 160, 172.

[144] Schreckenberg, *Tradition*, 77-79. For the sake of completeness Eustathius of Epiphaneia is also mentioned, who used Josephus in his Χρονικὴ ἐπιτομή (ad 503 CE) but is extant only in fragments; cf Allen, 'An Early Epitomator', 1-11.

became one of the most influential 'Christian' authors. The extent and manner of Eusebius' use of Josephus have been well documented,[145] but in various respects need to be further developed. We cannot here discuss the several hundred Josephus citations (most of which are only relevant for the emendation of Josephus' text), but must confine ourselves to the really significant cases.

It is conspicuous, first of all, that Eusebius, especially in his *Historia ecclesiastica* and *Praeparatio evangelica*, employs such a profusion of citations and excerpts from Josephus that the Jewish author thereby assumes the character of a primary source for Church history. By Eusebius' time at the latest the Church becomes conscious of its need to provide a historical foundation for its salvation-historical claims. To be sure, many Christian authors preceded him, but he was to be the first genuine Christian historian after Luke's beginnings in this area. And it was he who first fully recognized that Josephus' rich and manifold offerings for the history of the New Testament era were like a key unlocking the understanding of many texts in the gospels.[146]

Josephus offered the possibility to bridge the various gaps between the New Testament events and history at large, and provided a basis, so to speak, of scholarly proof for the incipient Christian salvation-history. At the same time the very account of this Jewish author allowed the history of the Jewish people to be understood as leading to their downfall. The result was a characteristic 'countermotion' between the Jewish history of rejection and the Christian one of salvation. Thereby, two important facts were ignored or suppressed. First, Flavius Josephus was a figure of only marginal importance within Judaism already in the first century, and at no time was he a representative purely and simply of Judaism; indeed, by Eusebius' time he was hardly known any longer in Jewish circles. This contrasts with the high significance he was given by the Christians, who made him into their principal witness from the enemy camp. Second, at no time was there an impartial inquiry into Josephus' own purposes, nor was it noted that his Jewish compatriots, who regarded him indifferently, made no attempt to protect him from Christian usurpation.

[145] Schreckenberg, *Tradition*, 79-88; id *Untersuchungen*, 16; 'Wirkungsgeschichte', 1120, 1133f, 1140, 1142, 1146f, 1180, 1183, 1193, 1204, 1213; id 'Works of Josephus', 318, 320; Grant, *Eusebius*, 29ff, 39ff, 100ff, 128ff, 147ff; Barnes, *Constantine*, 164-188; Hardwick, *Josephus*, 99-153, 173ff, 183. Gödeke, *Geschichte* provides little help for our question. Wallace-Hadrill, 'Eusebius' investigates the various forms of the *Testimonium* in Eusebius, concluding that the differing citations in his works show that several Christian versions already existed at his time. But the extant form does not originate with Eusebius.

[146] This is true e.g. for the so-called synoptic apocalypses Mark 13:2; Matt 24:2; Luke 21:6 and 19:40-44. Cf also Matt 23:38 and Luke 21:20ff; the figures of Theudas (Acts 5:36), Judas the Galilean (Acts 5:37), the Egyptian (Acts 21:38), and theHerodians, among the persons, events, places or regions, to which Josephus provides information.

As a matter of course, the line of thinking begun by Origen was continued: Josephus in his accounts 'was not far from the (Christian) truth' (*Contra Celsum* 1:47), indeed he somehow presaged and anticipated this Christian truth even though perhaps unintentionally. Therefore Christian theologians saw themselves as justified in including the works of Josephus within their own horizon of understanding. It seemed permissible, for example, to inflate a cursory, neutral mention of Jesus of Nazareth (probably the genuine basis for *Ant.* 18:63-64) into a witness of the *veritas christiana*, i.e., from a *testimonium de Jesu* to a *testimonium pro Christo*. Eusebius is the first Josephus traditionist to cite the text of *Ant.* 18:63-64, and there are several possibilities for its origin, just as in the case of the fictitious Josephus citations in Origen. Thus it could be that the Church father found the text already in his Josephus manuscript, perhaps in the margin. Support would be found in the fact that our medieval Josephus manuscripts also have it in 18:63-64, while the fictitious citations in Origen are missing in these same manuscripts. Neither can it be excluded, however, that Eusebius himself interpolated the text, thereby insuring its authority in the tradition, or took it over second-hand without verification. In that case he would, like Origen, be open to the charge of careless wishful thinking. Certainty today is hardly possible.

We will now examine such passages in Eusebius as deserve special attention.

Hist. eccl. 1:11 (*GCS* 9, p76-80). Here Eusebius treats first the account of John the Baptist, present both in the New Testament and Josephus (*Ant.* 18:116-119): because of his execution of John the Baptist, Herod Antipas' entire army was destroyed. Following that, Eusebius rehearses the *Testimonium Flavianum* in the same passage (*Ant.* 18:63-64).

In *Hist. eccl.* 2:23 (*GCS* 9, p166-72) Eusebius relates the story (according to Hegesippus) of James the Just the brother of the Lord in which James is thrown down from the battlement of the Temple, stoned and then killed with a club by a fuller. This man was so remarkable and righteous that many insightful Jews as well were of the opinion,

> ...that this was the cause of the siege of Jerusalem immediately after his martyrdom, and that it happened for no other reason than the crime which they had committed against him. Of course Josephus did not shrink from giving written testimony to this, as follows: 'And these things happened to the Jews to avenge James the Just, who was the brother of Jesus the so-called Christ, for the Jews killed him in spite of his great righteousness.

This is an expansion of *Ant.* 20:200: τὸν ἀδελφὸν 'Ιησοῦ τοῦ λεγομένου Χριστοῦ, 'Ιάκωβος ὄνομα αὐτῷ, 'a man named James, the brother of Jesus who was called the Christ'. A few lines further on in Eusebius' text, Josephus' *Ant.* 20:200 is cited a second time, this time correctly, without expansion.

Hist. eccl. 3:5,6 (*GCS* 9, p198, to *War* 6:425-428): Whoever will can read in Josephus' historical account the exact fulfillment of the prophecy in Dan 9:27 concerning the tribulation of Jerusalem. For, so Eusebius, Josephus reports that the approximately three hundred myriads (i.e., three million) of Jews, who had assembled in Jerusalem for the Passover Feast, were locked in as in a prison. For it was necessary that the door close on them, as in a prison, during that same season in which they had brought about the Passion of the Saviour of mankind, and thus, suffering the punishment sent from Heaven, perish in retribution. Eusebius uses Josephus to tell the suffering of the Jews in besieged, starving Jerusalem that his readers might learn,

> ...of how the punishment of God followed close after (οὐκ εἰς μακράν) them [the Jews] for their crime against the Christ of God. Come, then, take up again the fifth book of the history of Josephus and go through the tragedy of what was then done.

It must be noted here that the recommendation 'take up again' presupposes that Josephus' text was disseminated in Christian circles and available to interested readers.

Hist. eccl. 3:6 (*GCS* 9, p208-10): Eusebius relates the teknophagia of the Jewess Maria in besieged Jerusalem. The 'indescribable suffering' (ἀδιήγητα πάθη, p206:5; cf τὸ πάθος, p210:27) of the Jews, for whom this teknophagia stands as a significant example, is the punishment (ἐπίχειρα, *Hist. eccl.* 3:7; p210:14) for their mistreatment of the Christ of God, and the fulfillment of the prophecy of doom from Matt 24:19-21, Luke 19:42-44; 21:20, 23-24 which Eusebius expressly cites and connects with details from accounts by Josephus (*War* 6:417ff, 435), whom he describes – presupposing here acquaintance with Josephus – only as συγγραφεύς (i.e., author, historian; *Hist. eccl.* 3:7; *GCS* 9, p210; cf. 3:14, *GCS* 9, p220, etc).

Hist. eccl. 3:7 (*GCS* 9, p214): Eusebius explains that Heaven postponed the fall of the Jews for 'forty years' after their offense against Christ, in order to give them time to repent.

Hist. eccl. 3:8 (*GCS* 9, p214-20): Eusebius lists the portents which announced the doom of Jerusalem before its destruction (*War* 6:288-309).

Hist. eccl. 3:8 (*GCS* 9, p220): Eusebius relates the oracle concerning a world ruler arising in the East (*War* 6:312-313). He rebukes Josephus however for seeing in Vespasian the fulfillment of the oracle; for, so Eusebius, he only ruled over the Roman Empire, and not the entire world. It is rather Jesus Christ, he continues, who, according to Ps 2:8 and 19:5, is the true ruler of the world.

Demonstr. ev. 8, Proem 3 (*GCS* 23, p349): Referring to the year 70, Eusebius speaks of the 'destruction of Jerusalem and its Temple' and of the 'servitude of the entire Jewish people' under its enemies. Although he makes no special reference to Josephus, this is doubtless a reminiscence of the sale of the surviving Jewish prisoners of war into slavery reported by

Josephus (*War* 3:540; 6:414-419; cf. *War* 5:364: δουλεύειν [enslavement] of the Jews already before 70). Eusebius discusses the same topic extensively and with reference to Titus, Vespasian and the Romans in *Demonstr. ev.* 8:4 (*GCS* 23, p398f: δουλεύοντες 398:28; αἰχμαλωσία, 'captivity', 399:1), and connects this somewhat forcedly with texts from the Bible (Zech 11:2-3; 12:2, 10-13; 14:1-4, 9-10, 16, 19).

Demonstr. ev. 9:3 (*GCS* 23, p410f): Eusebius applies the curse of Num 24:9 to the Jews, who since their attack against Christ continue to curse him in their assemblies, and therefore remain to the present time under God's curse. For this reason also they behold even to the present time the destruction of their kingdom and their temple.

Demonstr. ev. 9:4 (*GCS* 23, p413): The Jews, to whom Matt 3:17 was directed in vain, will be overtaken by doom and destruction, and this was prophesied. It is evident how since the defeat of Jerusalem in the time of the Saviour the autonomy and rule of the Jewish people, which had stood until that time, has been destroyed and overthrown.

Demonstr. ev. 9:5 (*GCS* 23, p413): Eusebius cites *Ant.* 18:116-117 concerning John the Baptist: in the opinion of some Jews the Jewish army (τὸν 'Ιουδαίων στρατόν) was destroyed according to God's will as the just retribution for the death of John the Baptist (τισὶ δὲ τῶν 'Ιουδαίων - αὐτὸ φανεῖσθαι).

Demonstr. ev. 10:3 (*GCS* 23, p459): Ps 109(108):4ff is applied to the Passion of Jesus and in this connection the punishment of the Jews for their mistreatment of the Savior is seen as the fulfillment of the Psalm. For example, 'May his days be few', means 'the short time' that remained to the Jews after their offense until the siege and complete destruction of Jerusalem.

Theoph. 4:20-22 (*GCS* 11, p195-200). Here Eusebius sees the doom prophecies from Luke 21:20-24 fulfilled in the discernible dispersion of the Jews throughout the world – they are no longer permitted to enter Jerusalem – and also through the accounts of Josephus: whoever will may read the fulfillment of these things in Josephus. The lines of connection between Luke 21:20-24 and Josephus also extend to such details as the *teknophagia* of Maria (*War* 6:201-213):

> But how these things severally came to pass, and how that which was prophesied by our Saviour was fulfilled in actual fact, can be learned in the writing of Flavius Josephus, who also clearly shows and relates the fulfillment of our Saviour's prophetic word, 'Woe to those who are with child in those days, and to those who give suck,' as women roasted their children in fire and ate them because of the severity of the famine that had gripped the city. Even this, then, i.e., the famine that would come over the city, our Saviour prophesied, and admonished (therefore) his disciples to 'flee to the mountains' when the siege came upon the Jews... (*GCS* 11, 197:17-29).

> Whoever will may read the fulfillment of these [things] in the writings of Josephus... (*Theoph*. 4:20; *GCS* 11, p198:3-4)
> 'There will be at that time great tribulation such as has not been seen since the beginning of the world,' which, also prophesied by our Saviour, was confirmed by the author [Josephus] as fulfilled just forty years later in the time of the Roman king Vespasian (*Theoph*. 4:22; *GCS* 11, p199f).

We have already seen that the fictitious Josephus citations relating to early Christianity both in Origen and Eusebius present a problem for which it is difficult to find an unequivocal, convincing solution. Perhaps the *Testimonium Flavianum* was already present in Eusebius' Josephus text, or alternatively, as a marginal or interlinear gloss which eventually replaced the original form which from a Christian standpoint was less acceptable. Less probable is that Origen and Eusebius invented these accounts themselves, passing them off as Josephan. Presumably they found these fictitious witnesses present in one form or the other, possibly as elements within a theological argumentation in which the lines between citation and context had become somewhat blurred. After all, it was not uncommon during his time to cite an intermediary source or from memory. Moreover, it is no longer possible to determine how much Eusebius was influenced in this regard by Origen. Even a scholar of Eusebius' stature did not have Josephus' thirty books by memory and was either unable or unwilling to verify everything for accuracy. Where apologetic interests had come into play, carelessness was easy. Thus the 'destruction' of a given Jewish army (*Ant*. 18:116) could become, with a slightly altered reference, the very ruination itself of the Jews; or the 'deserved punishment' for the murder of a righteous man (*Ant*. 18:116; cf. 20:200: John the Baptist or James) which 'God' himself had brought about (*Ant*. 18:119), could easily become God's punishment on the Jews for the murder of Jesus. Given the gigantic task of verifying a citation without a concordance in a field of thirty books, even important theologians like Origen and Eusebius were probably tempted to disseminate such welcome witnesses, and yielded to the temptation. After all, no one in early Christianity took the trouble to investigate Josephus' text critically, as ancient exegetes did with Homeric texts. His text was, and remained almost to the present day, a quarry from which one helped oneself at need and pleasure for his own purposes.

For Josephus the prophecy of a world-ruler arising out of Judaea (*War* 6:312-313 – the interpreters point to Num 24:17-19, Dan 12:1, Gen 49:10 and Dan 7:13-14) had purely world-political rather than religious relevance or messianic importance. He had the historical development of his time culminating in Vespasian. Here Eusebius diverges expressly from Josephus, referring the logion to Jesus of Nazareth. He adds the eschatological dimension absent in Josephus; for Eusebius, Christ reigns universally and is the finisher of history, while Vespasian did not even rule the entire known world of his time. Here he cleverly underlays the theological significance with history and grounds rationally the *interpretatio christiana* from *War* 6:312-313.[147]

Historically unfounded, anticipatory theological wishful thinking is seen when Eusebius has 'the entire Jewish people' sent into slavery (*Demonstr. ev.* 8, Proem 3). To the contrary, the social and religious existence of the Jewish people were in no wise reduced after 70; for approximately three-fourths of all Jews lived, before and after 70, in the Diaspora away from the danger, and, by means of Caracalla's *Constitutio Antoniniana* in 212, attained full Roman citizenship.[148] Eusebius' statement then does not accord with the facts.

His arbitrary, indeed illogical, use of the sources is seen particularly clearly in the detail of the period between the death of Jesus and the destruction of Jerusalem. At one point the ἅλωσις occurs 'shortly after' the crime or, so to speak, follows closely on its heels (*Hist. eccl.* 3:5), and at another God 'postponed their destruction' for fully forty years in order to give them an opportunity to repent (*Hist. eccl.* 3:7; *GCS* 9, p214). Similarly arbitrary is the time for the punishment. Since Jesus was crucified during Passover, Eusebius has the Jews being closed up in Jerusalem 'during the same days' to suffer the punishment of Heaven (*Hist. eccl.* 3:5), whereby it is cleverly obscured that the actual fall of Jerusalem did not occur in the Spring, but on September 26, 70. For the sake of explaining the punishment therefore, i.e., for apologetic reasons, a chronological congruence of crime and punishment is suggested.[149] In the same text Eusebius rounds off the number given by Josephus for the number of Jews closed up within Jerusalem (*War* 6:425: 2.7 million) to three million – this too, to make Josephus' already impressive account even more effective, and thereby apologetically more useful.

[147] Schreckenberg, 'Wirkungsgeschichte', 1167.

[148] Cf Schreckenberg, 'Wirkungsgeschichte', 1211. See also Conzelmann, *Mitte*, 135: 'Der jüdische Krieg hatte keine spürbare Folgen für die allgemeine Stellung der Juden im römischen Reich'; and Smallwood, 'Jews', 235: 'The military defeat of the Palestinian Jews in the war of 66-70 did not affect the status of the Jewish religion or reduce the Jews' religious liberty; nor did the defeat of the North African Dispersion after their revolt at the end of Trajan's reign; nor did the second great defeat of the Palestinian Jews in the war of 132-5 led by Bar Cochba.' For the numerous pro Jewish laws of the *Codex Theodosianus* cf Schreckenberg, 'Wirkungsgeschichte', 1194, and 'Works of Josephus', 318: 'This collective servitude of the Jews is an unhistoric, apologetically motivated assertion; for the Jews of the Roman Empire ... remained, even under Christian Emperors, free citizens in principle, and their cult remained a *religio licita*.' Similarly Bein, *Judenfrage* 1, p19ff.

[149] Similar talion thinking (with 'rebounding punishment') is found in Josephus, *Ant.* 13:314-318: The blood of the murderer is shed at the scene of the crime over the blood of his victim. This is also the result of 'divine providence' (Attridge, 'Josephus', 219). Plutarch also reflects on the talion problem in this sense in *De sera numinis vindicta* 3-5 (Paton *et al.*, eds, *Moralia* 3:394-401): it is proper and sensible when punishment closely follows the crime so that the connection between the two is meaningful.

The treatment of the *teknophagia* of Maria (*War* 6:201-213) is an example of how Eusebius systematically enlarges the traditional correspondence between Old Testament prophecy and New Testament fulfillment, to include a further reference relationship between New Testament prophecy of doom for Jerusalem and Josephus' account of its realization. In certain respects therefore, Josephus is included in the customary procedure for establishing scriptural proof, and thereby becomes henceforth a new basic work for Christian apologetic.

Josephus' condemnation of the Jewish rebel groups in the war of 66-70 and many details of his historical account prepare the ground for the efforts of Christians since Eusebius at dramatizing the war and painting the colors even more lurid than they already are. The Jewish author's deeply moving eye-witness account already offered a suggestive, theological preliminary understanding that could be taken over with slight alterations. Since Eusebius' adoption of Josephus, it becomes not only an unshakeable certainty but an essential element of the Christian theology of history that the destruction of Jerusalem and the passion of Jesus represent a *propter hoc* rather than a *post hoc*. It seems that not before they read Josephus' account of the destruction, were Christian eyes really opened to the possible implications of this extraordinary event.[150]

Eusebius is of special importance for the discussion on the *Testimonium Flavianum*. He is the first to quote it and ascribe it to Josephus. Since Origen and others before him still do not know it, and Eusebius probably did not invent it himself, it must, as suggested above (p58), perhaps be seen as a clever forgery constructed around a small genuine nucleus. Although the extant medieval Greek Josephus manuscripts contain it, the Josephus codex used by Photius and the ancient *hypothesis* to book 18 of the *Antiquities*, more significantly, do not. But an especially telling argument against its authenticity is that Eusebius, whose treatment of Josephus is as arbitrary as Origen's, is the first to mention it.

There are no extant manuscripts of the Greek Josephus from the early Christian period, and we must therefore make do with medieval manuscripts to observe the characteristics of Christian interpolations and glosses *in situ*. But the habits of Christian copyists were little changed from a few centuries earlier. For example, in three Greek manuscripts (Laurentianus 69:10; Vindobonensis historicus gr. 20, Parisinus gr. 1419) at *Ant.* 9:64, δέσποτα ἐλέησον (Master, have pity) is changed by a Christian hand to δέσποτα κύριε ἐλέησον (Lord and Master, have pity). In Codex Beroli-

[150] Schreckenberg, 'Wirkungsgeschichte', 1213. Cf Bowman, 'Josephus', 363f: 'The role of Eusebius is pivotal in the canonization of Josephus as a source for Christian historical identity ... Eusebius' works became the major vehicle through which the Josephan corpus was transmitted to Byzantine chronographers for the next nine centuries'; and aptly, ib 367, 'Josephus was considered the ultimate authority for biblical history during the Byzantine period' and 'Eusebius gave to Josephus' collected works his imprimatur.'

nensis gr. 223, fol 208, there appears at *War* 5:442-443 the wrathful gloss of a Christian scribe:

> Νῦν ἄκων, ἀσεβέστατε καὶ τῆς ἀληθείας ἐχθρέ, εἴρηκας ὑπ' αὐτῆς ἐκείνης τῆς ὄντως ἀληθείας ἐλαυνόμενος, μήτε γενεὰν ἄλλην κακίας γονιμωτέραν γενέσθαι μήτε τὴν τηλικαῦτα κακὰ πεπονθέναι τινὰ πόλιν ἄλλην. καὶ γὰρ ἄλλων πολλῶν ἀγαθῶν τε καὶ κακῶν γεγόντων 'Εβραίων ὑμεῖς μόνοι τὴν ὑπερβολικὴν καὶ πασῶν κακιῶν ἐσχάτην κακίαν καὶ ἀθεῖαν εἰργάσασθε, τὸν κύριον ἡμῶν 'Ιησοῦν Χριστὸν καὶ σωτῆρα τοῦ κοσμοῦ παντὸς σταυρῷ προσηλώσαντες. καὶ διὰ τοῦτο ... τὴν δικαίαν ποινὴν ὑφίστασθε, ὡς ἐκεῖνός που φῆσιν· ἔσται θλῖψις ἐν τῇ ἁλώσει ὑμῶν, οἷα οὐ γέγονεν ἀπὸ καταβολῆς κοσμοῦ...
>
> Now, O most godless enemy of the truth, you have said – though forced to it by the truth! – that no other race has worked such evil and that no other city has suffered such ruin; for although there have been many other good and wicked Hebrews, you alone have committed the exceedingly godless crime: you nailed our Lord Jesus Christ, the Saviour of the whole world, to the cross. And therefore ... you have suffered the just punishment as was spoken by Him: There will be great tribulation, when you fall into the hands of your enemies, such as has not been from the beginning of the world until now ...

Glosses with alternative readings, indeed Christian interpolations of all kinds, are found, for example, at *Ag. Ap.* 1:92, 98; 2:166, 168, and in *Ag. Ap.* 2:163-217, where the original reading in the only relevant manuscript, Laurentianus 29:22, could hardly still be reconstructed without the help of the late Latin translation, and with the help of Eusebius and the Byzantine epitomizers. This situation must be kept in mind when the source use of Origen and Eusebius is discussed.

PSEUDO-HEGESIPPUS

So-called Hegesippus (Pseudo-Hegesippus), a Latin paraphrase of the Greek *War* written about 370 (making use also of 1 Maccabees, Lucanus, Suetonius and Tacitus) is preserved among the writings of Ambrose, but the identity of the author remains hypothetical.[151] By introducing a Christian standpoint, the paraphraser changes Josephus' own portrayal, indeed already in the prologue he distances himself from his source (*consortem se enim perfidiae Judaeorum exhibuit*, 'indeed, he shows himself to have shared in the unbelief of the Jews'; *Prologus*, p3). The fall of Jerusalem and the destruction of Jerusalem by Titus are, in the Christian view, the de-

[151] Edited by Ussani. Cf Schreckenberg, *Tradition*, 56-58, and *Texte* 1, p310f. Good information on questions of literary history in Bell, *Analysis*; 'Traditions'; and 'Josephus'. Cf also Callu, 'Le *De Bello Judaico*'.

served punishment for the *perfidia* of the Jews and the killing of Jesus. Hegesippus' comment to the *Testimonium Flavianum* is characteristic of his polemical attitude:

> If the Jews will not believe us, they should at least believe their own people [i.e., their Jewish brother Josephus]. This is said by Josephus [i.e., the witness to Christ], whom they themselves hold to be of great importance; and yet even at this very point, where he speaks the truth, he has so wandered from the way spiritually, that he does not believe his own words. Yet for the sake of historical truth he speaks, for he considers deception a sin, but he does not believe, for his heart is hard and his faith is false. To be sure, he does no disadvantage to the truth with his unbelief, but rather strengthens his testimony .... The eternal power of Christ Jesus was made clear, in that even the leaders of the synagogue, who dragged him to execution, confessed his divinity. (*CSEL* 66/1, p164)

(Ps.-)Hegesippus brings the charge against Josephus that, although he defected to the Romans, 'he did not distance himself from their [the Jews'] blasphemy [i.e., their unbelief and the killing of Jesus]', and, 'indeed, laments in a heart-rending manner the tribulation [of the Jews], but fails to grasp the reason for this tribulation' (*CSEL* 66/1, p3), i.e., the fall of Jerusalem and the destruction of the Temple are the deserved punishment for the false beliefs (*perfidia*) and the godlessness (*impietas*) of the Jews who rejected and killed Jesus Christ (*Prologus*; *CSEL* 66/1, p3). Whereas Josephus himself differentiates between the various rebel groups and the population of Jerusalem, part of which was in no wise hostile to Rome, here we have an unqualified reference to 'the Jews' who have themselves to thank for their doom and cannot escape the punishment they have earned. Again it is clear how particularly in the fourth century polemical patterns arise in which the Jews are attacked collectively.

Hegesippus still sees himself as a historian following the classical example, and not yet as an apologist or, like Eusebius, as author of an apologetically oriented church history. However, his understanding of history is already thoroughly Christian, and the distortion of Josephus' purposes continues.[152] Thus a Jewish recognition of the divinity of Jesus of Nazareth was never connected with the *Testimonium Flavianum*, neither by Josephus nor other Jewish personalities. But Hegesippus fails to recognize the *circulus vitiosus* in which he is travelling. His statement that the Jews consider Josephus of 'great importance' is also purely fictitious; for Josephus was apparently forgotten by his Jewish contemporaries soon after his death, his works being transmitted almost exclusively in Christian circles.

Among other new elements in Hegesippus, we find an almost aggressive

[152] For details see e.g. Schreckenberg, *Texte* 1, p310f; id 'Wirkungsgeschichte', 1126, 1131f, 1156f, 1165, 1170, 1199, 1213; id 'Works of Josephus', 318; Wright, *Vengeance*, 30-32.

missionizing intention: If the Jews will not believe us, they should at least believe their own people and adopt the Christian truth themselves. His work also testifies to the strong interest in the *War*, Josephus' most important work from the perspective of anti-Jewish apology. In addition, the language barrier to Greek, gradually increasing in the Latin-speaking West, made a Latin adaptation urgent – so urgent, that shortly thereafter Rufinus of Aquileia commissioned a literal translation of the *War*, which is still extant.

With the traditional title *De excidio urbis Hierosolymitanae*, under which Hegesippus' work still appears in MIGNE's *Patrologia latina* (vol 15, col 2061-2326), it becomes apparent that Christian interest, as was already clear from the title Ἅλωσις, is in shortening the war of 66-70 to its apologetically significant outcome. *Urbs Hierosolymitana* stands here as a synecdoche, a *pars pro toto* for Judaea and the Jewish people, the confirmation of whose end was contemplated with satisfaction. Later, Hrabanus Maurus writes his *De subversione Jerusalem* exactly in this sense.[153] The way had already been marked out by Eusebius. Here too, Hegesippus follows Eusebius, in that he prefers to apply his interpretations to the scenes which are particularly impressive from a historical point of view, among them the *teknophagia* of Maria (5:40,1-2; *CSEL* 66/1, p381-4; on *War* 6:201-213).

BASIL THE GREAT

Basil the Great (died in 379) recounts Maria's *teknophagia* during the famine of Jerusalem in the year 70 (*PG* 31, col 324 to *War* 6:201-213), thereby continuing a line of tradition stemming already from the second century:

> This drama is also shown by the 'Jewish history', which the excellent Josephus composed for us, to be a tragic event, when the horrible suffering befell those living in Jerusalem, who were justly punished for their sacrilegious crime against the Lord.[154]

[153] Cf Schreckenberg, *Texte* 1, p500f. Wright ib 32 notes correctly that Hegesippus 'seeks to identify the victory of Rome with the rise of the Church triumphant ... Whereas Josephus attributed the failure of the rebellion to the internal dissension among the Jews and their refusal to accomodate themselves to the rising fortunes of the new chosen nation in the West, Hegesippus unequivocally pronounces a new doctrine of vengeance, interpreting the fall of Jerusalem as God's just punishment of the Jews for their role in the crucifixion of Christ ... The war is understood less in terms of historical contingency than in terms of Christian theology: the Jews are condemned not for their failure to capitulate to Rome, but for their failure to be converted by the divine savior whose execution they devised.'

[154] See Schreckenberg, *Tradition*, 88. Basically, Josephus has been pocketed by Basil and other Church fathers in such a way that he becomes a kind of 'crypto-Christian Nicodemus-type' (Bilde, *Josephus*, 207).

It is striking that Basil describes Josephus' historical work as written 'for us' (ἡμῖν), i.e., Christians. He is reflecting here the actual situation of Josephan transmission history, in the course of which Christians came to regard the Jewish historian as one of their own. Eusebius' strong influence can still be seen in Basil's dramatization of the story, in which the outcome produces horror and dismay, as in a tragedy staged for the self-righteous satisfaction of Christian 'onlookers'.

AMBROSE

Ambrose (died in 379) employs Josephus' *Antiquities* in his Bible interpretation. However, his numerous references are usually very imprecise and of no particular use even for the textual criticism of Josephus' Greek text. It seems that the language barrier, which Greek presented to the Latin-speaking West, is already beginning to have an effect here.[155]

Fourth and Fifth Centuries

SYRIAN JOSEPHUS (5 MACC) AND 4 MACC (PS.-JOSEPHUS)

A Syrian translation of the *War* appeared perhaps around the end of the fourth or in the first half of the fifth century. Only the portion containing the sixth book is still extant. In the Syrian Vulgate it is found as the 'Fifth Book of the Maccabees'.[156] That a book of the *War* appears at the end of the Old Testament is somewhat astonishing, but it illustrates the high value placed on Josephus at this time. 'Here Josephus has truly become part of the canon', is HARNACK's amazed comment to this occurrence.[157] What has brought about this inclusion of the Jewish historian in the biblical canon? Obviously the great, almost suggestive, affinity of content between the *War* and the Old and New Testaments. Book Six (with its description of the capture and destruction of Jerusalem) rounds off the biblical story appropriately, so to speak, insofar as the year 70 signified the end of the Old Covenant and the end of the Jews as the people of God.

Of only peripheral interest here is the 'Fourth Book of the Maccabees', reckoned among the Old Testament Pseudepigrapha. This is a philosophical treatise, written in the form of a speech, dealing with the rule of the desires by reason, as the title Περὶ αὐτοκράτορος λογισμοῦ suggests. It is presumed to have been written already during the time of the Emperor Caligula (37-41), but in the fourth century became generally regarded as a

[155] For details of Ambrose's use of Josephus see Schreckenberg, *Tradition*, 88f.
[156] See edition by Ceriani vol 2, 660-79; and new edition by Bedjan vol 1, 770-837. Cf Schreckenberg, *Tradition*, 61f and 'Wirkungsgeschichte', 1168.
[157] Harnack, *Geschichte* 1, p859.

work of Josephus, and has been transmitted therefore in numerous Josephus manuscripts. Doubtless there are certain affinities between this work and Josephus; its author is a pious Jew, who, using historical examples (e.g., the martyrdom of Eleazar and the seven Maccabean brothers with their mother, 2 Macc 6:18-7:42), admonishes his Jewish brethren to be faithful to the Law. Like Josephus, he uses the conceptional world of the Stoics and/or Hellenistic popular philosophy to express his thoughts. For the author 'reason' is at bottom neither an autonomous authority, nor a pagan philosophical concept, but pious, rationally grounded faithfulness to the Law. The speech is probably not a synagogue lecture actually delivered, but a diatribe.[158] Despite some points of contact and points in common with Josephus, it is very different from his work in style and content. The actual extent of the linguistic differences ought to be checked once again with the help of RENGSTORF'S *Complete Concordance*.

CHRYSOSTOM

With the exception of Plato, John Chrysostom (died in 407) appeals to no other author as often as he does to Josephus. To be sure, he frequently seems to cite Josephus very freely from memory or from an intermediary source.[159] In view of the importance which Josephus held for Chrysostom it is not surprising that he draws the historical proof texts for his anti-Jewish apologetic from him. Thus, at one point he presses Josephus into service against his own people for the sake of convincing them that the destruction of Jerusalem and the Temple was irreversible (*PG* 48, col 897):

> Even though the man who wrote this [Josephus] was a Jew, he did not emulate your [the Jews] contentious maliciousness. He said that Jerusalem would be conquered (and destroyed), but was not so bold as to add to this that it would be rebuilt ... he wrote that Jerusalem and the Temple would be laid waste, but he adds no mention of an end to its desolation, for he found no such addition in Daniel [Dan 9:26-27].

Here Josephus' account of the end of Jerusalem has become a proof for the irreversibility of that end.

Like Basil, Chrysostom is also reminded of a 'tragedy' by Josephus' *War*; for Josephus is his witness 'that those horrible events were worse than any tragedy, and that never has a war of such severity afflicted the [Jewish] people' (*PG* 58, col 695, making free use of *War* 1:1, 22). Such conceptions (for which John relied on Josephus) lead him to a complete deprecation of the Jewish religion as a superstition, which, after Golgotha and the events

[158] Norden, *Kunstprosa* 1, p416-20; Williams, *Josephus*.

[159] Schreckenberg, *Tradition*, 90f, 'Wirkungsgeschichte', 1135, 1157, 1180, 1193, 1199, 1208; and cf *Texte* 1, p320-29.

of 70 has forfeited its right to exist: 'If the Jewish cult is venerable and significant, then ours can only be lies and deception' (*PG* 48, col 852).[160]

THE LATIN JOSEPHUS: RUFINUS AND CASSIODORUS

Besides Pseudo-Hegesippus, the language barrier between the Greek East and the Latin West which ever was increasing in late antiquity, soon gave rise to a further Latin version of the *War*, the most sought after of Josephus' works. Also, considerably later and already at the transition between antiquity and the early middle ages, a Latin translation of *Antiquities* and *Against Apion* appears which should be briefly mentioned for the sake of completeness.

Rufinus (died c. 410-411) is generally considered to be the author of the Latin translation of *War*.[161] This translation however should be differentiated both from Hegesippus' Latin paraphrase (c. 370) and from the Latin translation of *Ant.* 1-20 and *Ag. Ap.* 1-2 commissioned by Cassiodorus (died after 580). Cassiodorus mentions it explicitly (*Institutiones* 1:17,1; Mynors, p55):

> I commissioned my friends to translate him [Josephus] – for he is a very difficult and many-sided author – in twenty-two books [i.e., twenty books of *Antiquities* and two books of *Against Apion*], this requiring a great deal of labor. He also wrote an additional seven books on the captivity of the Jews [*Captivitas Judaica*], truly a most excellent work; the Latin translation of this work is ascribed by some to Jerome, others to Ambrose, and still others to Rufinus.

The absence of Josephus' autobiography is striking. Its special place in the history of transmission as an appendix after the twentieth book of the *Antiquities* perhaps explains its absence from Cassiodorus' Greek codex. At all events, the *Life* is the only one of Josephus' works not appearing in a Latin version from late antiquity. That Cassiodorus had only *Antiquities* and *Against Apion* translated had two reasons. One was the banal fact that there probably already existed sufficient copies of the Latin *War*, and the other was the inner affinity of the two works, which taken together presented an excellent compendium of Jewish history and religion.

In certain respects the path from the Greek to the Latin Josephus is comparable to that from the Septuagint to the Vulgate. If one adds the first Aramaic edition of the *War*, this would basically be a formal repetition of

[160] This line of thinking is still to be found among medieval theologians, for example, the anonymous author of a *Tractatus adversus Judaeum* (1166): 'Show me the Temple destroyed by Vespasian and Titus, and I will confess that Christ has (still) not come', says a Christian to his interlocutor, meaning that the Jew is unable to make the *adynaton* happen; for the Temple has been gone for over a thousand years. If it still existed, the messiahship of Jesus Christ could justly be disputed. See Schreckenberg, *Texte* 2, p205.

[161] See Schreckenberg, *Tradition*, 58-61; *Untersuchungen*, 27f; 'Wirkungsgeschichte', 1213.

the steps from the Hebrew Bible through the Septuagint to the Vulgate. A description of the manuscripts of the Latin translations has been provided by Blatt in the introduction to his critical edition of the *Antiquities*, Books 1-5; only these five books and the two books of *Against Apion* have hitherto been published.[162] Against the confusion regarding the number of Latin translations and their interrelationship, we can ascertain that there are three such versions: Hegesippus, Rufinus' translation of the *War*, and the translation of *Ant.* 1-20 and *Ag. Ap.* 1-2 commissioned by Cassiodorus.

Regarding Cassiodorus it must be further noted that he reckons Josephus (*Inst.* 1:17,1; Mynors, p55) among Church writers along with Eusebius, Rufinus, Socrates, Sozomen and Theodoret, i.e., among those who possess the *ecclesiastica gravitas* of a Church father or author. It would thus be completely consistent had Cassiodorus counted him among the *patres* (*CCL* 98, p1208; but the tradition is doubtful here). In his presentation the 'exceedingly cruel Jewish people' who killed Jesus are punished by the destruction of Jerusalem which coincides with the Passion, illuminating the appropriateness of the punishment, and by the continuing dispersion.[163]

JEROME

Jerome (died in 420) makes very extensive use of Josephus, like Eusebius in frequency, and likewise often failing to mention his name. Josephus' books are a very important reference work for him in questions pertaining to New Testament history and biblical exegesis. Characteristic for his judgement of the worth of this source is his occasional reference to Josephus as to a handbook, for example, *Lege Josephi historiam* (*Comm. in Matt.* 1:2,22; *CCL* 77, p16) or *Lege Josephi historias* (*In Esaiam* 5:19,18; *CCL* 73, p198). However, his relationship to Josephus is not so uncritical that he cannot occasionally doubt his statements (*Hebraicae quaestiones in Gen.* 32:28-29;

[162] Blatt, *Latin Josephus*; Boysen, *Flavii Josephi opera* 6. On the other hand, mere printed reproductions of individual Latin manuscripts were, since 1470, very numerous. For this see Schreckenberg, *Bibliographie* Supplementband, 163ff. Investigations on the translations by Rufinus and Cassiodorus are still almost completely lacking. But Witty, 'Book Terms' has directed a few remarks to the translation initiated by Cassiodorus. It is unclear why Feldman ignores Rufinus' Latin translation. Already in his *Studies*, 27 he writes, 'There are two translations of J. into Latin. The first is a free reworking of the fourth century attributed to a certain Hegesippus ... The other is the famous translation made under the direction of Cassiodorus.' There is no mention of Rufinus' translation. In 'Flavius Josephus Revisited', 770 Feldman repeats this statement uncorrected: 'There are two translations of Josephus into Latin' (i.e., Hegesippus and Cassiodorus), but shortly thereafter he mentions a Latin translation of the *War*, apparently without noticing the contradiction to 'two translations'. Feldman's 'Corrigenda' to *Josephus and Modern Scholarship* (*Supplementary Bibliography*, 689-91) also fail to correct 'two translations'. Nor does Bilde, *Josephus*, 63 appear to be aware of Rufinus' translation.

[163] *CCL* 98, p672f on Ps 74; *CCL* 97, p525f on Ps 59:12 (Vulgate 58:12, *ne occidas eos ... disperge illos*, 'slay them not ... disperse them'); cf *CCL* 98, p697 on Ps 76.

CCL 72, p40). At one point he notes what Josephus omits in his biblical account (*Comm. in Ps.* 105; *CCL* 72, p230). Only rarely does he cite his source more or less literally (e.g., *In Danielem* 1:2,1a; *CCL* 75/A, p783), generally preferring a free paraphrase. To be sure, Jerome knows Josephus well but often omits details, so that his references are to a greater or lesser degree unverifiable in Josephus himself. This problem is already well-known to us in early Christian authors, and we have raised various possible solutions: the Christian author may cite imprecisely from memory; he may use a Josephus codex that varies from the extant text; or he may cite an intermediary source that has altered the genuine text.

Moreover, the language barrier between Greek sources and authors writing in Latin seems also to play a certain role here. The translation of *Antiquities* and *Against Apion* commissioned by Cassiodorus was not yet available, and Rufinus' translation of the *War*, although completed during Jerome's lifetime, was perhaps still unavailable to him. Apparently then, he did not possess a Latin version of Josephus. Indeed, he had learned Greek as an adult and knew it well, and was thus certainly equal to a Josephus codex. Nonetheless, a Latin Josephus was a genuine desideratum during his lifetime, perhaps for himself as well. Thus it is not by chance that, in one of his letters, he must refute the mistaken belief that he himself had made a Latin translation of Josephus.[164]

Jerome's *De viris illustribus* deserves special attention. In this catalogue of Christian authors, which could also be called a history of Christian literature, chapter 13 (*PL* 23, col 662f) is dedicated to Flavius Josephus. This is typical of the high value that had been attached to Josephus in the intervening period: he has become, as it were, a Christian author. Since Josephus' Greek autobiography had not been translated by Cassiodorus' friends, presumably because of its special place in the transmission history as an appendix to *Antiquities*, it is absent from the older printings of the Latin Josephus.[165] In its place it was customary to print chapter 13 from *De viris illustribus*, where Jerome had presented a sketch of the life and work of Josephus, including the *Testimonium Flavianum* and the expanded text of *Ant.* 20:200 which he also adopted unverified: *propter interfectionen Jacobi apostoli dirutam Hierosolymam*, 'because of the killing of James the Apostle, Jerusalem was destroyed.' That Jerome relates these uncommonly

[164] Jerome, *Epist.* 71:5,2 (*CSEL* 55, p6): *Josephi libros et sanctorum Papiae et Polycarpi volumina falsus ad te rumor pertulit a me esse translata*, 'A false rumor has reached you to the effect that Josephus' books as well as the volumes of the saints, Papias and Polycarp, have been translated by me' (cf Cassiodorus, *Inst.* 1:17,1). For Jerome's use of Josephus see Schreckenberg, *Tradition*, 91-94; id *Untersuchungen*, 28f; id 'Wirkungsgeschichte', 1127, 1133, 1136, 1140, 1147, 1157, 1169, 1180, 1205, 1208; id 'Works of Josephus', 318; Baras, 'Testimonium Flavianum', 340; Feldman, 'Flavius Josephus Revisited', 823f. Good general information on Jerome's use of Jewish traditions and his view on Judaism is found in Stemberger, 'Hieronymus'.

[165] See Schreckenberg, *Bibliographie* Supplementband, 163ff.

valuable accounts concerning early Christianity only once, indeed, that he does not use them as anti-Jewish proof texts at all, might be due to his doubts about their genuineness, coupled with his reluctance to address that delicate question. Generally speaking he shows little respect for Josephus' text; even if he possessed no Greek codex of the *Antiquities*, he certainly could have had access to one somewhere.

AUGUSTINE

Augustine (died in 430) knew Josephus, but it was the Greek text which since the third century was transmitted in the Eastern Church. Hence if he had no access to a Latin translation, the language barrier must have played its role, for Augustine's knowledge of Greek was poor. Mentioning Josephus by name in a letter to Hesychius (*Epist.* 199:30; *CSEL* 57, p270), he remarks concerning the destruction of Jerusalem: 'Josephus, who wrote the 'Jewish History', says that such sufferings were visited on that people then, that they hardly appear credible'; which calls to mind accounts such as *War* 6:193ff; 201ff. Presumably he only knew the *War* in Latin translation, perhaps that of Hegesippus.[166] Regarding our subject here, it is certain that at the one place where Augustine really examines Josephus, he is impressed by the ἅλωσις account. It is thus not surprising that, albeit without directly referring to Josephus, he interprets the destruction of Jerusalem and the Temple in manner of conventional anti-Jewish apologetic.[167]

ISIDORE OF PELUSIUM

Isidore of Pelusium (died in 435) values Josephus highly. He considers him the historian *par excellence*: Ἰώσηπος ὁ ἱστορικώτατος (*Epist.* 3:19; *PG* 78, col 475). Once he speaks of him as a 'man famous for his literary education and his scholarly knowledge (ἀνὴρ ἐπὶ παιδεύσει καὶ εἰδήσει λόγων ἐπισημότατος, *Epist.* 3:81; *PG* 78, col 787).[168]

Particularly striking is Isidore's emphasis on Josephus' 'love of the truth', which incidentally is the most frequent *epitheton ornans* of the Jewish historian in the entire Christian Josephus-tradition.[169] Thus with reference to the *Testimonium Flavianum* Isidore says (*Epist.* 4:225; *PG* 78, col 1320):

> Understandably, the testimony coming from the opponents appears credible to Greeks, barbarians, and all men, but the Jews, in their unbounded wickedness, believed neither the prophets nor even God himself. But there once lived a certain Josephus ['Ἰώσηπος'], an

[166] Schreckenberg, *Tradition*, 96; for further correspondences between Augustine and Josephus, cf id 'Wirkungsgeschichte', 1180, 1200; Altaner, 'Augustinus', 207, 212f.
[167] Schreckenberg, *Texte* 1, p357.
[168] See also Schreckenberg, *Tradition*, 96f; 'Wirkungsgeschichte', 1157, 1165, 1181, 1200.
[169] See Schreckenberg, 'Wirkungsgeschichte', 1164.

> excellent Jew, zealous for the Law. He faithfully retold the story of the Old Testament, fought superbly for the Jews, and proved all their viewpoints superior [over against the pagans]. However, he believed it necessary to honor truth .... I admire greatly the love for the truth [τὸ φιλάληθες] so amply demonstrated by him, most of all where he says: 'Teacher of men, who receive the truth with gladness' (*Ant.* 18:63).

We also meet a direct recommendation to read Josephus (*Epist.* 4:75; *PG* 78, col 1136):

> If you wish to become acquainted with the punishment of the blasphemous Jews who raged against Christ, read the account by Josephus concerning the ἅλωσις; indeed he is a Jew, but one who loves the truth (φιλαλήθης). There you will see a historical account that has been inspired by God ... for in order that no one find the account of their unbelievable and incomprehensible suffering incredible, the truth raised up, not a non-Jew – for perhaps then one might be forced to doubt – but, much more, one of their own faith who was zealous [for the Jewish cause], to present that unprecedented suffering in an impressive way, in dramatic form (ἐκτραγῳδῆσαι).

Since Aristotle (*Poet.* 6:1449b, 24-27) two effects considered necessary to the 'tragedy' were 'commiseration and fear'. Already in Josephus' 'dramatic episode style' we see the influence of the ancient theory of literature and style, and the calculated effect of that theory is still echoed in Isidore. Often Christian reaction to Josephus' destruction account here as elsewhere is pity, horror and dismay, not infrequently mixed with satisfaction over the 'just' retribution visited on the criminal Jews. Elsewhere Isidore writes wholly in this sense, on the basis of a similar evaluation of the Josephus accounts (*PG* 78, col 968):

> Their [the Jews'] continued existence was permitted, that their endless suffering might serve as a tragic [ἐκτραγῳδεῖν] spectacle [for the world], and that they might wander the earth as prisoners of war [who had lost their freedom and homeland] and vagabonds, deserving nothing but blows, everywhere beholding the Crucified One highly exalted'.

Here, based particularly on the groundwork laid by Eusebius, the suffering and tragic fate of the Jews becomes an object of devotional instruction for Christians.

CYRIL OF ALEXANDRIA

Cyril of Alexandria (died in 444) apparently uses Josephus largely via an intermediary source. His mention of *teknophagiai* (*In Johannis Ev.* 8:28; *PG* 78, col 828) is a reference to the historiographical showpiece in *War* 6:201-213. The exaggerated plural *teknophagiai* for the singular episode (similarly, Eusebius in *Theoph*. 4:20-22) betrays a secret complacency with the suffering of the Jews. In his *Commentarius in Zachariam* 11:1-2 (*PG* 72, col 176) he sees the disobedience of the Jews prophesied for the time of Christ's incarnation, for which reason the Temple and Jerusalem had to be destroyed and the cities of Israel were laid waste. This happened 'at the hands of the Romans' and their generals Vespasian and Titus, because of their crimes against Christ. Whoever wishes to know everything in detail may read it in the writings of Josephus. Cyril writes in the same context (on Zech 11:6-7; *PG* 72, col 185):

> The disturbances of civil war in all Judaea, in Jerusalem, and in every city, have been presented in detail by him who recorded the unhappy fate of the Jews with tragic pathos, Josephus, a famous and wise man.

He continues (on Zech 12:11-14; *PG* 72, col 225):

> Because of their crimes against Christ they were delivered up to their enemies; Vespasian and Titus laid their land waste; Jerusalem was placed under siege, all inhabitants starved to death; and everywhere were misery and lamentation. Josephus bears witness to this. In the record of his books concerning the capture [of the city] he spoke in the following way about Jerusalem: for throughout the city they were bewailing the dead, there were loud shrieks of lamentation, and a dirge was conducted (κομμοὶ δὲ ἦσαν ἀνὰ τὴν πόλιν πανταχῆ, οἰμωγὴ δὲ διαπρύσιος καὶ θρῆνος ἐγκέλευστος).

Here the text from *War* 2:6 is torn from a completely foreign context (inner-Jewish disturbances after the death of Herod) and pressed into service as an anti-Jewish historical interpretation. Josephus' historical account is used here, as in other Christian authors, under the influence of theological aspects, and is changed to such an extent that the later epitomizers had a difficult time separating the *ipsissima verba Josephi* from their theological interpretation – an instructive example for the origin of a fictitious Josephan testimony *in statu nascendi* and *in situ*!

PROSPER OF AQUITAINE

Prosper of Aquitaine (died after 455) also comes to speak of the capture of Jerusalem by Titus in his *Epitoma chronicorum*:

> After the capture of Judaea and the destruction of Jerusalem, Titus put 600,000 men to death. Josephus writes that 110,000 died by the sword and starvation and a further 100,000 prisoners were sold [as slaves]. Passover is the reason that such a great number was present in Jerusalem. Therefore all those pouring into the Temple from all Judaea were shut up as in a prison: It was necessary then (*oportuit enim*), that they be killed in those same days [during Passover] in which they had killed the Saviour [i.e., in accordance with the *lex talionis*].Here as well, in a line of tradition we have already seen, the

genuine historical account (*War* 6:420-421, 423-428) is distorted and deformed. The historical event of 70 is regarded as the just punishment of the Jews for their crimes against Jesus. The death of the Jews is shifted to Passover time, even though, by Josephus' account, the fall of the city took place on September 26 (*War* 6:435), and this chronological congruity indicates a significant worsening of the talion. For the direct connection between crime and punishment would be especially mortifying for those being punished. Once again we see in *statu nascendi* how Josephus as a source is falsified by a Christian transmitter. Even the motif is obvious (*oportuit enim*...): the fate of the Jews shows how properly God directs history and punishes the wicked.[170]

FULGENTIUS FABIUS PLANCIADES

The aspect of punishment also dominates in a relevant section of the work *De aetatibus mundi et hominis* by the Christian author, Fulgentius Fabius Planciades (of uncertain date – probably belonging to the the fifth century). The author uses Josephus' *War* without citing him.[171] He is interested only in the *teknophagia* of Maria, who, faced with starvation in besieged Jerusalem, killed, roasted, and consumed her own child. Fulgentius, who leaves much to be desired as an author but in this respect is rather typical, believed that Christ himself chose the Roman general Vespasian as the avenger for the Jewish crime and their wickedness.

> However, this divine punishment [i.e. the *teknophagia*] against the rebels was just. For what patience had Judaea with her children, who led her own Salvation to the wooden cross; who instead of receiving the flesh of the Son of God despised it, and prepared for herself a meal from the flesh of her son...'

It is unclear what else Fulgentius knows from the work of Josephus and whether he had access to the original text. Perhaps he used an intermediary source which sufficed for his purposes of anti-Jewish theological argumentation.

THEODORET OF CYRRHUS

Theodoret of Cyrrhus (died in 457) consults Josephus most extensively in his biblical exegesis. He rates his value as a witness very high, but as a rule makes critical use of him.[172] It is thus not surprising that the text proliferation surrounding *Ant.* 20:200, regarding James the brother of the Lord, does not appear in his work. He does mention though the *Testimonium Flavianum* from his Josephus codex without any suspicion (*In Daniel.*

[170] Schreckenberg, *Untersuchungen*, 30; 'Wirkungsgeschichte', 1148, 1160.

[171] Chapter 14 in ed Helm; cf Schreckenberg, *Untersuchungen*, 31.

[172] Schreckenberg, *Tradition*, 98f; *Untersuchungen*, 16f; 'Wirkungsgeschichte', 1181.

12:14; *PG* 81, col 1544): 'He did not accept the Christian message, but did not want to hide the truth.' He also transmits unreflected the doctrine of the *servitus Judaeorum*: In 70 the Jews were 'scattered through all lands and over the sea, and though once free, became slaves' (*PG* 80, col 1525). Such recasting of socio-historical reality by Christian wishful thinking has already been seen above concerning the sale of prisoners of war (*War* 3:540; 6:384, 414-419); for there was no collective enslavement of the Jews after 70. On the contrary, as a *religio licita* Judaism was in an even better situation than Christianity, which suffered occasional persecution, and through Caracalla's *Constitutio Antoniniana* in 212 the Jews became fully enfranchised Roman citizens, which status they retained during the imperial period. Not until the fourth-fifth centuries did certain restrictions of social and civil rights resulting from Christian influenced imperial legislation come into effect, without however ever rescinding religious freedom.[173]

APPENDIX: EPITOME ANTIQUITATUM

The *Epitome Antiquitatum*[174] dates from the tenth century, but deserves to be mentioned in conclusion. In certain respects a Greek counterpart to Hegesippus' abbreviated *War*, it illuminates the great popularity of Josephus in the middle ages. *Epitomai*, abridged versions of larger works, were customarily only produced from works which were as voluminous as they were significant. This *Epitome* is also of some worth for the emendation of Josephus' Greek text, and therefore Niese edited it separately and consulted it throughout as a text witness in his *editio maior critica* of Josephus. Unfortunately, later editors of the Greek text of the *Antiquities* have extensively cited and used the *Epitome* incorrectly, an important circumstance which we cannot pass over in silence.[175]

[173] See Schreckenberg, 'Wirkungsgeschichte', 1179ff; *Texte* 1, p259ff.

[174] Edition by Niese, *Epitoma*.

[175] See my review of Feldman's *Josephus and Modern Scholarship*, 412; there, as an example, the list of errata from Feldman, *Josephus*, vol 9. Feldman, 'Postscript', 1299 has contradicted this criticism on the basis that 'ten of the alleged errors in my citations of the "Epitome" are not errors', but does not indicate which of his questioned references (in all, c. 70) are supposed to be correct. The incorrect evaluation of this important element of Christian transmission of Josephus has continued for decades: in order that it might finally be laid to rest, we list here all disputed citations from the *Epitome* in *Ant*. 18-20, using Niese's edition of the *Epitome*. The result proves that the objections raised to incorrect *Epitome* citations are indeed justified: *Ant*. 18:4 Γαυλανίτης δέ τις ἀνήρ; 18:32 ''Αννινος; 18:47 ἀνδραπόδῳ γὰρ ἀλλοτρίῳ; 18:78 ἐπεσήμανε; 18:82 ὁμοιοτρόπους and Φουλβίαν; 18:98 ἔπεσε; 18:107 τὸ πᾶν; 18:111 πύστεως; 18:118 τοῦ μεταβολῆς; 18:124 – here χειμαδιᾶν is omitted by the Epitome; 18:125 ἤ; 18:129 δὲ καί; 18:134 ἀδελφός; 18:138 ὁ 'Ελκίας; 18:157 Μαρσύαν; 18:192 παρ'; 18:205 περί; 18:226 κρίνοιεν; 18:230 καίνωσίν τινα; 18:234 θροεῖν; 18:264 θεωρεῖν; 18:296 ἀρετήν; 18:312 Νίσιβις; 18:339 αὐτῶν; 18:345 ἀρχήν; 18:376 σύμβασις; 19:12 λέγεσθαι; 19:34 Κυϊντιλίαν; 19:85 ἕωθέν τε and τῶν ἱππικῶν; 19:110 προκατειργασμένον; 19:130 θεραπείᾳ; 19:145 'Αρούντιος; 19:166 Σατορνῖνος and ἀρχῆς; 19:201 κακο-

Summary

Reviewing the role that Josephus plays in early Christian texts, we see that the *War* gradually assumed a dominant role, above all since Eusebius. To be sure, many early Christian authors found *Against Apion* useful at first, since the argument for the antiquity of the Jewish religion and its superiority to Greek wisdom could be extended to Christianity as its successor. And the accounts in the *Antiquities* concerning Jesus and early Christianity were certainly a stimulating factor for Christian Josephus transmission. But the *halosis* account, once recognized as such, caused far and away the greatest interest; for, 'The fall of Jerusalem is not an arbitrary historical event; it belongs of necessity within the context of salvation history, indeed as a seal upon the 'Old Covenant', verily ended and fulfilled through 'Christ's' cross and resurrection.'[176]

Early Christianity learned from anti-pagan apologetic in *Against Apion* and adapted it to its own apologetic interests. But for the Church's historical self-definition over against Judaism, the *War* proved itself to be the most useful in the long run. Josephus' judgement on the Zealots and other rebel groups could, as an inner-Jewish critique, easily be generalized. Instead of naming individual militant groups in distinction from portions of the population thinking otherwise, as did Josephus, it sufficed to speak of 'the Jews' – and a principal witness from the enemy camp proving the fulfillment of the New Testament doom prophecies over Jerusalem was ready to hand. The inherent circular reasoning was not recognized; that these prophecies were not formulated until after 70 as statements ex eventu, so to speak, was first recognized by exegetes of the nineteenth and twentieth centuries. And the fact that in the year 70 at least three-fourths of the Jews in the Roman Empire already lived in the Diaspora, safely survived the catastrophe and were in no wise subjected to servitude, but since 212 had enjoyed full Roman citizenship, was too easily suppressed by Christian historiography since Eusebius.

The authors of a new history of salvation and of the church saw Josephus as one of their own, indeed a man of *ecclesiastica gravitas* (above, p77) and inspired by God above (above p80). He documents the fulfillment of New Testament prophecies, as the New Testament does the realization of Old Testament promises. 'Josephan accounts supplied all the credentials of

τροπίας; 19:226 συμφράξαντές τε; 19:230 ἡσσώμενον; 19:246 ἔργῳ-προκεισομένης; 19:264 οὐ μεθ'; 19:268 ἑταίρους; 19:299 εἰς αὐτὸν ... ἑκάστης; 19:323 ἀπολουμένην; 19:324 ποριζόμενος; 19:338 Κότυς; 19:339 παρουσίᾳ; 19:347 ἄρτι μου; 19:355 'Αντιόχου; 19:366 ἐπαρχίας; 20:4 'Αννίβας; 20:18 Βαζαῖος; 20:22 'Αβεννήριγον; 20:23 Συμμαχώ; 20:35 διδαχθεῖσαν; 20:43 ἀκριβής; 20:44 ἀναγινώσκειν; 20:59 ἐκστήσομαι; 20:86 ἔχων ... ἑξακισχιλίους; 20:158 δυνάστου; 20:159 δεκατέσσαρας; 20:180 οὐδὲ ἕις; 20:186 ἐπικαμπέσι ... σίκαις; 20:190 πάλαι and 'Ασαμωναίου; 20:203 Δαμναίου; 20:216 φυλή; 20:231 'Ιωσαδάκην; 20:232 τετρακοσίων; 20:256 ἠθῶν.

[176] Von Campenhausen, 'Entstehung', 199.

historical authenticity and convincingly allowed New Testament prophecies to appear fulfilled. The relationship between his 'Jewish War' and the New Testament is in some respects like that between the New and the Old Testament, i.e., a kind of verifying commentary or key to prove the fulfillment of prophecy.'[177] The typological relationship between the Old and New Testaments, known in early Christianity particularly since Justin Martyr, could be turned into an unassailable apologetic bulwark via the correspondence between the New Testament and Josephus. Josephus is as it were conscripted into the established methods of proof-texting, and even canonized, as seen not least of all by his reception into the Syrian Vulgate. Viewed this way, New Testament, Old Testament and Josephus form a relational triangle, which made a rich treasure of theological argumentation and religious edification available.

The more an author was read and his work transcribed, the greater the probability that his text would undergo distortions. This is particularly true for Josephus. He was not subject to a standardizing text control comparable to that applied on the New and Old Testaments, albeit with varying success. Thus it happened that even important theologians disseminated and thereby sanctioned cleverly invented falsifications, apparently with no thought of first verifying them. To be sure, the absence of indices and concordances limited the possibilities for verification. But the decisive factor was the lack of motivation: for by then the rejection of spurious texts was no longer new in the history of scholarly criticism, and it had already been practiced successfully by Alexandrian literary and textual critics. In any case, Hellenistic Alexandrian scholars already worked more or less critically, without theological interests or prejudice.

[177] Schreckenberg, 'Wirkungsgeschichte', 1131.

Chapter Four

Josephus in Medieval Christian Art

As we have seen, Josephus was passed on almost exclusively in the Christian sphere. It appears that he was forgotten soon after his death by his fellow Jews. Since no Jewish transmission of Josephus manuscripts exists, either ancient or medieval, neither are there miniatures to his work from the hands of Jewish artists. Thus we might well have omitted the 'Christian' from the title of this chapter. 'Josephus' in the title requires some qualification. The numerous illustrations in manuscripts of the *Antiquities* could not be taken into account here, since these are mostly concerned with biblical scenes in Josephus' extensive Bible paraphrases, pictures which, as a rule, are untypical for the Jewish historian and which can also be found in medieval biblical manuscripts. The situation is similar, for example, with depictions of Herod in manuscripts of the *Antiquities* or *War*: they could also be found in New Testament manuscripts. Moreover, Deutsch has already published numerous examples of such pictures.[178] Indeed, he has searched out extensive pictorial material and made it available for Josephan research also in the area of the Early and High Middle Ages. His impressive contribution is by no means diminished by our recognition that it is incomplete because its focal point is in the Late Middle Ages, and that in this area there is still much *terra incognita*. Further developing work published elsewhere on medieval iconography concerning Jews,[179] the present contribution intends to describe the specific representation of Josephus in medieval Christian art.

Portraits of Josephus

BERN, BURGERBIBLIOTHEK, COD. 50 **(pl. 1)**

Miniature in one of the Latin manuscripts of the *Antiquities* and the *War* from the first half of the ninth century (Bern, Burgerbibliothek, Cod. 50,

[178] Deutsch, *Iconographie*; regarding Jean Fouquet especially, Deutsch seems to have overlooked the study by Thomas, *Buchmalerei*, 80f; see also Deutsch, 'Illustration', 398-410.
[179] Schreckenberg, *Texte* 2, p447-635: 'Ikonographie des Judenthemas bis zum 4. Laterankonzil'.

fol 2r; plate: DEUTSCH, 'Un portrait de Josèphe').[180]

This portrait of Josephus is the earliest that can with certainty be determined. As all others, it is an imaginative product with no claim to likeness to the author; as DEUTSCH assumed, it portrays him in Parthian dress. He is identified in the superscript: Υωσυππος 'Υσϑωρυωγραφος (Josephus the Historian). He produces a somewhat exotic effect, but not as DEUTSCH thinks, dark and frightening ('le barbare hirsute et infernal', p63) and comparable with the ancient oriental god of doom, Nergal – in short 'le magicien oriental Josèphe'.[181] The dark facial color seems rather to have been caused by natural damage. A more likely indication could be the round head covering with the extended side pieces depending downwards and somewhat outwards (a kind of Phrygian cap?). It also appears on persons who on other grounds as well should be described as oriental.[182] But by no means does this suggest an affinity to doom, evil, and the Infernal. DEUTSCH's interpretation is also erroneous at another important point, i.e., that Josephus wears a soldier's helmet and therefore is meant as a warrior. rather, his further appearance identifies him as a messenger or herald, a function that he had often actually had (*War* 5:114, 261, 361ff, 541; 6:94ff, 129, 365). Accordingly, he carries the customary herald's wand in his right hand in this picture, as the emblem of this office (κηρύκειον, *caduceus*).

PARIS, BN, GR. 923

Miniatures in a ninth century manuscript of the *Sacra Parallela* of John of Damascus, probably of Palestinian provenance (Paris, BN, Cod. Gr. 923, fols 74r, 192r, 226v, 296r: Flavius Josephus; fol 208r: Philo and Josephus as double portrait).[183] Each of the author portraits appears in a medallion. Josephus wears shoulder-length hair and a beard. This giant florilegium contains numerous other portraits, mostly stylized, among others of Philo, Justin Martyr, John Chrysostom, Ezekiel, and the Evangelists. Similar author portraits of the most varying kinds, above all of the Prophets, Evangelists, Church fathers, and pagan authors of antiquity, can be found

[180] Blatt, *Latin Josephus*, 47; Homburger, *Burgerbibliothek*, Tafel XXXIV; Deutsch, 'Un portrait de Josèphe'; id, *Iconographie*, Fig. 4; id, 'Illustration', 400-404; Schreckenberg, *Texte* 2, p462f. We mention only in passing the 'supposed head of a Roman statue of Flavius Josephus' in Copenhagen, *Ny Carlsberg Glyptotek* (frontispiece in Eisler's *Iêsous basileus*, vol. 2), since the findings are uncertain here; cf Schreckenberg, *Tradition*, 174.

[181] Gutmann's objections ('Josephus' Jewish Antiquities', 440) to Deutsch are justified: 'The evidence he presents for a Greek Josephus of Syro-Iranian origin is not convincing.' Moreover, Deutsch has incorrectly read the superscription: Υωσσιππος instead of Υωσυππος.

[182] Ehrenstein, *Das Alte Testament*, 817 pl. 2, a Christian fresco of the fourth century: the three young men in the fiery furnace (Dan 3); a French wall painting from c. 1100 depicts David's father Jesse wearing a similar oriental cap, the pointed side pieces of which also curve lightly outwards (Waterman-Antony, *Romanesque Frescos*, fig. 339).

[183] Weitzmann, *Miniatures*, fig. 717-20, 751; cf Deutsch, *Iconographie*, 62.

1. Josephus as oriental messenger
9th cent. ms. of *Antiquities* and *War* (p87)

in numerous medieval manuscripts, often at the beginning of the work or of a section.

BRUSSELS, BR, MS. II 1179 **(pl. 2)**

Miniature to the prologue of the *Antiquities* in a Latin Josephus manuscript from the Stavelot abbey, at the end of the eleventh century (Brussels, BR, Ms. II 1179, fol 1v; plate: GASPAR – LYNA, *Les principaux manuscrits* 2, pl. XIII).[184]

Within the miniature of the initial *H(istoriam)*, Josephus sits upon the crossbar of the letter as upon an armchair, in exactly the same way as the Church father Jerome in the miniature of the initial *H(ieronymus)*.[185] He is richly gowned, and is shown just dipping his quill into an inkwell with his right hand, while the left holds a penknife over the book in which he is writing. This is the same depiction that we find elsewhere with Old Testament Prophets, the Evangelists, or the Church fathers. The picture illustrates something of the *ecclesiastica gravitas* which Cassiodorus attributed to Josephus.

CAMBRIDGE, ST. JOHN'S COLLEGE, A 8 **(pl. 3)**

Minature in the initial C of the prologue of a Latin *War* (c. 1130; Cambridge, St. John's College, Ms. A 8, fol 103v; plate: KAUFFMANN, *Romanesque Manuscripts*, fig. 118).[186]

The Jewish historian, for whom the adscript *Iosephus* is provided, stands in rich raiment, exactly as a genteel Hebrew of the twelfth century, before a seated scribe (adscript: *Samuel*). The scribe, wearing tonsure and cowl, is depicted as a monk at his duties in a cloister scriptorium. Josephus holds an open book showing the beginning of the *Testimonium Flavianum* (*Fuit autem*...), and here appears like one of the biblical prophets (e.g., Isaiah) who in medieval illustrated Bibles are frequently depicted as presenting the Christ prophecy contained in their own text. Josephus' stature, almost that of Church father, is due not least of all to his accounts about Christ and Christianity.[187] In this role, moreover, he is the final link in a chain of authorities: Old Testament – New Testament – Josephus. He confirms as it were the *veritas christiana*. The tonsured *notarius* probably represents the thankful Christian public. Additionally, Josephus is bearded and his luxu-

[184] Blatt, *Latin Josephus*, 82f; Gaspar and Lyna, *Principaux manuscrits* 2, Pl. XIII; Deutsch, *Iconographie*, fig. 5; Schreckenberg, *Texte* 2, p517f.
[185] Gutbrod, *Initiale*, Pl. 106.
[186] Blatt, *Latin Josephus*, 89; Kauffmann, *Romanesque Manuscripts*, fig. 118; Deutsch, *Iconographie*, fig. 6; 'Illustration', 404f; Schreckenberg, *Texte* 2, p518.
[187] Cf Schreckenberg, 'Wirkungsgeschichte'.

2. Josephus as ecclesiastical writer
Miniature, late 11th cent. Latin ms. of *Antiquities* (p90)

3. Josephus as a genteel Hebrew with monastic scribe
Minature, Latin ms. of *War*, c. 1130 (p90)

4. Josephus with oversized Jews' hat
Miniature, 12th cent. Latin ms. of *Antiquities* (p94)

riant hair is stylized in locks in the manner often found in personal depictions from late antiquity and the Early Middle Ages.[188]

PARIS, BN, LAT. 5047 (pl. 4)

Miniature in the initial *P(rincipio)* at the beginning of a twelfth century Latin manuscript of the *Antiquities* (Paris, BN, Lat. 5047, fol 2r, col 2; plate: GUTBROD, *Initiale*, p107, pl. 65).[189]

The bearded, long-haired Josephus forms with his body the shaft of the letter P. The belly of the P is formed by an unrolled scroll held in the historian's hand; it bears the inscription, *Iosephus Antiquitatum*. 'What we have here is an author portrait comparable to the initials of the Prophets and the Evangelists'.[190] Being a Jew, Josephus wears the conventional symbol of recognition, an immense Jews' hat, which, with its curved tip, appears similar in form to a Phrygian cap. This Phrygian cap (*mitra*, *tiara phrygia*) is the predecessor of the actual medieval Jews' hat: a pointed hat, often with upper shaft and round knob. In the visual arts of the High Middle Ages, the biblical prophets, for example, still wear the Phrygian cap.[191] That Josephus is here wearing an oversized Jews' hat has a good reason: in such cases the Jewishness of the person depicted is especially emphasized. In Josephus' case, it is his very Jewishness which increases his value for Christian apologetic: he is the principal witness from the enemy camp. Thus also is the gesture to be understood, in which he indicates the picture of Christ placed directly beside him (see below, pl. 21). Here the role often written for him in early Christianity is singularly illustrated: Josephus the Jew becomes a prophet of Christianity.[192]

[188] See, e.g., Weitzmann, *Age of Spirituality*, Plate on p533; Hobson, *Große Bibliotheken*, Plate on p54; Ferguson, *Miniatures*, 101, fig. 8.

[189] Blatt, *Latin Josephus*, 64; Lauer, *Enluminures*, pl. XLIII, Nr. 4; Gutbrod, *Initiale*, Pl. 65; Schreckenberg, *Texte* 2, 552.

[190] Gutbrod, *Initiale*, 107.

[191] For the Phrygian cap which marked the medieval Jews as an oriental 'alien group' see Schreckenberg, *Texte* 2, p701 (index, s.v. 'phrygische Mütze'). Cf Chapeaurouge, *Einführung*, 144f who remarks that this cap marked its wearers already in pre-Christian antiquity (above all Persians and Trojans), and says aptly (144): 'Noch in der christlichen Kunst sieht man die Magier phrygische Mützen tragen, um ihre östliche Herkunft kenntlich zu machen.' The oversized Jews' hat in this picture links up with other medieval portrayals showing immense Jews' hats, as for example the picture of Moses in an anonymous twelfth century world chronicle (Schreckenberg, *Texte* 2, p571) or a line drawing in a twelfth century Augustine manuscript (ib p600f).

[192] It is thus not surprising that the historian is even once depicted with a halo, in the miniature of a Latin Josephus manuscript written in the Bonne Esperance abbey in Flanders (Faider, 'Un Manuscrit', 141-4).

STUTTGART, LB, HIST. 418 **(pl. 5)**

Initial miniature at the beginning of the prologue of the *Antiquities* in a twelfth century Latin manuscript from the monastery at Zwiefalten, (Stuttgart, LB, Hist. 418, fol 1; plate: GUTBROD, *Initiale*, p164, pl. 107).[193]

Josephus, half-sitting and half-leaning on the crossbar of the initial *H(istoriam)*, is beginning to write in a scroll with his quill. He is respectably but not expensively clothed, and, wearing relatively short hair and no beard, gives almost a youthful appearance. Accordingly, we find here no prophetic gesture or attitude.

CHANTILLY, MC, MS. 1632 **(pl. 6)**

Miniature of the initial *H(istoriam)* to the prologue of the Latin *Antiquities* from a manuscript produced in the Flemish abbey St. Trond in 1170 (Chantilly, MC, Ms. 1632; plate: DAMMERTZ, *Benedictus*, p204, pl. 161).[194]

Josephus sits on the crossbar of the initial H while writing in a codex with a quill in his right hand and holding a penknife in his left. He is richly gowned, longhaired, bearded, and wears a conical Jews' hat, the distinguishing feature for Jews in twelfth century Europe.[195] DAMMERTZ' evaluation of the writing figure as a 'scribe at work' is completely erroneous; he fails to recognize the function and type of the so-called author portrait in medieval manuscripts.

ADMONT, MS. 25 **(pl. 7)**

Portrait within the initial A at the beginning of the fourteenth book of the Latin *Antiquities*, in a manuscript from the Admont Stiftsbibliothek (Admont, Ms. 25, fol 2; plate: BUBERL, *Die illuminierten Handschriften*, p52, fig. 50).[196]

Josephus, looking like a scribe in a scriptorium, is seated upon the crossbar of the initial A, which is depicted as a bench. He is shown sharpening his quill with a penknife. He is bearded and wearing the conical Jews' hat of the twelfth century as a head covering.

PARIS, BN, FR. 247

Initial miniature by Jean Fouquet (1415/20 – 1477/81) to the prologue of a fifteenth century French translation of the *Antiquities* (Paris, BN, fr. 247,

193 Blatt, *Latin Josephus*, 40f; Gutbrod, *Initiale*, Pl. 107.
194 Dammertz, *Benedictus*, Pl. 161; Schreckenberg, *Texte* 2, p518f.
195 Numerous examples of this hat type can be found in Schreckenberg, *Texte* 2, p693 (index, s.v. 'konischer Judenhut').
196 Buberl, *Illuminierte Handschriften*, fig. 50 and also fig. 79 of Philo; cf also *EJ* 9 (Berlin 1932) 410; and Schreckenberg, *Texte* 2, p518.

5. Josephus as a youthful writer
Miniature, 12th cent. Latin ms. of *Antiquities* (p95)

6. Josephus in rich gown and Jews' hat
Miniature, Latin ms. of *Antiquities*, c. 1170 (p95)

7. Josephus with Jews' hat
Miniature, late 12th cent. Latin ms. of *Antiquities* (p95)

fol 1).[197] A sitting Josephus is depicted as a kind of 'savant humaniste' (DEUTSCH).

PARIS, BN, LAT. 5060

Portrait within an initial at the beginning of a fifteenth century Latin manuscript (Italian provenance) of the *War* (Paris, BN, Lat. 5060, fol 1).[198] DEUTSCH's interpretation is probably correct: 'Un peintre italien de manuscrits semble avoir retrouvé la tradition antique et paléochrétienne de l'écrivain inspiré. Assis de face, Josèphe tient le livre en son giron de sa main droite; deux doigts de sa main gauche sont tendus comme pour bénir ou pour argumenter. L'auteur apparaît là comme la personnification de son texte dans lequel il trouve sa justification. Il est promu au rang d'organe de l'Esprit, incarné entre les pages du livre.' Less certain is DEUTSCH's interpretation at another point ('Illustration', 405) of the figure 'as a town councillor or magistrate, or as an Oriental magus wearing conical hat with a wide and curving brim'. Given the lack of clarity and poor quality of the picture, it is perhaps better to content ourselves with a *non liquet*.

PARIS, BN, LAT. 5051, FOL 1

Initial miniature to the prologue of a fifteenth century Latin manuscript of the *Antiquities* from Italy (Paris, BN, Lat. 5051, fol 1).[199] Josephus, apparently bearded, is seated on a bench at a large writing desk under the crossbar of the initial H. He is looking like an important scholar or 'mage oriental' (DEUTSCH), since he wears the high conical hat with raised front and rear brims which in contemporary French and Italian portrayals customarily identifies its wearer as Oriental, and above all, as Jewish or Israelite actors in New and Old Testament scenes.

PARIS, BN, LAT. 5051, FOL 2

Initial miniature at the beginning of the Genesis paraphrase in Book One of the Latin *Antiquities*, in a fifteenth century manuscript of Italian provenance (Paris, BN, Lat. 5051, fol 2).[200] Josephus is apparently wearing a high conical hat, as in fol 1 of the same manuscript. Here again DEUTSCH recognizes in Josephus the 'mage oriental'.

[197] Deutsch, *Iconographie*, fig. 20.
[198] ib, fig. 14; id, 'Illustration', 405.
[199] id, *Iconographie*, fig. 15; 'Illustration', 405.
[200] id, *Iconographie*, fig. 16.

Incipit prologus sancti Jeronimi in Josephum

Osephus mathie filius ex iherosolimis sacerdos/a vespasiano captus cu tito filio eius relictus:hic romam ueniens septem libros iudaice captiuitatis imperatoribus patri filioque obtulit qui et bibeliothece publice tradite sunt et ob ingenij gloriã statuã quoque rome meruit. Scripsit aut et alios viginti antiquitatu libros:ab exordio mundi usque ad quartu decimum annu domiciani cesaris. hic in octauo decimo antiquitatum libro manifestissime ofitet propter magnitudinem signorum xpm a pharisseis interfectu & iohannem baptistã vere prophetam fuisse et propter interfectionem iacobi apli iherosolimam dirutam. Scribit aut de dño in hunc modum. Eo tempore fuit ihesus sapiens vir:si tn uirum eum oportet dicere Erat enim mirabilium patrator opm et doctor eorum qui libent vera suscipiut plurimos quoque tã de iudeis q de gentibus sui habuit sectatores et credebat esse cristus. Cumque inuidia nrorum principu cruci eum pilatus addixerit nichil ominus qui pmum dilexerut. perseuerauerunt. Aparuit enim eis tercia die uiuens:multa hec et alia mirabilia carminibus prophetarum de eo vaticinantibus Et vsque hodie cristianorum gens ab hoc sortita vocabulum non defecit

Explicit prefacio

ISTORIAM conscribere disponentibus non vnam nec eandem uideo eiusdem studij causam sed multas existere:et ab alterutro plurimum differentes. Nam quidam eorum sui sermonis pandere uolentes ornatu et ex hoc gloriã aucupãtes ad partem huius discipline accedunt alij vero illis grãm deferentes. de quibus ipsam descriptiõez esse otigerit in eodẽ opere vltra virtutem coacti sunt laborare. Quidam aut ipsarum rerum necessitate vim passi sunt. vt ea quibus interfuerunt cum agerent scripte declaratione colligerent. Multos aut rerum vtiliu magnitudo in oculto iacentiu muitauit ut historiam ex hijs ad utilitatẽ deberent pferre cõmunem Harum itaque qs pdixi causarum. due nouissime michi etiam puenerut. Bellu nãque quod int romãos et nos iudeos fuit. et q actus qque finis accesserit experimento ipse cognoscens. narrare coactus sum. propter eos qui veritatem in ipa oscripcõe corrumpũt. Presens autẽ opus assumsi credens dignu studiu eciam grecis apparere oibus. Continebit itaque omnẽ antiquitatem nostrã:et couersacionis ordinem ex ebraicis libris interpretatum Dudum siquidem cu bella conscriberẽ pposuerã declarare q fuerint in initio udi. et quibus usi sint fortunis et per quem legislatorem sint eruditi. hoc quod ad pietatem aliamque virtutis

8. Josephus as scholar and prophet
Woodcut in incunabulum containing Latin Josephus, Lübeck 1475 (p101)

WOODCUT, LÜBECK 1475 **(pl. 8)**

Woodcut in an incunabulum containing the *Hystoria de antiquitate* (the *Antiquities*) and the *Hystoria de judaico bello* (the *War*), published in 1475 by Lucas Brandis in Lübeck (plate: KUNZE, *Geschichte*, pl. 201).[201]

This portrait, the first of those published by KUNZE at the beginning of the prologue of the *Antiquities*, takes the form of a scholar seated at a writing desk underneath the crossbar of the initial *H(istoriam conscribere)*. The second picture, accompanying the short biography authored by Jerome (see above p78), is apparently also a portrait of Josephus. Here he is perched on the capital of a pillar, in the manner often found for biblical prophets in the portal architecture of medieval churches, dressed as a humanist scholar, and holding a scroll in his left hand while pointing with his right to the text printed beside him:

> *Hic in octavo decimo antiquitatum libro manifestissime confitetur, propter magnitudinem signorum Christum a Pharisaeis interfectum et Johannem Baptistam vere prophetam fuisse et propter interfectionem Jacobi apostoli Iherosolimam dirutam. Scribit autem de Domino in hunc modum: Eo tempore fuit Ihesus sapiens vir...*
>
> In the eighteenth book of the *Antiquities* he makes abundantly clear that because of the greatness of his miracles Christ was put to death by the Pharisees, and that John the Baptist was in truth a prophet, and that in consequence of the death of James the Apostle, Jerusalem was destroyed. Concerning the Lord, he also wrote in this wise: 'There was at that time a certain Jesus, a wise man...'

The result here is a unique mutual reference of picture and text since Josephus' right hand is actually pointing to Jerome's *manifestissime profitetur* in the text. Once again, Josephus' role is rather that of a prophet to Christ.

PARIS, BN, FR. 405

Miniature by Jean Colombe (died in 1529) to the prologue of a late fifteenth century French translation of the *War* (Paris, BN, fr. 405, fol 1).[202] The author is clothed in the garb of a fifteenth century scholar, sits upon a canopied chair, as fifteenth and sixteenth century university professors are often depicted, and dictates to a scribe who is seated apart. In this period Josephus increasingly dons the habit of a learned author of important works, rather than that of the Prophet, Evangelist, or Church father. Here the gradually increasing influence of critical theology can be seen, which tended to regard Josephus' text as a high-ranking theological source.

[201] Schreckenberg, *Bibliographie* Supplementband, 164; Kunze, *Geschichte*, pl. 201.
[202] Deutsch, *Iconographie*, fig. 19.

9. Josephus presents his work to Titus and Vespasian
Miniature, late 11th cent. Latin ms. of *War* (p103)

PARIS, BA, COD. 5082

Miniature to the prologue of a French translation of the *Antiquities* from the workshop of Alexander Bening (died in 1519): Josephus dictating his works (Paris, BA, cod. 5082, fol 1).[203] Here also Josephus is depicted as 'erudit humaniste' (DEUTSCH).

PARIS, BN, FR. 11

Miniature by Bening (see above) to the prologue of the *Antiquities* in a late fifteenth century French translation (Paris, BN, fr. 11, fol 1).[204] Once again as the 'savant humaniste', Josephus is seated in a contemporary scholar's study at a large round table while dictating to a scribe sitting apart at a writer's desk. A look through the window draws the landscape into the scene.

Josephus as Dramatis Persona in His Own History

PARIS, BN, LAT. 5058 **(pl. 9)**

Miniature in a Latin manuscript of the *War* written in Toulouse at the end of the eleventh century (Paris, BN, Lat. 5058, fol 2v and fol 3r; plate: ROBB, *Illuminated Manuscript*, p173, fig. 112).[205]

This impressive work of French Romanesque book illumination is bipartite: the left half (fol 2v) shows Titus and Vespasian enthroned, and clothed in imperial raiment with crown and scepter; in the right half Josephus is approaching on a paved street, offering his historical work which is bound in a wooden cover and presented deferentially on a cloth. It is known from Josephus' writings that he actually did present the finished *War*, which he had written during the seventies of the first century, to Vespasian and Titus (*Ag. Ap.* 1:51; *Life* 361). Josephus' Jewishness is here not yet recognizable by means of a group symbol. The careless or awkward miniaturist has drawn Josephus' right leg too long and apparently eliminated the left arm altogether. However, this does not seriously reduce the grandeur of the total effect. The Christian historical view of the capture of Jerusalem (as God's judgement against the Jews and confirmation of Christian truth) is supported above all by this book of the principal witness from the enemy

[203] ib, fig. 17; id, 'Illustration', 405.

[204] id, *Iconographie*, fig. 18. We cannot here examine further portraits which often appear as the frontispiece in early printings of his works and in many older printings as well. As one example, the fictitious portrait in the English translation of Josephus by Court (London, 1733) can be named; cf Schreckenberg, *Bibliographie* Supplementband, 190.

[205] Blatt, *Latin Josephus*, 113; Porcher, *Buchmalerei*, pl. XIX; Robb, *Art*, fig. 112; Mazal, *Buchkunst*, pl. 68; Durliat, *Romanische Kunst*, pl. 131; Deutsch, *Iconographie*, fig. 2-3; 'Illustration', 404; Schreckenberg, *Texte* 2, p520f.

10. Titus, Josephus, and the *teknophagia* of Maria
Miniature, 12th cent. Latin ms. of *War* (p105)

camp. Moreover, the strong Christian interest is reflected in these verses which accompany the miniature and interpret it:

Quod vates bellum crevit non esse duellum,
edidit et multis vobis qui cernere vultis.
Est Josephus dictus, fert librum corpore pictus.

(Because the prophet-like author did not view the war as a mere skirmish between two opponents, he published [his work] for those of you as well, who, in great numbers, wish to examine it. We speak of Josephus, and he is here depicted in person as he presents his book.)

A verse written over the heads of the two enthroned rulers reads: *stemate vestitus praefulget cum patre Titus*, 'At the head (of the *War*), richly arrayed and crowned, Titus appears with his father'. Perhaps Titus seated at Vespasian's right hand represents Christianity or the Christian rulers of the West; this is indicated in that he already holds the scepter, that his father is handing him the sphere (*globus*), symbol of the universe and world rule, and that his throne is larger than that of his father, who would then represent the pre-Christian imperium. We have already seen that in the Josephan tradition Vespasian and Titus, with their actions against Jerusalem and the Jews, are often seen as predecessors of the Christian rulers of the West, indeed in Christian legend they even become Christians.

This interpretation would accord with a certain ambivalence in this 'dedication picture'. We know that Josephus actually worked as a kind of court historian in the Flavian household, and presented his completed *War* in this capacity (*Ag. Ap.* 1:51; cf. *Life* 363: Titus gives Josephus his 'imprimatur'). But at a second level of interpretation, which to our artist certainly was the more important, the *War*, as stated by the second of the three hexameters, is a book for a Christian readership and strengthens the early medieval conception of the Christian rulers of the Occident as continuing the ancient imperial tradition, and, particularly in the case of Charlemagne, the tradition of the biblical kings David and Solomon. In this view Josephus becomes a kind of representative of Judaism, which, albeit in the role of a servant, attains a place in this new Christian imperium.[206]

PARIS, BN, LAT. 16730 (pl. 10)

Initial miniature to the seventh book of the *War* in a twelfth century manuscript from Corbie (Paris, BN, Lat. 16730, fol 262v; plate: DEUTSCH, *Iconographie*, fig. 143).[207]

Jerusalem appears as the architectural background in iconographic re-

[206] For this type of dedication picture compare the depiction of Pliny the Elder presenting a finished book (*Historia naturalis*) to the Emperor Vespasian in an early twelfth century manuscript from South-West Germany: Vienna, Österreichische Nationalbibliothek, cod. 9, fol 1r (Mazal, *Buchkunst*, pl. 71).

[207] Blatt, *Latin Josephus*, 73; Deutsch, *Iconographie*, fig. 143.

11. Josephus before Vespasian
Miniature, Latin ms. of *Antiquities*, c. 1181/88 (p107)

duction; Maria stands directly on the city wall with her child, while Josephus, standing beside her, points to her with his left hand as the historiographical showpiece of his work. Outside the city, the mounted Titus rides while swinging his sword at the city. The limitation to the most necessary elements is noteworthy: the Roman as the conqueror, the most fearful scene of the *halosis*, the author of the *halosis*, and the city (depicted with the iconographic cipher of city wall and tower). Maria is in some respects here an allegory of conquered and humiliated Judaea. Josephus, who was actually outside the city with the Romans observing the siege as an outsider, is integrated here in singular manner into the fall of Jerusalem. From within the city he points[208] – and medieval legends also depict him similarly – in admonition and warning to the most ghastly occurrence of all those reported in his *War*.[209]

FULDA, LB, COD. C 1 (pl. 11)

Miniature in a Latin manuscript of the *Antiquities* written prior to 1188 in the Weingarten monastery scriptorium (Fulda, Hessische Landesbibliothek, Codex C 1, fol 1v; plate: *Illuminierte Handschriften Fulda*, p441, cat. nr. 47).[210]

Josephus appears here as the leader and representative of the Jews who stand assembled behind him in a group. All are wearing the funnel-shaped Jews' hat of the twelfth century, including Josephus himself, who moreover is provided with the superscript *Iosephus*. The book roll in which he is writing and the writing desk with inkwell emphasize his authorship of the *War*. *Vespasianus* (so the superscript) sits enthroned over against the Jewish group with his retinue behind him. Thus this miniature combines elements of an author portrait with those of a dedication picture; the author is depicted as he writes his work, along with the emperor, the recipient of

[208] Schreckenberg, *Untersuchungen*, 53ff, *Texte* 2, p165-8 (referring to the twelfth century 'emperor chronicle': Josephus is within the city during the siege, but he finally flies from the Tower of David to the Roman siege camp by means of two shields under his outspread arms).

[209] Deutsch, *Iconographie*, 63 remarks, probably correctly : 'Il est le témoin (un peu comme le choeur de la tragédie antique) qui désigne d'un doigt réprobateur la mère cannibale.' Deutsch, 'Myth', 27 also provides a similar reduction to two highpoints of the *War* in the miniature of a thirteenth century Italian manuscript: in the divided picture the upper half shows Maria devouring her child and the lower shows the bound *Judei* being led away. This last was just as important an event, albeit of a different type; for this is the basis for the Christian view of the *servitus Judaeorum*. The pictorial statement of Josephus admonishing and warning the Jews has parallels in the*War*, for example, in the form of his warning speech (*War* 5:391-393), where, standing outside the city wall, he acts like a Jeremiah redivivus (see Cohen, *Josephus*, 232; Neusner, *A Life*, 116).

[210] Blatt, *Latin Josephus*, 41; *EJ* 9 (Berlin 1932) p403f; Swarzenski, *Berthold Missal* 2, fig. 9; *Suevia sacra*, pl. 176 (the editor's supposition that the figure seated before Vespasian is a scribe, is incorrect); Köllner, *Illuminierte Handschriften* 1, fig. 47; Deutsch, *Iconographie*, 188 (no plate).

12. Titus and Josephus in Jotapata
Miniature, French ms. of *War*, last quarter 15th cent. (p109)

the dedication (cf. *Ag. Ap.* 1:50-51). Again the pagan Vespasian is portrayed as a Christian emperor, a witness to the truth of Christianity even as Josephus is the principal witness from the Jewish camp.

CHANTILLY, MC, FR. 1061 (pl. 12)

Miniature in the French translation of the *War* by Guillaume Coquillard made in 1460-1463 (Chantilly, Musée Condé, Ms. fr. 1061, fol 151; plate: MEURGEY, *Les principaux manuscrits*, pl. LXXXIV).[211]

The capture of Josephus after the fall of Jotapata is repesented here (*War* 3:392ff). As the storming of the city continues in the background, Vespasian is apparently being enthroned as emperor (extreme upper left corner), while Titus and Josephus meet in the foreground of the picture, the one with a large retinue, and the other, bound and led between two Roman soldiers. Josephus, with long hair and beard, is not humiliated, apart from his bonds. Although smaller in stature he is depicted rather with a dignity similar to that of Titus. It seems that his appearance is meant to indicate in advance the prophecy of Vespasian's exaltation to emperor (*War* 3:399-408), which is then portrayed in the upper left corner as a vision.

It should also be remembered that in medieval poetry Vespasian and Titus often appear as predecessors to the Christian emperors who as crusaders march to the Holy Land in order to redress the deplorable situation. Similarly medieval legend has them punish the wicked Jews with a large crusader army for their crimes against Jesus of Nazareth. Consistently then, they also become Christians, in which circumstance the healing power of Veronica's *sudarium* plays an important role.[212]

Since early Christian days Josephus was seen as a witness to the victorious truth of the Church. Thus his prophecy of Vespasian's enthronement could easily be associated with his role as herald to Christianity. Accordingly, this picture of the fall of Jotapata points both to the fall of Jerusalem which occurred somewhat later, and to the end of Judaism whose leading representative – as Josephus is seen in medieval legend – is defecting to the victors. In any case, the Eastern campaign of the Roman commanders, portrayed in Christian legend as a divinely ordained Occidental expedition to punish the Jews in the Orient, belongs to the intellectual climate of the Crusades.

[211] Meurgey, *Principaux manuscrits*, Pl. LXXXIV; Deutsch, *Iconographie*, fig. 127. For Guillaume Coquillard cf Schreckenberg, *Bibliographie*, 103.

[212] See Schreckenberg, *Untersuchungen*, 53-68: 'Heilungserzählungen und das Thema der Vindicta Salvatoris'; cf id, *Texte* 1, p463-5.

13. Capture of Jerusalem by Titus
'Franks casket', runic chest, c. 700 (p111)

Depictions of Josephus' Historical Highpoints

LONDON, BM, FRANKS CASKET **(pl. 13)**

Bas-relief on a whalebone chest inscribed with runes, perhaps originating in Northumberland c. 700 (London, BM, donated by Sir A.W. Franks; discovered in Auzon, Département Haute-Loire; plate: BAUM, *Malerei und Plastik*, p30).[213]

Inscriptions, primarily runic but partly in Latin, explain the pictures: Wieland saga, Romulus and Remus, homage of the three Eastern Magi, destruction of Jerusalem by Titus. The interpretation of the runes is disputed. The picture that interests us, the capture of Jerusalem, reflects a theme that is also treated in poetry and legend during this period, so that a certain response could be expected in the observer. There is no doubt that the picture formulation has been at least indirectly influenced by Josephus' *War*. In any case, the chest bears witness to how much interest there was in the European sphere, already c. 700, in a theme that had great significance for the self-understanding of Christianity and its relationship to Judaism.

PARIS, BN, GR. 923

Teknophagia of Maria (*War* 6:201-213). Miniatures in a ninth century manuscript of the *Sacra Parallela* of John of Damascus (Paris, BN, Gr. 923, fol 227r)[214] Besides the accounts concerning Christ and early Christianity, *War* 6:201-213 is the most frequently cited and discussed passage in Josephus' works. Accordingly, it has strongly influenced Christian posterity. Since the early Christian period almost until the present day this tale has been recounted in order to demonstrate the fearful suffering of the Jews in besieged, starving Jerusalem; Maria's desperate act has been regarded as a particularly memorable sign of God's judgement on the Jews.[215]

Codex 923 relates the Josephan account as a picture story in four parts: the starving Maria holds her child in her arms; she kills the child; she roasts it over a fire; she offers it to the soldiers who have broken in seeking food. 'The picture story can be "read" without the text', remarks WEITZMANN correctly (p247). DEUTSCH (p408) sees in Maria a negative Jewish counterpart to the mother of Jesus and concludes: 'To the Christians this rapidly became Mary's sacrifice, with all the connotations which can be derived from the name. It condensed, in a striking form, the relationship between the pitiful mother and the over-possessive one, between the sacrifice on the

[213] See Grant, *Morgen*, 158; Williamson, *Introduction*, fig. 3; Becker, *Franks Casket*, 63-71, 110-114; Schreckenberg, *Texte* 2, p460.
[214] Weitzmann, *Miniatures*, fig. 715f; Deutsch, 'The Myth of Maria', plate on p28; *Iconographie*, fig. 1; 'Illustration', 408; Schreckenberg, *Texte* 2, p469.
[215] Cf Schreckenberg, *Tradition*, 190 (index); *Texte* 2, p687 (index).

14. Jesus weeping over the impending destruction of Jerusalem
Miniature, evangelistary of Otto III, c. 1000 (p113)

cross and the Eucharist, and between Christianity and Judaism, considered to be the wicked stepmother.' But in order to be persuasive, this interpretation would need to be supported with proofs drawn from early and medieval Church history. At all events Fulgentius Fabius Planciades (whom DEUTSCH does not mention) cannot be ignored here: he says that Judaea rejected the flesh of the Son of God, however there was prepared for her a meal from the flesh of her own son (above, p82). But even here Maria is not typified as a counterpart of Mary the mother of Jesus, but is rather seen as representative of the Jewish people; she does penance vicariously, as it were, for the crimes of the Jews against Jesus. It is not even certain whether with his portrayal Josephus wanted to call to mind the biblical examples of cannibalism (Deut 28:53; 2 Kgs 6:29; Lam 2:20; 4:10; cf Lev 26:29).

MUNICH, SB, LAT. 4453 (pl. 14)

Miniature in the so-called evangelistary of Otto III, originating c. 1000, from the Reichenau school of painting (München, SB, Clm 4453, fol 188v; plate: DUBY, *Die Kunst des Mittelalters*, p53).[216]

The theme of this masterpiece of Romanesque book illumination is the prophetic scene from Luke 19:41-44 and its realization in the year 70. In an ingenious iconographic reduction the miniaturist omits everything extraneous, condensing the complex event into a few scenes. Jerusalem consists only of a small city wall enclosure, or more precisely, a part of it, and two buildings. Jesus, highlighted by the customary cross nimbus, stands at the head of four apostles upon a terrace ground or a cloud, and all within an arcade framework. His hands are held in a ritual gesture of mourning, under the garment and raised to the face, as he beholds in a vision the anticipated fulfillment of his prophecy, i.e., Titus' capture of Jerusalem in 70.

The original prophecy of Luke was probably intended eschatologically, but was historicized and understood in light of the events of the year 70, as also occurred in other relevant New Testament passages. Colors and details of this depiction were found in the eye-witness account from Josephus' *War*. There can therefore be little doubt about the identity of the woman in the lower half of the miniature who is pictured wielding a knife against a child. It is not the personified Jerusalem killing her prophets (cf Matt 23.37) as was earlier thought, but Maria slaying her child prior to eating it (*War* 6:201ff). This description represents an iconographic scene which was stylized during the Middle Ages and admits of no other interpretation; the parallel with the Paris Codex Lat. 16730 alone (above p105) confirms this. As is the case there, the unspeakable suffering of the starving mother stands

[216] Leidinger, *Miniaturen* 1, pl. 41; Duby, *Kunst* 1, plate on p33; Schreckenberg, *Texte* 2, p497f.

15. *Teknophagia* of Maria as punishment of Hell
Miniature, *Hortus deliciarum* by Herrad von Landsberg, c. 1185 (p115)

for the suffering of the Jews under the deserved punishment for their crimes against Jesus. The miniature uniquely illustrates how medieval Christianity saw the fall of Jerusalem, with Josephus' help, as a historical proof for its own victorious truth and the rejection of the Jews.

PARIS, BN, LAT. 16730

Titus before the Temple in Jerusalem. Initial miniature at the beginning of the fifth book of the *War*, in a twelfth century manuscript from Corbie (Paris, BN, Lat. 16730, fol 251).[217] Here the iconographic reduction is taken still further: Titus rides towards the Temple, representing the Romans who are executing God's commission to destroy Jerusalem, while the Temple represents Jerusalem and the Jews. There is clearly a certain affinity to the behavior of the crusaders, particularly since Titus does also appear elsewhere as a medieval Christian ruler.[218] All he lacks is the cross on his garment.[219]

HERRAD, HORTUS DELICIARUM **(pl. 15)**

Miniature in the *Hortus deliciarum*, completed c. 1185, by the abbess Herrad von Landsberg, fol. 255r (plate: GILLEN, *Herrad von Landsberg*, p145).[220]

The only manuscript of this work was destroyed in Strasbourg in 1870, but most of the miniatures are extant in copies made before that year. Here, individuals representing the various categories of malefactors are being punished in a Hell full of red, leaping flames. Among these is a child-murderess, shown holding the child before her mouth like a large roast, preparing to eat it. Given the widespread *teknophagia* motif from *War* 6:201-213, this is with near certainty an allusion to that passage. The Jewess Maria would here be in good company, for directly below her a group of *Judei* (identified by the inscription and by their large Jews' hats) is being punished; these, it should be noted, are not being punished for any specific misdeed, but for being Jews. It is well-known that in the medieval view of things Jews were necessarily reckoned with the *damnati* as Jews. In the

[217] Deutsch, *Iconographie*, fig. 135.

[218] See for example Deutsch, *Iconographie*, fig. 133: a crowned Titus with the three-tailed *gonfanon*, the medieval war banner.

[219] Cf Deutsch, *Iconographie*, 177: 'Pour le monde chrétien, il est le prototype du *miles christianus*, le bras armé de l'Église.' See also Schreckenberg, 'Wirkungsgeschichte', 1150ff for the talion correspondence 'Jesus – God the Father = Titus – Vespasian', according to which the Jews, having denied God the Father and God the Son, are appropriately punished by the father (Vespasian) and the son (Titus). In this sense, Titus and Vespasian carried out God's will as actual *milites christiani*. That they convert and undergo baptism as a regular feature of the medieval legends is thus only consistent (cf Schreckenberg, *Untersuchungen*, 53ff).

[220] Edited by Green; cf Schreckenberg, *Texte* 2, p601-4.

16. Capture of Jerusalem by the Romans
Miniature, ms. of the Rhyming Bible by Jacob van Maerlant, dated 1332
(p117)

Hortus deliciarum they are being boiled by gleefully sadistic devils in a metal caldron over a flaming fire. Maria's everlasting punishment seems to consist in continual repetition of the crime of eating her child.

PARIS, BN, LAT. 11560

Vespasian and Titus defeat the Jews. Miniature in a thirteenth century *Bible moralisée* (Paris, BN, Lat. 11560, fol 6).[221] BLUMENKRANZ correctly identified the two crowned figures as Vespasian and Titus, who with mighty swords are hewing a group of people wearing Jews' hats. Jesus, identifiable by his cross nimbus, surveys the scene from above with complacency, while below where the drama unfolds two praying men, one of them a haloed saint, greet the deed with gestures (or invoke it through prayer?). This depiction is either directly or indirectly suggested by Josephus' *War*.

That Titus and Vespasian are explicity named in the accompanying text of the *Bible moralisée* of the Codex Vindob. 2554, fol 27v, supports this interpretation. They correspond to the two bears of 2 Kgs 2:23-24 that mauled the boys who had ridiculed Elisha. Thus these boys are the biblical antitype of the New Testament Jews. In this typological relationship the round picture directly to the left shows Jews with pointed hats ridiculing the crucifix with words and gestures. Thus crime and punishment stand together in striking polemical iconographic connection. This supplements and confirms Blumenkranz' interpretation.

THE HAGUE, MMW, MS 10 B 21 **(pl. 16)**

Miniature in a manuscript of the Rhyme Bible by Jacob van Maerlant dated to 1332 (The Hague, Museum Meermanno-Westreenianum, Ms. 10 B 21, fol. 152v; plate: Catalogus *Noordnederlandse miniaturen*, pl. 1).[222]

This multi-scene picture depicts the warrior Romans besieging the city and its defenders, some of whom are wearing the medieval funnel-shaped Jews' hat. The miniaturist here is known: Michiel van der Borch.

[221] Blumenkranz, *Juden*, pl. 52. The miniature in Ms. L.A. 139, fol 13, of the Museu Calouste Gulbenkian in Lisbon has a similar character. Here important elements of the Josephan tradition (in the adaptation of the *Vindicta Salvatoris* legends) are presented pictorially: ' Vespasian sold thirty Jews for a penny, as we see in the illustration, where a man standing before the Emperor reaches into his purse to pay for the Jews bound and shackled at his left ... In the illustration we see the weeping women lamenting the Roman massacre of Jews at the far left, while the figure of the Lord presides over the scene' (Lewis, 'Gulbenkian-Apokalypse', p562; to fig. 24, p561).

[222] Sokolová, *Paysage*, pl. 22; Catalogus *Noordnederlandse miniaturen*, pl. 1; Byvanck, *Miniature*, pl. V, fig. 11; cf fig. 12, a further miniature of the same theme in a manuscript of the poems of Jacob van Maerlant, in Groningen, Universiteitsbibliotheek, Ms. 405 (dated 1339), fol 148a verso.

VIENNA, ÖN, COD. 12766

Teknophagia of Maria. Minature in an early fifteenth century manuscript of Boccaccio's *De claris mulieribus* (Vienna, ÖN, Cod. 12766, fol 275v).[223] The miniaturist, drawing from the account of *War* 6:201-213, portrays the relevant section 209ff: The soldiers force their way into Maria's house and see her eating the arm of her child, the armless body of which is fastened on a spit and being roasted over a fire.

BRUSSELS, BR, MS II 591 (pl. 17)

Miniature in an early fifteenth century manuscript of Hegesippus' Latin paraphrase of the *War* (Brussels, BR, Ms. II 591, fol 13v; plate: GASPAR – LYNA, *Les principaux manuscrits*, vol. 2 pl. CV).

Jerusalem, depicted architecturally as a medieval city, is being consumed by flames; its inhabitants are being killed by the swords of the attacking Romans. The survivors are being led away into slavery (below right), while (below left) a single bound prisoner – apparently Josephus – is being brought before the Emperor. With the historical inaccuracy necessitated by artistic reduction, the events consist of three scenes: the end of Jerusalem (and thereby the Jewish state and people); the *servitus Judaeorum*; and the pardoning of Josephus who as an eyewitness is able to record the important event for Christian posterity.

PARIS, BA, MS 5193 (pl. 18)

Miniature in a French manuscript of Boccaccio's *De casibus virorum illustrium*, produced c. 1409/1419 (Paris, Bibliothèque de l'Arsenal, Ms. 5193, fol 305; plate: MARTIN, *Le Boccace*, pl. CIX).[224]

The upper half of the bipartite picture shows Jerusalem being stormed by the Romans and the Jews being killed. In the lower left, Titus sits on his throne. Like a Christian ruler, he holds the imperial orb (*globus*, *sphaira* as representing the world) in his left hand, and a sword in his right. In the lower center, money changes hands for the sale of Jewish prisoners, who are shown in the lower right being led away, bound together with a long line in a sort of 'chain gang', by a cudgel-wielding menial. This recalls the Josephan accounts of the sale of Jewish prisoners of war (*War* 3:540; 6:384, 414-419). MARTIN's interpretation that here 'the surviving Jews pay tribute to their conqueror' (p64) is incorrect. This is rather a depiction of the ἄγειν ἀνάγκῃ, widespread in antiquity and already found in Homer, i.e., the

[223] Deutsch, 'Myth', plate on p26; *Iconographie* fig. 144.
[224] Martin, *Le Boccace*, fig. CIX.

17. Fall of Jerusalem, capture of Josephus and the Jews
Miniature, early 15th cent. ms. of Latin *War* paraphrase by Hegesippus
(p118)

18. Fall of Jerusalem and capture of the Jews
Miniature, French ms. c. 1409/19 (p118)

leading away of prisoners of war in bonds.[225] We have already recognized this above as an important impetus for the Christian doctrine of the *servitus Judaeorum*. This Boccaccio miniature is iconographically remarkable moreover because some of the actors wear oriental hats – in part conical, turban-shaped, with ball, and in part in apparently completely fictitious forms – to situate the event in the Orient.

PARIS, BA, MS 5193, FOL 309

Teknophagia of Maria. Miniature in a manuscript of Boccaccio's *De casibus virorum illustrium*, Book 7, Chapter 9 (c. 1409/1419; Paris, BA, Ms. 5193, fol 309v).[226] Chapter 9, from which this miniature is taken, is not concerned with historical events, but contains exclusively anti-Jewish apologetic argument. Herein, all the sufferings of the Jews, for which the most prominent example is the *teknophagia* in starving Jerusalem, are seen as the just punishment for the crucifixion of Jesus.

GENEVA, BIBL. PUBL. ET UNIV., MS FR 190

Teknophagia of Maria. Miniature in a fifteenth century manuscript of Boccaccio's *De casibus virorum illustrium* (Geneva, Bibliothèque publique et universitaire, Ms. fr. 190, fol 101).[227] The depiction here is similar to those in BA, Ms. 5193, and Vienna, ÖN, Cod. 12766.

GAND, MUSÉE DES BEAUX-ARTS, ALTAR SCENE

Capture of Jerusalem. Fifteenth century altar scene (Gand, Musée des Beaux-Arts).[228] The two scenes of this panel form the predella, the lower part of an altar painting depicting the Calvary motif. The arrangement of the individual pictures within the larger picture shows a causal connection between the crucifixion of Jesus and the destruction of Jerusalem. The two multifigured pictures show many of the individual scenes described in Josephus' *War*, among these apparently the *teknophagia* (fig. 147, lower center).

[225] See Schreckenberg, *Ananke*, pl. IIIff; cf *die fuort man an den seilen*, 'they are led [bound] by ropes', in a medieval poem, with reference to the transport of bound Jews who had survived the capture of Jerusalem (in Schreckenberg, 'Wirkungsgeschichte', 1197).
[226] Martin, *Le Boccace*, fig. CX; Deutsch, *Iconographie*, fig. 146.
[227] Deutsch, 'Myth', plate on p25; *Iconographie*, fig. 145.
[228] Deutsch, *Iconographie*, fig. 147f.

19. Battles within besieged Jerusalem
Woodcut in incunabulum, Paris 1492 (p123)

PARIS, BN, FR. 21013, FOL 191

Vespasian, mounted on a war horse wearing the insignia *SPQR* (*Senatus populusque Romanus*),[229] rides at the head of his army before Jerusalem. Miniature (to *War* 3:1ff) by Jean Fouquet (died c. 1477-81) in a manuscript of a French translation of the *War* (Paris, BN, fr. 21013, fol 191).[230]

PARIS, BN, FR. 21013, FOL 262

Roman attack on the Jerusalem Temple. Miniature by Jean Fouquet (Paris, BN, fr. 21013, fol 262v).[231]

WOODCUT, PARIS 1492 (pl. 19)

Woodcut in an incunabulum of the *War*: Antoine Vérard, *Josephus de la Bataille Judaïque*, Paris 1492 (plate: GOFF, 'Antoine Vérard', fig. 1).[232]

The scene is apparently of rival Jewish groups fighting among themselves within besieged Jerusalem. In the foreground stands the High Priest (with bishop's hat, frequently seen in Christian portrayals), in the background a woman, perhaps Maria from *War* 6:203, rushes out of her house.

PARIS, BA, MS 5083

Siege of Jerusalem. Miniature from the workshop of A. Bening (died 1519) to the sixth book of the *War* in a late fifteenth century manuscript (Paris, BA, Ms. 5083, fol 292v).[233] Jerusalem is represented as a medieval occidental city with Roman war tents standing before it.

LONDON, COLL. SOANE, MS 1

Siege of Jerusalem. Miniature in a late fifteenth century Flemish translation of the *War* (London, Coll. Soane, Ms. 1, fol 305).[234]

[229] This *SPQR* appears in many late medieval depictions of the crucifixion of Jesus in order to differentiate the participating Roman soldiers from the Jews. The Jews on the other hand are frequently identified with a scorpion.
[230] Omont, *Antiquités*, fig. 22; cf fig. 24: 'Sac de Jérusalem par les Iduméens' (to *War* 4:305ff) and fig. 25: a battle scene of the storming of Jerusalem. A miniature by Jean Fouquet less relevant for our purposes refers to *Ant.* 12:246-247 (the capture of Jerusalem without resistance by Antiochus Epiphanes); see Mazal, *Buchkunst der Gotik*, pl. 45. For Fouquet cf Schreckenberg, *Bibliographie*, 144, 152.
[231] Deutsch, *Iconographie*, fig. 141.
[232] Goff, 'Vérard', 345, fig. 1.
[233] Deutsch, *Iconographie*, fig. 137.
[234] ib, fig. 140.

VIENNA, ÖN, MS 2538

Titus before the burning Jerusalem Temple. Miniature in a late fifteenth century French translation of the *War* (Vienna, ÖN, Ms. 2538, fol 141v).[235]

FRONTISPIECE, 1722 **(pl. 20)**

Title picture of Josephus translation by W. Sewel, *Alle de werken van Flavius Josephus*, Amsterdam 1722 (photo H. Schreckenberg).

This frontispiece serves to illustrate the uninterrupted continuance of the iconographic tradition at issue long after the the Middle Ages:[236] A bound woman, pressed by attacking Roman soldiers, sits against a background of Jerusalem and the Temple burning. She is a late iconographic echo of the sitting *Judaea capta* (so also the inscription) on the post-70 coins, and of the allegorical female figure *Jerusalem* that is beset and dethroned by *Ecclesia* in the Carolingian ivory reliefs.[237] The 1722 picture shows in three medallions above Noah's ark, Heaven, and the Tabernacle. At the feet of the bound woman lie the vestments of the High Priest unheeded, booty of the victor even as the defenceless Judaea-Jerusalem whose fate is captivity and slavery. The text to the picture provides the interpretation: 'De vreesselykste straf, gevolgd op zwaare zonden, word door den Joodschen Staat, hier als een Maagd verbeeld in Ketenen geboit ...en ziet haar Staat en Tempel in den brand...' (The most dreadful punishment, the consequence of grave sins, is visited upon the Jewish state, here portrayed as a maid in chains ...seeing both her state and her Temple in flames...).[238]

Christian Theological Themes in Miniatures from Josephus Manuscripts

PARIS, BN, LAT. 5047 **(pl. 21)**

Title miniature to the first book of the *Antiquities* in a twelfth century Latin manuscript (Paris, BN, Lat. 5047, fol 2, col 1; plate: LAUER, *Les enluminures romanes*, pl. LXXXV).[239]

Josephus' portrayal of the Creation is given a wholly Christian interpretation. This accords with a tendency, already well-known to us, to see

[235] ib, fig. 142.
[236] Sewel, *Alle de werken*, frontispiece.
[237] Schreckenberg, *Texte* 2, p450ff.
[238] Cf the frontispiece to the second edition of Leusden's *Philologus*: 'Destruction of the temple, with Israel represented as a queen being carried off into captivity' (*EJ* 9 [1971] col 63). As a final example of this pictorial tradition we mention the copperplate engraving in Basnage, *République*, shown in Gidal, *Juden*, pl. on p22.
[239] Schiller, *Ikonographie* 4, 1, pl. 174; Deutsch, *Iconographie*, fig. 21, 'Illustration', 406; Schreckenberg, *Texte* 2, p609.

20. Capture of Jerusalem
Frontispiece, Amsterdam 1722 (p124)

21. Christ as Creator-Logos and Cosmocrator
Miniature, 12th cent. Latin ms. of *Antiquities* (p124)

22. Typologies
Miniature, Latin ms. of *Antiquities*, c. 1180 (p128)

Josephus as a prophet of Christianity. Jesus, provided with the traditional cross nimbus, appears here as Creator-Logos. *Sapienta-Ecclesia* (in the central medallion) is already present in the six day work. The six border pictures show the individual days of Creation (cf. Gen 1:1-27). Of these six days, five are shown as allegorical personifications with the work of each day entrusted into their hands. The sixth day (lower right) shows Adam with Eve just emerging from his side. Christ stands upon the *sphaira* (*globus*), symbol of the earth, or the world and the cosmos. In its way this miniature documents the gradual Christian appropriation of Josephus' works. Here he is already a classic of Church history with the stature almost of Church father. Compare the depiction of Josephus pointing to Christ, above p100f.

STUTTGART, HIST. FOL. 418 **(pl. 22)**

Miniature of the initial *I(n principio)* to *Ant.* 1:27, in a manuscript produced c. 1180 in the Benedictine monastery at Zwiefalten, Baden-Württemberg (Stuttgart, LB, Hist. fol. 418, fol 3r; plate: LEGNER, *Deutsche Kunst der Romanik*, pl. 477).[240]

The crucifixion is depicted here, not on a cross, but on a double-stemmed, stylized grapevine. It is decorated, not with the customary allegorical personifications *Ecclesia* and *Synagoga*, but with various biblical scenes, already christologically interpreted in early Christian literature, and here depicted iconographically in an impressive way. Thus Abraham's ram is a reference to the christological sacrifice typology of Gen 22:1-19 (SCHILLER's interpretation of the ram as a 'Jewish sacrificial animal' and symbol for 'conquered Judaism' is incorrect). Further, the widow of Zarephtha appears from 1 Kgs 17:12. The Vulgate translates the Hebrew text's 'a few sticks' with *duo ligna*, 'two sticks' – these are held by her in the form of a cross; hence this is the starting point of the cross typology. A further cross typology is found in the iron serpent (compare John 3:14 on Num 21:4-9; Moses is provided here with the medieval Jews' hat!). Adam and Eve are at the very bottom, where, since the Carolingian ivory reliefs, those who have been saved through the cross customarily appear as resurrected. They appear once again at the very top in a scene of the Fall. Directly below this is Noah's saving ark (with dove) as a type of salvation through the wooden cross; the *tertium comparationis*, as is often the case, is the wood (wooden ark – wooden cross). The soteriological program is already developed literarily in early Christianity, but does not appear in the medium of art until some time later.

[240] Schiller, *Ikonographie* 2, pl. 431; Mellinkoff, *Horned Moses*, fig. 124; *Suevia sacra*, pl. 172; Legner, *Deutsche Kunst*, pl. 477; Schreckenberg, *Texte* 2, p597f.

PARIS, BN, LAT. 16730

Christ enthroned. Initial miniature to the words *F(uit autem)* at the beginning of the *Testimonium Flavianum* in a twelfth century Latin manuscript of the *Antiquities* from Corbie (Paris, BN, Lat. 16730, fol 165v).[241] Christ as Cosmocrator enthroned, his throne being the globular symbol of the earth and heavens (*sphaira*, *globus*). Here too Josephus plays the role of prophet of Christianity.

PARIS, BN, FR. 247

The Jerusalem Temple as Christian cathedral. Miniature by Jean Fouquet (died c. 1477-81) in manuscript of a French translation of the *Antiquities* (Paris, BN, fr. 247 [and 21013], fol 163).[242] Nine miniatures of this manuscript are considered to be by Fouquet, among them the idealized picture of the building of Solomon's temple, from the eighth book of the *Antiquities*. The building style is Gothic, as particularly seen in the multisectional portals. The modelling of the temple architecture in the likeness of a contemporary cathedral is not without a specific purpose: biblical Judaism is, so to speak, the forerunner of Christianity and the Bible is the retrospective extension of the New Testament. Since Justin Martyr (*Dial.* 11:5) early Christianity considered itself *verus Israel* and interpreted biblical history as Christian pre-history. Not only was Christ the pre-existent Logos always there, but *Ecclesia* also reaches far back into the past, typologically at least. We have seen above that not only Christ, the Creator-Logos, is assigned to the *hexahemeron* of Genesis, but that *Ecclesia* also appears. Perhaps this clarifies why Solomon's temple can be portrayed as a Christian cathedral as a matter of course. Josephus, with his *ecclesiastica gravitas*, was a kind of ideal 'Sitz im Leben' for the development of such radical christianizations of the Jewish tradition.

Summary

The results of our iconographic investigation confirm and supplement on every hand the Christian assessment of Judaism within the literary Josephus tradition.[243] It is striking, above all, that it took several centuries before Josephus and his works became a theme of pictorial art. There are two basic reasons for this. First, the legends and poetry from the early and high

[241] Deutsch, *Iconographie*, fig. 110.
[242] Ehrenstein, *Das Alte Testament*, p646 pl. 18; Ring, *Century*, pl. 79; Haussherr, 'Templum', 116; Deutsch, *Iconographie*, fig. 62. For Codex fr. 247 see above p95.
[243] Cf as a reference point of our investigation in extenso, Schreckenberg, *Tradition*; *Untersuchungen*; 'Wirkungsgeschichte'.

middle ages were necessary for many names and themes of learned theological discussion to become widely known. Legends and poetry made use of dominant theological themes and thus already reflect a high measure of recognition and acceptance. Pictorial art does not take up a theme until it has established a wide basis of recognition. The second reason is somewhat banal: the Carolingian Renaissance in the European sphere gave a great impulse to book illumination, out of which were first developed certain artistic techniques necessary to the elaboration of its themes.

Josephus portraits are numerous in illuminated books, generally as 'author portrait' to his works, but otherwise are not found in sacred art, e.g., in cathedral sculpture, or stained glass, or in church frescos. This indicates an ongoing consciousness of Josephus' Jewishness, despite his being regarded almost as a Church father. He remained in some respects the alien; indeed, this was probably necessary. The reason, to be sure, is less a disinclination to assimilate him completely into Christianity, than that his very Jewishness made him a valuable witness to the *veritas christiana*. This can be compared with the indispensible Jewishness of the Jews in numerous medieval portrayals of Helena discovering the cross; here as well, Judas, or the entire group of Jews, wear the Jews' hat as a differentiating mark.[244] That of all possibilities a Jew, the Levite Judas, should make the discovery of the cross possible was a decisive proof of the truth of Christianity. Judas, however, reveals his knowledge only under coercion, while Josephus offers his testimony voluntarily.

It is not surprising that there are no Jewish portraits of Josephus, notwithstanding the slight acceptance of personal portraits within the Jewish sphere, which in the Middle Ages however did permit pictures of Moses, Elijah, or even the Messiah. This is because there was no Jewish manuscript tradition of Josephus and thus no relevant miniatures. Josephus, like Philo and the LXX, was transmitted only by Christians.

Josephus' wearing the medieval Jews' hat is not, as is often the case elsewhere, a derogatory group symbol. Rather, Josephus is seen here in clear affinity with others who wear the hat for whom Jewishness carries no negative connotation, as, e.g., the biblical prophets or Joseph, the husband of Mary.[245]

[244] Examples in Schreckenberg, *Texte* 2, p561f, 583; for the Helena legend see, e.g., Keller, *Lexikon*, 279-81.

[245] Numerous examples of the differentiating and typifying valuation of the Jews' hat according to the affiliation of the wearers with the various groups in the Old and New Testaments can be found in Schreckenberg, *Texte* 2, p522-629.

Chapter Five

Epilogue

Retrospect: Josephus Christianized

The almost universal ignoring of Josephus in the Jewish literary tradition and, on the other hand, the almost total assimilation of his works by the Christian tradition are the most striking features of the Josephus tradition since the early Christian period. Further, it is striking that, as the Middle Ages progress, the Western, Latin Josephus tradition becomes on the whole richer and more varied than that in the Byzantine sphere. The iconographic portrayal of both the author himself and his accompanying themes is much more pronounced and differentiated in the European sphere. This is perhaps due to theological discussion in the West since Ambrose, Jerome, and Augustine being more lively and fruitful than in the Eastern Church.

The history of Josephus' influence in Christianity begins in the second half of the second century, i.e., at about the time that relevant Christian texts became the New Testament canon. Here a kind of comparison becomes possible of relationships, similarities and common elements: e.g., the content of *Against Apion* and the claim raised in the New Testament to co-possession of the biblical tradition, or the affinity between the *War* and the New Testament prophecies of Jerusalem's destruction. We have already seen that the events of 70 caused redactional alterations in New Testament texts.[246] There now follows a further step. The possibility of reading the Jewish and Christian texts side by side suddenly revealed that the so-called synoptic apocalypses[247] actually had been realized. For it was the detailed comparison of the New Testament texts, already 'historicized' by redactional adaptation to the historical events, with the even more richly

[246] See Schreckenberg, 'Wirkungsgeschichte', 1116-1119.

[247] Matt 24:2 (and parallels): 'There will not be left here one stone upon another;' Luke 19:40-44: 'Your enemies will cast up a bank about you ... and they will not leave one stone upon another in you;' Luke 21:20ff: 'But when you see Jerusalem surrounded by armies, then know that her desolation has come near ... For great distress shall be upon the earth and wrath upon this people; they will fall by the edge of the sword, and be led captive among all nations; and Jerusalem will be trodden down by the Gentiles, until the times of the Gentiles are fulfilled.'

detailed eye-witness account in Josephus that first allowed the full measure of agreement to be seen.

For example, Luke 21:24 ('they will be carried captive into all countries') fits hand in glove with *War* 3:540; 6:384, 414-418 (the sale of captured Jews into slavery), a possibility already realized with much generalization and exaggeration by Eusebius, when he has 'the entire Jewish people' (ὁ πᾶς Ἰουδαίων ἔθνος) being sent into Roman slavery (δουλεία; *GCS* 23:349, 17-20). Other Christian theologians referred Luke 21:23 to the shocking *teknophagia* by Maria (*War* 6:201-213). Once Christian eyes had been opened to these possibilities, they divined the fall of Jerusalem already from the Old Testament (e.g., Dan 9:26); just as in general since early Christian days or at the latest by the Middle Ages, New Testament words of doom and judgement of the most various kinds were seen as fulfilled in the events of 70 (e.g., Matt 21:19-20, 33-46; 22:1-14).

After the second half of the second century the synoptic comparison between Josephus and the New Testament reached a kind of 'critical mass', making a new situation possible. 'Receptor' passages such as the synoptic apocalypses seemed to be only waiting for the appropriate connection to their Josephan counterparts. They formed complex projections, so to speak, which could mesh with the indentations of the key, i.e., the relevant Josephan texts. The bridges between Josephus and the New Testament, however, connected not only affinities at single points, but also entire complexes, such as the question of guilt as it was treated in Josephus (the guilt of the Zealots, Sicarii, etc. for the Fall of Jerusalem), and in the New Testament. As opposed to Josephus' differentiated intentions, it is to be noted, already the New Testament shows the tendency to place the blame for the Fall of Jerusalem on all Jews collectively, and thus to see them as deserving collective punishment. This was apparently encouraged by the fiction of the Jews' collective guilt for the death of Jesus. In truth, the social and religious existence of the Jews, three-fourths of whom were living in the Diaspora already before 70, remained unendangered, indeed, even improved after they acquired Roman citizenship via Caracalla's *Lex Antoniniana* in 212.

The abundance of Josephan accounts concerning New Testament figures and events acted in fact as a key to a deeper understanding of the New Testament. We can recognize a temporary conclusion to this development in Eusebius. His anti-Jewish apologetic and theological conception of history operate in the reference triangle, Old Testament – New Testament – Josephus. The stature thereby ascribed to Josephus is reflected in the author portraits made of him – for the manuscripts reserve these as a rule for such figures as the Prophets, the Evangelists, Church fathers, and specially revered authors.

With Eusebius a new phase of Christian evaluation of Judaism begins. Since his time, and not least of all through his work, early Christianity acquired both a distinctive consciousness of its historical identity and, through its connection with the Roman empire, a leading position in world history. As a result, the sphere of existence for Judaism became narrower. Christian-Jewish polemic intensified markedly, indeed actually began in earnest at this point.

What Origen introduced, i.e., putting a Christian interpretation on Josephus' historical accounts, Eusebius completed. He only had to reverse and remodel the inner-Jewish self-understanding of Josephus through relatively unobtrusive and seemingly trivial changes of emphasis. As a result the Jewish historical account became a Christian historical legend. It is not always clear to what extent the falsifications it entailed were consciously intended. It had not yet become customary to identify citations with quotation marks, and it was time-consuming and troublesome to verify citations in long texts without the help of indices or concordances. Therefore it probably occurred not infrequently that unverified citations were made from memory and via intermediary sources, whereby wishful thinking could prevail. This was already known in antiquity.[248]

Since in any case correct scholarly citation in the modern sense was virtually unknown, and apologetic interests were everywhere dominant, the temptation was great simply to pass on what was considered to be the genuine text. In this process, it was possible for marginal and interlinear glosses to be included, i.e., text-traditional elements which, intentionally or not, could be easily incorporated into the genuine text. Moreover, there was already a theological 'secondary literature', in which bits of text from Josephus were cited and disseminated, the genuineness of which, although unverifiable, was never doubted. The verification possibilities were further reduced because of the growing difficulty which the Latin Western church had in reading the Greek manuscripts of the Eastern church. The seriousness of this barrier is illustrated by the production of several Latin translations or paraphrases from the fourth-sixth centuries.

It is a trivial insight of literary theory that the desired effect of an author's work is often very different from its actual effect. GADAMER even went so far as to assume a 'structural bias' of understanding and to speak of a 'fusion of two horizons', that of the text and of the reader.[249] In other words, the true sense of a text first surfaces in its historical influence as expressed in successive interpretation. This accords with the elementary fact of experience that texts can say more than their authors intended, and that even

[248] Cf Caesar, *De bello Gallico* 3:18,6 (ed Seel, 89): *Quod fere libenter homines id, quod volunt, credunt*, 'In general, men believe gladly what they want to believe'; Caesar, *De bello civili* 2:27,2 (ed Klotz 2, p77): *Nam quae volumus, ea credimus libenter*, 'We gladly believe what we want to believe'; thus already Demosthenes in the third Olynthian speech, c. 19 (Butch et al., ed., *Demosthenes: Orationes*, 1:33): ὃ γὰρ βούλεται τοῦθ' ἕκαστος καὶ οἴεται, 'Every man believes what he wishes'.

[249] Gadamer, *Wahrheit und Methode*.

interpretations based on opposite viewpoints can attain to a consensus of understanding.[250] However, even if applicable to certain philosophical, theological, and poetic texts, such hermeneutical views cannot be applied to literature of all kinds. In the case of Josephus, who as an historian describes and evaluates historical events within the framework of his world view and personal position, the text understanding quickly reaches a limit beyond which falsification of the author's intent begins. For this Jewish author the Tora stands unchallenged at the center of his convictions, while for early Christianity, from the very beginning, Jesus of Nazareth is decisive for salvation.

Doubtless, Josephus became in many respects the schoolmaster of early Christianity, which presumably made thankful use of his texts and regarded them as a gift from Heaven. He was welcomed as a principal witness from the enemy camp, with whom moreover a spiritual and theological affinity was felt, and who offered ample resources for strengthening nascent Christianity in its apologetic battle against pagans and Jews.

His double role as Jew and Hellenist greatly strengthened the effect of his works in early Christianity. In this respect, there are good reasons for understanding 'the hellenization of ancient Judaism as *praeparatio evangelica*',[251] and the comparison with Josephus' example seems to advance our understanding of the hellenization of early Christianity – the different points of departure, Tora or Jesus Christ, being taken into account. For regarding goals, Josephus and early Christianity had significant elements in common: both were concerned with demonstrating their own to be the true religion and philosophy over against Paganism. With the help of arguments taken from Josephus, Christianity successfully attempted to prove itself as the true and better Judaism, and to take advantage of the openness of many pagans to Jewish monotheism.[252]

As we have seen, Josephus sold his works to Jews and Gentiles (*Ag. Ap.* 1:51 concerning the *War*, but maybe also for other works), writing not only to awake interest and understanding for his religion among Gentiles, but also to give his compatriots a perspective for their future existence within the Roman Empire, and to fortify their religious self-confidence. This is comparable with many later Christian apologists, who often wrote primarily to strengthen faith within Christianity.[253] Here we have another reason for Josephus' attractiveness to early Christianity, for both Jews and pagans were targeted by the Christian mission, and many of Josephus' accounts

[250] id, *Gesammelte Werke* 1, 311, e.g.

[251] Hengel, *Hellenisierung*, 1-30.

[252] Cf, for example, Schreckenberg, *Texte* 1, p242-7 to Commodianus, and the illuminating explanation by Cohen, *Maccabees*, 49-58: 'Philo-Judaism'.

[253] Troiani, 'Lettori' attempted to show that Josephus wrote more for Hellenistic Diaspora Jews than for a Gentile public. This is not convincing, as we have seen: Josephus targeted Jews and Gentiles as his intended audience.

and arguments could (even while serving inner-Christian purposes) appeal to both. Good arguments were at all events welcome, precisely when they came from the opposing side. That Christian theologians in their disputations with Jews felt themselves in need of proof can be seen in the numerous extant tractates *Contra Judaeos* and *Adversus Judaeos*. Indeed, during the Middle Ages Christians often express the concern at being inferior and appearing ridiculous in their discussion with Jews.[254] Josephus was just the man to fill this need for solid proof, and thus he has served, almost to the present day, as a quarry for pro-Christian and anti-Jewish arguments of every sort.

Josephus' works became a handbook of apologetic for ancient Christianity. They contributed to the development of the Church's self-definition and helped to mediate an understanding of her historical role. Jewish circles were certainly aware of this, and it may have contributed to the obscurity of this Jewish historian and theologian among his own people, even when the teachers of the third to sixth centuries developed the edifice of their religious tradition. Judaism lost sight of him; but neither did it need him to hold its own in the face of expanding Christianity.

Selective Bibliography of Josephus Research

Bibliographical information for all areas of Josephan research can be found in SCHRECKENBERG, *Bibliographie*; FELDMAN, *Scholarship (1937-1980)*, and *Supplementary Bibliography*. RENGSTORF's *Complete Concordance* is a versatile *instrumentum laboris*.

The most dependable edition of the Greek text of Josephus with the best information on the manuscripts and the indirect tradition is still NIESE, *Flavii Josephi opera*, even though the evaluation of the witnesses and resulting text are unsatisfactory and inadequate. NABER, *Flavii Josephi opera omnia*, is outdated as well. The most widely used edition today is THACKERAY, *Josephus with an English Translation*. NABER and THACKERAY offer no tradition-historical advance on NIESE and make eclectic use, according to the views of each editor, of the text critical materials in NIESE's textual apparatus. A similar approach is employed by the partial editions of REINACH-BLUM, *Flavius Josèphe, Contre Apion*; MICHEL-BAUERNFEIND, *Flavius Josephus, De Bello Judaico*; PELLETIER, *Flavius Josèphe, Autobiographie*; VITUCCI, *Flavio Giuseppe, La Guerra Giudaica*; PELLETIER, *Josèphe, La Guerre des Juifs*. One serious defect of all editions since NIESE is their failure to take cognizance of several hundred changes to the *editio major* which NIESE made in his *editio minor*, published in 1888-95 (*Flavii Josephi opera recognovit*), making this his 'final edition'. Therefore

[254] Schreckenberg, *Texte* 2, p688 (index).

the *editio minor* should henceforth be regarded as the 'NIESE text'. Moreover, the numerous new tradition-historical materials and aspects published in Schreckenberg's *Tradition* and *Untersuchungen* make a new critical edition a pressing need for Josephan scholarship.

The intensity of current research on Josephus is documented by the number of important monographs and essays on Josephus in general, his life and his works. Among these are COHEN, *Josephus in Galilee and Rome*; RAJAK, *Josephus*; ATTRIDGE, 'Josephus'; and FELDMAN, 'Flavius Josephus Revisited'. Of the encyclopedia articles, special attention is still deserved by HÖLSCHER, 'Josephus'; good, up-to-date information can be found in MAYER, 'Josephus Flavius'.

A study of early Christian literature in connection with our theme is imperative. Old, but still indispensable are the classics by HARNACK, *Geschichte*; and BARDENHEWER, *Geschichte*. Among the works that discuss the reception and historical influence of Josephus in early Christianity, special attention should be given to SCHRECKENBERG'S *Tradition, Untersuchungen*, and 'Wirkungsgeschichte'. Several valuable contributions to this theme are contained in FELDMAN-HATA, *Josephus, Judaism, and Christianity*. Finally, the questions which interest us have been thoroughly and convincingly investigated by HARDWICK, *Josephus as a Historical Source*.

Certain individual aspects of our theme have been impressively discussed by VAN UNNIK, *Flavius Josephus als historischer Schriftsteller*; HENGEL, *Zur urchristlichen Geschichtsschreibung*; and MOMIGLIANO, *Die Juden in der Alten Welt*. PLÜMACHER, *Lukas als hellenistischer Schriftsteller*, and 'Lukas als griechischer Historiker', deals especially with the affinities between Josephus and the Lukan writings.

The portrayal of the Jew in medieval Christian art is for the most part still terra incognita, especially Josephus' role in this area. The Jew motif in general is only given scant attention in the otherwise important handbook by SCHILLER, *Ikonographie der christlichen Kunst*. The little book by BLUMENKRANZ, *Juden und Judentum in der christlichen Kunst* broke new ground in this area. However, Josephus' importance in this relatively young field of research was first given special attention by DEUTSCH, *Iconographie*, albeit with a focal point on the late Middle Ages. DEUTSCH's foundational work has been supplemented in the intervening period by Schreckenberg, *Adversus-Judaeos-Texte* 2, 447-629 ('Ikonographie des Judenthemas bis zum 4. Laterankonzil').

Further advances in our knowledge can be expected, both here and in Philo research. In any case it must be recognized that the influence of certain Hellenistic Jewish texts on Christian art is at least as significant as that on the literature. It would be arbitrary and inappropriate to draw a line here between Antiquity and the Middle Ages. For in analogy to the influence on Christian literature which occurred earlier, the influence on art first required a certain gestation period, but then, bursting forth in a most impressive way, began to develop following the thought patterns of the Church fathers.

Desiderata for Further Study

1. A continuation of FELDMAN'S *Scholarship* for the period following 1981.
2. A new critical edition of the entire Greek text of Josephus – preferably, with international cooperation; building further on NIESE'S flawed text would be methodologically unsound.
3. The completion of the critical edition of the Latin Josephus, begun by BOYSEN and continued by BLATT.
4. A commentary on all thirty books of Josephus which includes relevant parallels from Rabbinic, Greek and Latin sources, including Philo and the New Testament. Simultaneously, a 'Commentary on the New Testament from Philo and Josephus' could be prepared, for the current New Testament commentaries cover Josephus only occasionally and incompletely. Even the newly revised edition of BAUER'S *Wörterbuch* yields this impression.
5. An investigation dealing with all passages in Josephus relating to himself and his work, directly or indirectly; not the least interesting of these would be those that cast light on Josephus' understanding of himself as person and author.
6. A reappraisal of THACKERAY'S theory, rejected by most, that not only did Josephus use assistants for the sake of Greek style when composing the *War*, as he himself concedes (*Ag. Ap.* 1:50), but that also his other works and above all the *Antiquities* entailed the help of several 'assistants', whose work could be identified in specific portions (theory: 'Josephus & Co'). Among those who have more or less distanced themselves from THACKERAY'S theory are SCHRECKENBERG, *Bibliographie*, 208, 212f; LADOUCEUR, *Studies*; RAJAK, *Josephus*, 233-6; ATTRIDGE, 'Josephus', 212; and BERNARDI, 'Sémitismes'. A conclusive clarification, above all with the help of RENGSTORF'S *Complete Concordance*, still remains to be done. Significant results could be expected from an investigation of the distribution frequency of individual Greek words, or their specific connotations, throughout the thirty books. At the same time results could be expected here regarding the history of composition of Josephus' works. This could be relevant to the special position of the *War*, or even its seventh book specifically, which was perhaps composed at a later date than books 1-6.[255]

[255] Even a cursory glance in the *Concordance* reveals spoors to be followed. For example, συντυγχάνω (to meet someone or something) is completely absent in *War*, but occurs in the other works 47 times; στολή (clothes, dress, garment) occurs 65 times in the *Antiquities* but

7. An investigation to determine all the sources used by Josephus. Work has been done in this area already for many decades, but much is still uncertain. Here as well the *Complete Concordance* could be useful. The results of this investigation should appear in a source apparatus in a new critical edition.
8. A history of research on the *Testimonium Flavianum* still remains to be done, in which among other things the very numerous textual conjectures should be collected and analyzed.
9. Extensive investigation of the affinities of language and content between Josephus and the New Testament; apart from a few relevant attempts, e.g., that of SCHLATTER, almost nothing has been done in this area. There is a dearth of comparative studies of all kinds.
10. In addition to the attempts by DEUTSCH and myself, both of which yield only partial results, exhaustive investigations and analyses of the iconographic use of Josephus in medieval manuscripts and early printed works should be made. There remains a rich yield to be harvested here.

never in *War*; συγχωρέω (to agree, permit, arrange, yield) is found in *War* only once (7:44), but in the other works 126 times; ὥρα (season, time of day, hour) occurs 46 times in Books 1-6 of the *War*, but not once in the seventh book (cf similarly ῥίπτω, 'to throw, hurl', and στίφος, 'crowd, mass, storm, troop'). Computer technology can produce statistics here that can perhaps facilitate the solution of some problems. A step in this direction has already been made by Michaelson-Morton, 'Stylometrie', 97f.

II

Kurt Schubert

Jewish Pictorial Traditions in Early Christian Art

Detailed Table of Contents

Introduction

Theoretically one might ask whether early Christian illustration was a completely new phenomenon, or whether in addition to Greco-Roman traditions it was also influenced by Jewish exemplars. On the other hand, Judaism has been seen traditionally as opposed to images in principle. However, after the discovery of ancient Jewish picture cycles the dependance of early Christian illustrations on Jewish exemplars was frequently suspected.

Exod 20:4 was long seen as the proof that Judaism had remained fundamentally opposed to images, until the impact of emancipation and assimilation since the nineteenth century began to make itself felt. This view was encouraged by the complete rejection of images by Josephus Flavius, who was in effect the primary source of information for the early, formative period of Judaism. Thus, the pioneering publication of *Die Aggadah von Sarajevo* (Vienna, 1898) by D.H. MÜLLER and J. v. SCHLOSSER was a surprise. This was a well served, late fourteenth century Catalonian Pesah Haggada, richly illustrated with biblical scenes. Although Christian collectors such as the famous Italian theologian and Hebraist, Giovanni Bernardo DE ROSSI (1742-1831), had gathered important collections of both illuminated and non-illuminated manuscripts, Jewish book illumination was unknown by scholarship until the end of the nineteenth century. Even the pioneering work of Müller and Scholler found few followers. Nevertheless, a beginning had been made. David KAUFMANN, Bruno ITALIENER and a few others continued with the research of Jewish book illumination. But although the existence of significant Jewish book illumination even during the eighteenth century was mentioned in a few journals of Jewish studies and introductions to facsimile editions, art historical research took no notice. In general, we may say that a systematic investigation of Jewish figurative art did not begin until after World War II.

The new interest in research in this area was fueled not only by increasing attention being paid to Hebrew book illumination, whether by Jews or Christians, but above all by the surprising discovery in 1932 of the biblical cycles (often with Rabbinic interpretations) in the third century synagogue of Dura Europos on the Euphrates. This was complemented by the discovery of floor mosaics with figurative depictions in Palestinian synagogues dating from the fourth through sixth centuries. The inescapable conclusion to be drawn from these initially surprising facts was that in late antiquity, at least in the Syro-Babylonian sphere and probably beyond, synagogues decorated with pictures were the rule, and thus the synagogue at Dura Europos was no exception. This can also be seen from its location. Dura was a provincial border town on the Euphrates whose function was to protect Roman territory against invaders from the East. It is highly improbable that the rich picture program of the synagogue originated in such a small town. It is much more likely that this was adopted from one of the contemporary metropolises such as Antioch on the Orontes, or Seleucia-Ctesiphon.

The ideologically most important panel above the Tora shrine niche in the Dura Europos synagogue was repainted twice within seven years. This fact supports the thesis that an established picture program was taken over. The original layer depicted the Tree of Life, doubtless corresponding to the exemplar, since Tora and Tree of Life belong together in Rabbinic thought. The two repaintings however emphasize the element of messianic expectation. This means that those who commissioned the painting had additional wishes as compared with the original.

The discoveries between the two world wars persuaded art historians such as K. WEITZMANN, C.O. NORDSTRÖM and others to investigate early and medieval Christian picture cycles for elements of Jewish iconography. The research area suggested itself because early Christian art manifests more Old Testament than New Testament picture cycles. That such cycles were adopted from Jewish pictorial exemplars seemed a reasonable conclusion particularly since such cycles were attested in Judaism since the third century. In addition, these picture programs contained clear elements from Jewish midrashic and aggadic traditions. Research of this type dominated the first two decades following World War II. The findings were supported by specialists in Rabbinic literature. They were able to prove from Rabbinic writings that the proscription of images in a universal sense, as it had hitherto been understood, no longer existed after the second and third centuries CE.

Of course the joy of dicovery also leads to overstatement. The investigations of H. HEMPEL in articular are open to this criticism. Others, too, have incautiously ignored the *Sitz im Leben* of the individual traditions. Apocryphal and Rabbinic traditions were not distinguished methodologically and thus it was overlooked that the Old Testament Apocrypha were disseminated in the Christian, not the Jewish, realm. Nor was the question asked concerning whether, when and to what extent a given tradition was also known to the Church fathers. The understandable result was a tendency to see the adoption of Jewish traditions by Christian artists as depending on oral transmission rather than pictorial exemplars. Thus, since the mid-sixties a clear counter-current has existed that fundamentally denies the relevance of Jewish pictorial exemplars for early Christian art. It is significant however that, with the exception of J. GUTMANN, the advocates of this view are not Judaic scholars, but Christian archeologists. On the other hand, the majority of art historians and archeologists familiar with Rabbinic literature continue to hypothesize the existence of Jewish pictorial exemplars -- properly so!

The following essay attempts to avoid extremes on both sides. There are pictorial depictions whose *Sitz im Leben* can be found nowhere outside Rabbinic interpretation of Scripture, and which cannot be accounted for either by the Apocrypha or the Church fathers. To deny Jewish pictorial exemplars here would be methodologically false. The situation is otherwise where the Apocrypha and Church fathers agree with Rabbinic tradition. Here the question must remain open, a clear pronouncement being possible neither one way nor the other.

Chapter One

Jewish Art in the Light of Jewish Tradition

Exod 20:3f, generally reckoned within the Elohist tradition, is the biblical text which seems to determine Judaism's relationship to graphic depictions: 'You shall not make for yourself a graven image (פסל), or any likeness of anything that is in heaven above, or that is in the earth beneath, or that is in the water under the earth; you shall not bow down to them or serve them; for I the Lord your God am a jealous God.' This stipulation, directed against the idolatry of the cultural environment surrounding ancient Israel, has often been exegeted and understood as though Israel had always and fundamentally been averse to every form of figurative representation. In fact, however, this verse means no more than that no images should be produced which, as idol statuary, could then serve as cultic images for the Israelites. The commandment was still not recognized even in this sense in the early period, the so-called period of the Judges. Jdg 17:3, 18:14-31 relates a quite unembarrassed account of a small shrine containing an idol (פסל) and other objects of veneration owned by a certain Micah from the hill country of Ephraim; Israelites from the tribe of Dan were so interested in these that they stole them. Even Solomon's Temple, the central sanctuary in Jerusalem, was not without its images. According to 1 Kgs 6:23 two olive-wood cherubim were found in the Holy of Holies in the Jerusalem Temple, and according to 1 Kgs 7:25 the 'bronze sea' rested upon twelve oxen, three each facing in the directions of the four winds. Even the erection of calf statues in the two national sanctuaries of the Northern Kingdom – first interpreted redactionally as the 'sin of Jeroboam' by the Deuteronomist – is proof that carved images were originally regarded neutrally insofar as they themselves were not the objects of divine veneration. The calf idols of Dan and Bethel were probably regarded as the bearers of the invisible divinity (whose invisibility thus admitted no possibility of representation), in the same way as the cherubim of the Temple in Jerusalem.

The proscription of images therefore referred from the very beginning only to such images as might become the objects of divine worship. Stemming from the Elohist source it bears the stamp of prophetic theology and can be dated to c. the eighth century BCE. The naive assumptions attested for the pre-national period by Jdg 18 no longer accorded with the standardizing notions of the later period, when the cultic ideology of Jerusalem and prophetic teachings also determined the relationship to figurative representations. In popular religion, however, the older structures continued to exist, as can be seen by, among other things, the Canaanite and syncretistic elements in the cult of the Jewish emigrants to Elephantine in Egypt, still into the fifth century BCE.[1] However, the standardizing movements reflected in Exod 20:3f led to the proscription of images being taken more and more seriously after the Babylonian exile in the sixth century BCE, in order to ensure Israel's distinction from surrounding Paganism. The Priestly author of Gen 1 also showed his concern for this differentiation when he characterizes sun, moon and stars worshipped as gods in his surroundings as God's creation. At a time and place in which the preservation of Jewish identity was only possible through a conscious distancing from the heathen environment, it was necessary for the leading circles to interpret the proscription of images ever more stringently. That even Herod permitted only geometric patterns in the finishing of his mosaic pavements in Masada is further evidence of this.[2]

An examination of how Exod 20:3f was understood in the first century CE reveals a very narrow and strict interpretation of the proscription of images. This was in reference to the desecration of the Temple at Jerusalem by the erection of a statue of a Roman emperor, or to prevent the setting up of imperial emblems within the city. Thus Flavius Josephus reports (*War* 2:195 [10,4]) that the erection of Caligula's statue in the Temple at Jerusalem was successfully hindered by appealing to the Jewish law against images. The narrow interpretation of this proscription led also to an infuriated crowd tearing down a large golden eagle that, by Herod's order, had been fastened above the largest Temple gate during his renovation of the Temple (which amounted in fact to building a new temple). Josephus gives as the reason for this: '... the Law forbids those who propose to live in accordance with it to think of setting up images or to make dedications of (the likenesses of) any living creatures' (*Ant.* 17:151 [6,2]).[3]

Josephus was a typical reprentative of the trend of hostility towards images in the first century CE.[4] Even King Solomon falls under his criticism, not only for marrying foreign women (*Ant.* 8:191 [7,5]) but also for fashioning bronze bulls for the bronze sea and lions for his throne. He also pursued this radically hostile attitude towards images during his tenure as commander-in-chief of the Galilean forces at the beginning of the rebellion against Rome (66-70 CE). He relates that he ordered the palace of Herod Antipas to be razed because it was decorated with animal figures, 'such a style of

[1] Sachau, *Aramäische Papyrus*; Cowley, *Aramaic Papyri*; Vincent, *Religion*; Kornfeld, *Onomastica*.
[2] Yadin, *Masada*.
[3] Cf also *War* 1:650 [1:33,2].
[4] Gutmann, 'Second Commandment'.

architecture being forbidden by the laws' (*Life* 65 [12]). These clear statements from Josephus the Pharisee make it extremely improbable that before c. 100 CE images with biblical content were produced in the Syro-Palestinian sphere.

As ever in Jewish history, Judaism consisted of various groups. The present state of our knowledge[5] about them lets us assume that all groups officially supported the commandment forbidding images. And yet there were such representations. Thus Josephus reports (*Ant.* 15:25-27 [2,6]) that members of the Hasmonean family in the first century BCE did not refrain from having human representations fashioned. Alexandra sent portraits of her children, Aristobulus and Mariamne, to Antony in Egypt. Likewise, the events following on the death of Agrippa I in 44 BCE show clearly that statues of his two daughters had been produced at his behest. Josephus relates that Agrippa's palace was broken into immediately after his death, and the plunderers, 'seizing the images of the king's daughters carried them with one accord to the brothels, where they set them up on the roofs...' (*Ant.* 19:357 [2,1]).

Before we can examine the relationship of the Rabbinic Sages to the question of images in the period after the second century CE, we must first examine the importance of Hellenism for Judaism and the absorption and adaptation of Hellenistic thought structures.[6] From the third century BCE there existed such groups as the Tobiad family, for whom the Hellenistic lifestyle and proximity to the High Priestly family were not at all incompatible.[7] A certain Hyrcanus of the Tobiad family built in 200 BCE a residence in Trans-Jordan that according to Josephus 'had beasts of gigantic size carved on it' (*Ant.* 12:230 [4,11]). This information was confirmed by the excavations at Araq el-Emir where a large lion frieze was actually found.[8] Following the incorporation of Judaea into the Seleucid empire at the beginning of the second century BCE, these strongly hellenized circles of the Jewish upper class, in which there was an interest above all in maintaining harmony with the Hellenistic rulers and Hellenistic society, were increasingly prepared to abandon their own identity in favor of further integration into the Seleucid state. The Maccabean rebellion (168-164) followed in reaction to this and the Hasidic movement arose, resulting in the development of the Jewish religious parties attested since the middle of the second century BCE. Although these were also influenced by Hellenism, the Pharisees and Essenes at least succeeded in adapting Hellenistic

[5] Among others, K. Schubert, 'Religionsparteien'; Baumbach, *Jesus*; id, "Volk Gottes"; Stemberger, *Pharisäer*.

[6] Tcherikover, *Civilisation*; Liebermann, *Hellenism*; Hengel, *Judentum*; K. Schubert, 'Israel im Altertum'.

[7] Mazar, 'Tobiads'; Tcherikover, *Civilisation*, index: Tobiads.

[8] McCown, 'Araq el-Emir'; Cornfeld, *Daniel*.

thought models to express their own identities, whereas members of the Hasmonean High Priestly family, already since the last decades of the second century BCE, regarded themselves as Hellenistic rulers rather than bearers of the Jewish spirit.[9] It is therefore not surprising that the attitude towards images in these circles was far more liberal than, for example, among the Pharisees, who were concerned for the retention of Jewish identity even within altered external structures. However, the extent to which public opinion sided with the opponents of images is shown by Herod's Masada palace as already indicated above. For in avoiding the use of figures in Masada, Herod showed his concern for public opinion, which he had no desire to provoke any further than he already had.

In Syro-Palestinian Judaism then there were several varieties of Hellenistic integration. There were Jews who accepted Hellenistic thinking as a means of self-expression, and those who were prepared to abandon their own identity for the new and alien. These various nuances could be found in even greater number in Alexandria, the center of Hellenistic Judaism. Aristobulus and Philo,[10] for example, were both concerned to express Jewish teaching and Jewish lifestyle as the highpoint of the creative power of God's Wisdom in this world.[11] According to Philo, the Jew faithful to the Law follows the Law of Nature most consistently, the law according to which the Stoic also strives to live. The opposite extreme as well is seen in Philo's family: Josephus relates of Philo's nephew, Tiberius Julius Alexander, that he 'did not stand by the practices of his people' (*Ant.* 20:100 [5,2]). According to a further report, he also ordered a bloody pogrom in Alexandria, when, as a result of the Jewish rebellion against Rome (66-70) in Palestine, riots also broke out there (*War* 2:87ff [18,7-8]).

A positive Jewish attitude towards images developed only in environs where images were appreciated. Pagan culture of Late Antiquity fulfilled this condition perfectly. Statues, mosaics and frescos were ubiquitous. It is thus not surprising that scholars at first supposed the Septuagint to have encouraged the proliferation of images.[12] It was thought that from a formal point of view Alexandrian Judaism was the most advanced in the hellenization process and thus had the fewest objections to an illustrated Greek Bible. A possible attestation of Alexandrian painting with biblical themes would be found in a fresco from Pompeii, assuming that its interpretation as

[9] K. Schubert, 'Religionsparteien'.

[10] Heinemann, *Bildung*; Wolfson, *Philo*; Goodenough, *Introduction*; Walter, *Aristobulos*; Haase, *Philon und Josephus*.

[11] Cf the parable of the architect in Philo, *Opif.* 3:16-20.

[12] Weitzmann, 'Die Illustration' (cf 'The Illustration'); Weitzmann-Kessler, *Frescos*. However, Weitzmann locates the originals of his pictures not in Alexandria, but in the area around Antioch.

23. The judgement of Solomon (?)
Fresco, Pompeii (p150)

the 'Judgement of Solomon' is correct **(pl. 1)**.[13] A judge accompanied by two associates sits on a pedestal; standing behind are soldiers with bushy helmets holding lances and shields. In front of the pedestal a soldier raises a cleaver to slice through a child being held by a woman in such a way as to give the soldier better access. At the right kneels a second woman who is raising her hands beseechingly to the judges. The raised left hand of the middle judge apparently indicates that, having heard the pleading of this woman, he hinders the slaying of the child. To the left five more observers are standing, some of these obviously children. This picture may well be a representation of 1 Kgs 3:16-28, but also shows signs of being a caricature.[14] Indeed, it could be interpreted as a portrayal of 'stage scenery'.[15]

The assumption of the emergence of Jewish figurative art in Alexandria for the purpose of illustrating the Septuagint can therefore neither be fully proved nor disproved in the present state of our knowledge. But even assuming that it existed, this figurative art did not influence early Christian biblical painting. The rebellion against Rome in 115-117 interrupted the political and cultural importance of Alexandrian Judaism for centuries. Jewish figure painting cannot be assumed before the second century CE, being first attested in the synagogue at Dura Europos from around the mid-third century CE.[16] Both the iconographic motifs in Dura Europos and those connected with early Christianity, insofar as these reveal similarities with Jewish interpretation traditions, point unequivocally to the Syro-Palestinian sphere. It was not the Philonic, Alexandrian allegorical interpretation of scripture, but that of the Rabbis reflected in the Talmud and the Midrashim that influenced both Dura Europos and early Christian depiction of biblical scenes and sequences. Therefore we must first of all examine the attitude of Rabbinic scholars to the problem of figurative representations.[17]

After the Temple had been destroyed by the Romans in 70 CE, its desecration with the statue of a Roman emperor ceased to be a threat. This made possible a liberal attitude towards images already at the beginning of the second century. The attitude of Gamaliel II (c. 100 CE) typifies the change. The following episode is related in the Mishna:

[13] Frey, 'Les juifs', pl. XXII; Goodenough, *Symbols* 3, pl. 854. Against interpreting this fresco as the 'Judgement of Solomon' is Gutmann, 'Was There a Biblical Art?', who sees the influence of 'stage scenery' here.

[14] These caricature-like signs indicate Egypt as the likely origin of the models for this fresco, where, since Manetho, the biblical tradition of the Exodus from Egypt had, for polemical reasons, been modified to an expulsion of anti-social elements. See Reinach, *Textes*, 20-34; Stern, *GLAJJ*; Schwabl, 'Notizen'.

[15] Gutmann, 'Was There a Biblical Art?'

[16] Kraeling, *Synagogue*; Goodenough, *Symbols* vol 9-11: *Symbolism in the Dura Synagogue*; Weitzmann-Kessler, *Frescos*.

[17] Blau, 'Archaeology'; Urbach, 'Rabbinical Laws'; K. Schubert, 'Problem der Entstehung'.

> Proklos ben Pilosphos [i.e., the philosoper Proklos] asked Rabban Gamaliel in Acre while he was bathing in the Bath of Aphrodite, ...Why [then] dost thou bathe in the Bath of Aphrodite? He answered, One may not make answer in the bath. And when he came out he said, I came not within her limits: she came within mine! They do not say, Let us make a bath for Aphrodite, but, Let us make an Aphrodite as an adornment for the bath. Moreover if they would give thee much money thou wouldest not enter in before thy goddess naked or after suffering pollution, nor wouldest thou make water before her! Yet this goddess stands at the mouth of the gutter and all the people make water before her. It is written, *Their gods*, only; thus what is treated as a god is forbidden, but what is not treated as a god is permitted. (mAZ 3:4)

The final statement shows clearly that Gamaliel II applied the proscription of images only to such images as could be the object of cultic veneration. He did not consider even the statue of the goddess Aphrodite a cultic image because it had been placed at the mouth of the gutter. Gamaliel clearly takes a position on images here different than that of Josephus, although the two were contemporaries!

The basically liberal attitude of Gamaliel II prevailed over the hostility to images, as shown by numerous texts in Rabbinic literature. To begin with, a distinction was made between cultically neutral images and idols, which were never tolerated. The goal of the Rabbinic proscription of images was to prevent the emperor cult. This can clearly be seen in the Mishna chapter:

> All images (צלמים) are forbidden because they are worshipped [at least] once a year. So R. Meir. But the Sages say: Only that is forbidden which bears in its hand a staff or a bird or a sphere. Rabban Simeon b. Gamaliel says: That which bears aught in its hand. (mAZ 3:1)

To these forbidden attributes, the Tosefta adds sword, crown, a stamped image and snake, and the Babylonian Talmud in addition specifies a seal ring. In the continuation, the Tosefta informs us: 'Rabbi Eliezer b. Zadok said: There existed all types of images in Jerusalem, not just human images.'[18] This information would be particularly valuable since Eliezer b. Zadok lived in the decades preceding and after the destruction of Jerusalem in 70 CE. But as can be seen from the context, this is apparently only concerned with figurative representations of seal rings. Therefore Eliezer b. Zadok's statement cannot be taken to contradict the witness of Josephus.

The Jerusalem Talmud as well shows clearly that the proscription of images was directed exclusively against idol cults.[19] Statues serving only decorative purposes were not regarded in this sense as idols. In a city where

[18] tAZ 5:1-2 (p468); bAZ 41a.
[19] yAZ 3:1, 42a bottom.

Jews and pagans lived together – and this was almost everywhere the case – Jews could not avoid walking by statues. Thus we read in the same chapter:[20]

> 'All graven images are forbidden' etc. – R. Hiya bar Abba said: Because they are worshipped in the great city of Rome [at least] twice in seven years. From this it follows that they are forbidden only where they are worshipped, but where they are not worshipped they are permitted. R. Yose said: Because they are forbidden in one place, they are forbidden everywhere. What is in fact at issue? When it is clear that the images are from kings,[21] all agree that they are forbidden. When however it is clear that they have been erected by the authorities [for the beautification of public places], all agree that they are permitted. At issue, in principle, are all graven images. R. Meir says, in principle those of kings; but the Sages say, in principle, those set up by the authorities.

This discussion between second and third century scholars is proof that it was possible to differentiate between images relevant for cultic use and those that served only aesthetic purposes.

The discussion in Mishna Avoda Zara 4:4 yields the same impression: 'The idol of a gentile is straightway forbidden, but that of an Israelite is not forbidden unless it has been worshipped.' This means that a statue produced by an Israelite can only benefit an Israelite (e.g., by its sale) if it has not already been worshipped by a gentile; in other words, an Israelite can produce and sell them. This interpretation of the Mishna finds both agreement and disagreement in the Babylonian Talmud:[22]

> The idol of an idolater is not prohibited until it is worshipped; but if it belonged to an Israelite it is prohibited forthwith; such is the statement of R. Yishmael. But R. Akiva says the opposite: The idol of an idolater is prohibited forthwith; but if it belonged to an Israelite it is not prohibited until it is worshipped.

As was often the case, the two scholars (early second century) were not of the same opinion. The liberal opinion of R. Akiva prevailed in the Mishna, according to which only that which had been worshipped by a Gentile was considered to be an idol. R. Yishmael regarded the possibility of cultic veneration of a statue by an idol worshipper as so grave, that no Israelite should occupy himself even with their production and sale. However, R. Akiva opined that an idol worshipper, in the production and marketing of images, did not differentiate between sacred and profane use. For this reason, the images produced by him must *eo ipso* be considered idols. A Jew, on the other hand, is able to differentiate here. Moreover, one need not assume that from the outset he intended to produce an idol. Therefore

[20] yAZ 3:1, 42 b-c.
[21] A reference to the emperor cult.
[22] bAZ 51b below.

the image was considered an idol only after it had been cultically worshipped by a Gentile. We find here basically the same attitude: no opposition to images lacking pagan cultic relevance.

It might be objected that, as is often the case in the Talmud, only theoretical speculations without practical relevance are being discussed. Against this, it must be pointed out that the question concerning what could be produced and sold was of vital interest for the Jews of Palestine, who increasingly became a small town population after the disastrous consequences to agricultural production in the wake of the Bar Kokhba rebellion.[23] In this social situtation artistic crafts provided a welcome source of income. Particularly informative on this point is a tradition in Sifrei Deuteronomy.[24] The interpreted Bible verse is taken from the Song of Moses and reads: 'They sacrificed to demons, which were no gods, to gods they had never known, to new gods that had come in of late, whom your fathers had never dreaded' (Deut 32:17). The midrash reads:

> 'They sacrificed to demons, which were no gods' – if they had worshipped the sun, moon, stars, constellations and things necessary to the world and which are a blessing to the world, the wrath would not have been doubled; but they worshipped things that, rather than blessing, brought evil on them.
>
> 'To demons' – what does a demon do? He invades man and overpowers him.
>
> 'To gods they had never known' – such as the peoples of the world do not know.
>
> 'To new gods that had come in of late' – whenever one of the Gentiles sees such a one, he says: this is a Jewish idol (צלם יהוד[יי]ם הוא זה). And likewise, he says: 'As my hand has reached to the kingdoms of the idols whose graven images were greater than those of Jerusalem and Samaria' (Isa 10:10). This teaches that Jerusalem and Samaria produce the model (דפוס) for the entire world.

Of course, in interpreting this text one must allow for the possibility of exaggeration. What concerns us here is that the statement placed in the mouth of the Gentiles, 'this is a Jewish idol', arises from the particular artistry and imaginative richness of the Jewish artisans. In this sense, the reference to Isa 10:10 and its interpretation can be clarified in the given context that Jerusalem and Samaria, in other words, Judaism in the Syro-Palestinian sphere, produced the models for the entire world. This then is clearly dealing with Jewish models which were being used in a non-Jewish sphere.

However, biblical illustrations, produced exclusively for internal Jewish use, held a special position. That they existed we know today from the

[23] Schäfer, *Bar Kokhba-Aufstand*.
[24] SifDeut 318 (p364); see Urbach, 'Rabbinical Laws', 161.

frescos of the synagogue at Dura Europos and other archaeological sources. These will be treated extensively in the following sections, but for the present we will examine the written sources. According to bYoma 54a, the fourth century Babylonian scholar, Rav Aha bar Yaakov, could no longer imagine a Temple without figurative representations. If there were no longer three-dimensional cherubim, which had been burned in the destruction of the First Temple in 587 BCE, the Second Temple contained at least 'painted cherubim' (כרובים דצורתא). Apparently, synagogues with mosaic pavements and frescos provided his optical stimulation. The mitigation of Lev 26:1 in Targum Yonatan must be mentioned in this connection. According to the biblical text idols and graven images (פסל ומצבה) as well as 'hewn stones' or 'pillars' (אבן משכית) were forbidden. The latter phrase, אבן משכית, acquired the meaning 'mosaic' but continued to be understood in the Targum as 'hewn stone' in order that this limitation could be applied: 'However you may make your synagogues like halls provided with figures and pictures in the floor, but you may not worship them, for I am the Lord your God'.

There were of course Rabbinic circles in favor of a consistent interpretation of the biblical commandment against images. Thus we read in the Mekhilta:[25]

> 'You shall not make for yourselves' – You may not say: Because the Tora permitted [such images] to be made in the Temple, I will make them in the synagogues and study houses. For it says: 'You shall not make *for yourselves*'.

This midrash obviously reflects a polemic fitting the situation of the second century CE, when the Rabbinic scholars were attempting to prevail over synagogue leaders and members whose attitude towards images was positive. That they were unsuccessful in this can be inferred from a note in the Jerusalem Talmud:[26]

> When Nahum bar Simai [early third century Palestinian] died, they covered the images with mats. It was said: Even as he refused to view them in life, so let him not be forced to view them in death.

The behavior of third century Babylonian scholars indicates the same thinking. These were very reserved in their attitude to both alien and Jewish graphic decoration. However, it can be clearly seen from the texts that they had to reconcile themselves to this or that occurrence, since even within the Jewish congregations they were unable to muster enough influence and power to direct things as they wished.[27] Thus we read in the Babylonian Talmud:[28] 'There was a Shafweyativ synagogue in Nehardea, in which stood a statue. Rav and Shmuel and the father of Shmuel and Levi entered therein

[25] Bahodesh 10 (p241; Lauterbach 2, p283).
[26] yAZ 3:1, 42c top.
[27] Neusner, 'Rabbis'.
[28] bRH 24b; the statue probably was of the Persian monarch.

and prayed there.' That Shmuel, at least, cannot have been enthusiastic about such a statue can be seen elsewhere in the Babylonian Talmud, where the Mishna which prohibits statues images *expressis verbis* includes the statues of kings: 'Rav Yehuda said in the name of Shmuel: The teaching of the Mishna refers to the royal statues.'[29] The Babylonian synagogue leaders could be more liberal in this case since a Sassanid royal statue would not be connected with ritual worship as were Roman emperor statues.

Figurative representations, which to all appearances reproduced salvation-historical scenes from the Old Testament, were also rejected by Rav, who however was unable to hinder them. The Babylonian Talmud relates:[30]

> Rav came to Babel during a time of public fasting. He stood up and read from the Tora. At the beginning he spoke a blessing, at the end he spoke no blessing. All those present bowed down. Rav however did not bow down. Why did Rav not bow down? There was in that place a [mosaic] stone floor, and Scripture says: 'You shall not make for yourselves a stone floor in your land in order to bow down upon it' (Lev 26:1).

The situation seems very clear. The synagogue in question contained a mosaic floor with figure representations. Bowing down upon them might have been understood as bowing down *before* them. Apparently, Rav had nothing against figure representations in principle, but refused at least to bow down upon or before them.

A few decades after Rav, who lived in the first half of the third century, Rabbinic scholars were forced to abandon their resistance to figurative representations. The Jerusalem Talmud reports:[31] 'In the days of R. Yohanan [bar Nappaha; died 279] they began to paint on the walls, and he hindered them not.' The text clearly reflects a given situation to which R. Yohanan had to reconcile himself. A fragment of this tractate from the Leningrad National Library contains the further remark: 'In the days of R. Abun they began to produce mosaics with figures, and he hindered them not.'[32] R. Abun lived approximately one generation after R. Yohanan and thus can be dated to c. 300 CE.

These two citations fit perfectly with our extant archaeological witnesses. The frescos of the synagogue at Dura Europos can be dated to the time of Yohanan bar Nappaha, and the oldest mosaic pavement of Hammath Tiberias, which depicts the signs of the zodiac and was commissioned by a high official from the court of the Jewish patriarch, can be dated to the beginning of the fourth century.[33] The frescos at Dura Europos were by no means entirely new inventions in a garrison town on the extreme Eastern

[29] bAZ 40b.

[30] bMeg 22b.

[31] yAZ 3:3, 42d middle.

[32] Quoted in Sukenik, *Synagogues*, 27.

[33] For the Dura Europos synagogue see p163ff; for the Hammath Tiberias mosaic p167ff.

edge of the Roman Empire. Rather, they were probably copies of exemplars found in more important Jewish centers from Asia Minor, Syria, and Mesopotamia.[34] This justified assumption agrees with the evidence of the Rabbinic statements. It may therefore be assumed that by the second half of the second century a Jewish figurative art had developed, of which the mid-third century frescos of Dura Europos are the earliest evidence.

Regardless of what served as models for the Dura Europos synagogue frescos, whether illustrated Bibles in whatever language, illustrated Targums, or model books used for synagogue decor, it can be accepted with certainty that figurative appointments for synagogues of the third through the sixth century were the rule rather than the exception. The numerous mosaic pavements in Palestinian synagogues of this period support this conclusion. An inscription reveals that the synagogue at Sardis contained a ζωγραφία, i.e., a figure painting – probably on the ceiling.[35] A certain Eudoxios, by profession a ζωγράφος – 'figure painter', was buried in the Jewish catacombs in the Vigna Randonini in Rome.[36] It may be assumed then that such figure painters in Rome took their models from the Syro-Babylonian sphere. Thus, Jewish tradition and inscriptional sources fully justify the conclusion that Jewish figurative art was widespread in the Talmudic period.

Since the latest instances of such art date from the sixth century, after which Jewish iconoclasts carried out their work,[37] it is not improbable that the stricter Rabbis ultimately prevailed ideologically over against the positive attitude towards images. This may be connected with an inner development within Judaism. At the beginning of the sixth century the monumental work, the Babylonian Talmud, had been completed, and Hebrew liturgical poetry in Palestine was also at a highpoint in the sixth-seventh centuries.[38] According to the book *Yetsira*, which is also to be dated in this period, it was thought that the Hebrew characters possessed metaphysical-cosmic meaning and that the cosmic order accorded with them. The catacomb inscriptions show that Western European Judaism, in contrast to its oriental counterpart, was hellenized to the extent that individual Jewish congregations celebrated their liturgical services in Greek and Latin. From the sixth century these Western Jewish congregations could be visited by

[34] As emphasized by Weitzmann in Weitzmann-Kessler, *Frescos*. A further, more important Rabbinic reference to murals in the Syro-Palestinian area is found in the interpretation of 1Sam 2:2 in bMeg 14a: '"There is no rock צור like our God" – there is no painter/artist צייר like our God: a man draws a form on a wall but cannot provide it with spirit, soul, organs, and bowels; but the Holy One, blessed be He, draws one form in another and provides them with spirit, soul, organs, and bowels.'

[35] Robert, *Inscriptions*, 49; Kraabel, 'Diaspora Synagogue', esp. 486.

[36] *CII* 1, p76 no. 109.

[37] This can be seen, for example, from the synagogue at Naaran and Biram.

[38] The liturgical poets, Yannai and Elazar Hakkalir.

emissaries from the Syro-Babylonian sphere, who desired to acquaint them with the new developments in the Jewish centers of the East. A clear indication of this is the edict of Justinian I, Novella 146, enacted in 553.[39] The preamble to this edict mentions a disturbance among the Jews that had arisen as a result of some congregation members, apparently influenced by a revival of Hebrew originating in Palestine, insisting on the liturgical Bible reading being conducted in Hebrew, whereas others preferred Greek. The Emperor decreed in §1 that the Bible could continue to be read in Greek and in all other local languages. Likewise, Justinian prohibited the Jews using a δευτέρωσις and in §3 issued a warning against the Jewish scribes. The word δευτέρωσις is the Greek equivalent of משנה, *mishna*, which in the context of the warning against the scribes probably means here the entire Rabbinic tradition. Justinian intended, by means of this intervention, to encourage Jewish assimilation; however the powers which Judaism derived from its tradition and which enabled its transition into the Middle Ages proved to be stronger.

Chapter Two

The Holiness of the Synagogue and its Figurative Decoration

There are several theories concerning the age and origin of the synagogue, and concerning the content and essence of the synagogue worship service, which it is not our purpose to investigate here in detail.[40] Already in the third century the synagogue at Stobi in Macedonia (Yugoslavia) was described as ἅγιος τόπος, 'holy ground'.[41] This appellation gained such general acceptance that it can be described as characteristic for Late Antiquity. The Aramaic equivalent, found in the mosaic pavements of Palestinian synagogues, is אתרא קדישא,[42] and where Latin prevailed, we even find *sacra sinagoga*, 'holy synagogue'.[43] The understanding of the synagogues as 'holy ground' probably resulted from the destruction of the Jerusalem Temple in 70 CE. The holiness formerly reserved for the Temple was henceforth transferred to the individual synagogues. The synagogue became in certain respects then the 'representative and esteemed replacement of the Temple'.[44] The last traces of this in modern synagogues are contained in the words ארון for the Tora shrine (ark), an allusion to the Ark of the Covenant, and פרוכת, the curtain shielding the Tora shrine, originally the Temple curtain.

The Temple-like worth ascribed to the synagogue was also strengthened by the sayings of third and fourth century Rabbinic scholars. In the opinion of some Rabbis, the Shekhina or the Divine Presence, whose place had until then been the Temple, forsook the Holy City and accompanied Israel into exile. Thus, in the saying of a second century scholar:

> R. Shimon ben Yohai said: Come and see, how dear are the Israelites to the Holy One, blessed be He. Wherever they are in exile the Shekhina is with them. They were exiled to Egypt, the Shekhina was with them, for it says: "I appeared to the house of your father when they were in Egypt" (1 Sam 2:27). They were exiled to Babylon, the

[40] K. Schubert, 'Sacra Sinagoga'; Levine, *Synagogue*, esp 7-31.

[41] Hengel, 'Proseuche'; id, 'Synagogeninschrift'.

[42] E.g., the fourth century synagogue at Hammath Tiberias; see Hüttenmeister-Reeg, *Synagogen*, 167.

[43] Renan, 'Les mosaïques'; Goodenough, *Symbols* 2, p91; 3 pl. 887, 888, 894; Kraabel, 'Synagogue', esp 502.

[44] Schrage, 'Synagoge', esp 821.

> Shekhina was with them, for it says: "For your sake I sent to Babel" (Isa 43:14). Even when they are saved in days to come will the Shekhina be with them, for it says: "For the Lord your God will return with your captives" (Deut 30:3). It does not say, "He will bring back", but, "He will return". This teaches that the Holy One, blessed be He, will return with them from exile.[45]

After the destruction of the Temple then, the Shekhina was no longer regarded as attached to the Temple site. According to most Rabbinic teachers it could just as well be in one place as another, both in the Western Wall of the destroyed temple and the individual synagogues. For example, we read in Midrash Psalms:

> As long as the Temple stood the Shekhina dwelled within; but after it was destroyed because of our sins it vanished into Heaven, for it says: The throne of the Lord is in Heaven. R. Eliezer ben Pedat [third century] said: Regardless of whether it is destroyed or not destroyed, the Shekhina does not depart from its place, for it says: The Lord is in His holy Temple. Although His throne is in Heaven, his Shekhina is in the Temple. R. Aha [fourth century] said: The Shekhina never departs from the Western Wall.[46]

The tradition we have just quoted, according to which the Shekhina accompanies Israel in exile as well as in her return from exile, continues: 'Where is the Shekhina in Babylon? Abaye said: In the synagogue at Huzal and in the Shafveyatif synagogue at Nehardea. But do not say: Both here and there, but: At one time here, at another time there.'[47] Even more clearly, the place of prayer is associated with the Shekina in the following tradition: 'Whenever ten men come together in the synagogue to pray the Shekina is with them, for it says: "God is found in the assembly of God" (Ps 82:1).'[48] The Shekhina is found then wherever a *minyan* prays together in a synagogue.

The dispersion of Judaism therefore meant that the Shekhina was no longer conceived of as attached to the holy site. In the Diaspora the synagogues were considered its dwelling place because there the Tora scrolls were preserved and there the congregations met to pray. Certain statements by third and fourth century Rabbinic teachers place this beyond doubt. Thus we read in the Jerusalem Talmud:[49]

> R. Huna said: Whoever in this world does not enter the synagogue, will not be able to enter a synagogue in the [eschatological] future.... R. Abba said, R. Hiya said in the name of R. Yohanan: A man must pray in a place that is especially determined for prayer.... R. Pinhas said in the name of R. Hoshaya: Whoever prays in a synagogue is as

[45] bMeg 29a.
[46] MidrPs 11,3 (49b). Cf Goldberg, *Untersuchungen*, 176-88.
[47] bMeg 29a.
[48] Mekh dRY, Bahodesh 11 (p243; Lauterbach 2, p287).
[49] yBer 5, 8d below.

> one who offers a pure sacrifice... R. Yirmeya said in the name of R. Abbahu: Seek the Lord where he may be found (Isa 55:6). Where then may he be found? In the synagogues and study houses.

Similarly we read in the Babylonian Talmud: 'Rabin, son of Rav Ada, said, R. Yitzhak said: From where do we learn that the Holy One, blessed be He, dwells in synagogues? It says: "God is found in the assembly of God" (Ps 82:1).'[50] This is followed by the opinion, already quoted in part, that the Shekhina is also with a *minyan* of ten praying men, a group of three judges, as well as with two who are engaged in intensive study of the Tora.

The Temple in Jerusalem was regarded as the dwelling place of the invisible God. The description *Shekhina*, derived from the Hebrew root שכן or 'to dwell', reflects this belief. Now since after the destruction of the Temple the Shekhina was regarded as mobile, no longer attached only to the holy site, it followed necessarily that the synagogues came to be understood as 'holy ground' where the Shekhina would bind itself to the praying congregation. The conception of the synagogue in Late Antiquity as ἅγιος τόπος or *sacra sinagoga* was the logical consequence of the Jewish conviction that, despite the Roman destruction of the Temple in 70, the Presence of God had not departed from Israel. This 'nearness' intensifies and crystallizes at the very place where the Law of God is studied and handed down, and where, in accordance with this Law, the congregation comes together for common prayer.

The Dura Europos Synagogue (pl. 24-25)

The synagogue at Dura Europos is approximately contemporary with (or only slightly earlier than) that at Stobi, and acquired its figurative decoration in 245; it was destroyed by the Persians in the course of their war with the Romans already in 256.[51] That the synagogue was considered 'holy ground', even though no explicit inscription has been found in that sense, can be safely concluded from the portrayals directly above the niche for the Tora scrolls (**pl. 24**).[52] From left to right these are a *menora*, the seven-branched candelabrum, with *etrog* and *lulav*, a Temple façade resembling that pictured on the coins of the Bar Kokhba period,[53] and a depiction, unique in kind, of Abraham's sacrifice of Isaac. All three representations are intended to express the worship service of the synagogue in analogy to that of the Temple cult. The seven-branched candelabrum was an important part of the furniture of the Second Temple, both before and after Herod's renovation, otherwise it would not have been carried to Rome in triumph after the fall of Jerusalem, as depicted on the Arch of Titus. The

[50] bBer 6a; cf Mekh dRY (n48).
[51] See n16 above.
[52] K. Schubert, 'Bedeutung des Bildes'.
[53] Kraeling, *Synagogue*, 59.

24. *Menora*, *etrog* and *lulav*; Temple façade; Binding of Isaac
Fresco over Tora niche (detail of no. 25), Dura Europos synagogue,
c. 250 (p163)

25. 'A tree of life for all who hold fast to her'
Fresco over Tora niche, Dura Europos synagogue, c. 250 (p166)

Temple façade speaks for itself, just as does Abraham's sacrifice of Isaac to everyone who was familiar with the Jewish identification of the Temple mount with Mount Moriah, upon which Abraham had prepared to sacrifice Isaac. It could already be read in 2 Chr 3:1 that 'Solomon began to build the house of the Lord on Mount Moriah'. This identification survived at all levels of Jewish tradition and continued to be generally acknowledged. It is also seen in Jubilees (18:13), a book originating from priestly circles who were kindred to the Qumran community. Likewise Josephus writes in *Ant.* 1:226 [13,2] that Abraham 'proceeded with his son alone to that mount whereon king David afterwards erected the temple'. In Rabbinic literature the identification of Moriah with the Temple mount can be found, e.g., in the Targums to Gen 22:2 and 2 Chron. 3:1. According to Genesis Rabba,[54] R. Shimon bar Yohai, in a discussion concerning the worth of Mount Moriah, suggested that it might even be situated over against the heavenly temple.[55]

Above the area directly over the niche for the Tora scrolls, in the first and oldest layer, a representation of the Tree of Life was found **(pl. 25)**, apparently corresponding to an exemplar used for the decoration of such Tora scroll niches.[56] The identification of the Tree of Life with the Tora or its eschatological significance was a commonplace of Jewish interpretation of Scripture: 'Shimon bar Yohai said: The tree is none but the Tora, for it says: "She [Wisdom identified with the Tora] is the tree of life for all who hold fast to her" (Prov 3:18).'[57] In an eschatological context, the Targum tradition to Gen 3:24 also refers to the significance of the Tree of Life as symbol for the Tora. Targum Neophyti paraphrases Gen 3:24 by first referring to the tradition according to which the Tora had been created 2000 years before the creation of the world. Next the rewards and punishments for the righteous and the wicked at the judgement are mentioned. The Targum concludes with the words:

> For the Tora is the tree of life for everyone who occupies himself with it. Whoever keeps its commandments in this world lives and endures, like the tree of life, for the world to come. To obey the Tora in this world is to be compared with [eating] the fruits of the tree of life.

Targums Yerushalmi and Yonatan are similar here.

Therefore, when the Tree of Life was originally depicted as growing out of the Tora scroll niche in the Dura Europos synagogue, it signified the Tora to its full extent, both as the instrument of God's creation and the

[54] GenR 55,7 to Gen 22:2 (p591; Mirqin 2, p262f).

[55] For the special iconography of Abraham's sacrifice of Isaac, see K. Schubert, 'Bedeutung des Bildes', 13-15.

[56] The theses of Goodenough and Kraeling are disputed by Schubert, 'Bedeutung des Bildes', 15f. Kessler (in Weitzmann-Kessler, *Frescos*, 158f) has recently rejected the interpretation as the Tree of Life, suggesting instead a messianic significance.

[57] GenR 12,6 to Gen 2:4 (Mirqin 1, p86, as in printed editions, see Theodor-Albeck p104).

norm for the life of the Jewish people.[58] The Tora scroll niche with *menora*, *etrog* and *lulav*, the Temple, and Abraham offering Isaac, and the Tree of Life representing the Tora, clearly belong together. In the nature of things, the Temple and the sacred Mount Moriah belong to Tora and the Tree of Life. The Tree of Life, as representative of the Tora, is also meant to depict the heavenly Paradise. The two repaintings of this eschatological panel above the Tora scroll niche, carried out between 245 and 256, are a sign that those who commissioned the frescos desired that the eschatological dimensions be further emphasized.[59] This will be examined in greater detail in the following section. The illustration above the Tora scroll niche in the Dura Europos synagogue is therefore clear and certain proof that this synagogue was considered 'holy ground'.

Hammath Tiberias and Beth Alpha Synagogues (pl. 26-27)

As did the painting above the Tora scroll niche in the Dura Europos synagogue, the mosaic floors of Palestinian synagogues emphasized the character of these houses of God as 'holy ground'.[60] We give only two examples here: Hammath Tiberias **(pl. 26)** and Beth Alpha **(pl. 27)**. In each case the depiction of a Tora shrine, flanked both by seven-branched candelabra and the religious symbols of Judaism, is found in a floor mosaic directly in front of the Tora scroll niche. In front of this mosaic, and leading to it, are the signs of the zodiac.[61] Although initially it seems surprising that an originally pagan motif was used in a Jewish synagogue, we may take it as certain that the Jews did not adopt such a motif before it was possible to understand it in the sense of their own religious traditions.[62] According to a Greek dedicatory inscription, the mosaic in Hammath Tiberias (ca. mid-fourth century) was donated by a leading official in the Patriarchate, the mention of which guaranteed the donor's orthodoxy.[63] The design of this mosaic accords well, both in content and the time of its construction, with the saying concerning R. Abun mentioned above, i.e., that he was unable to withhold his consent to mosaics consisting of figurative representations. Whatever sense the zodiac signs in a synagogue might have had – most probably, as in the *Hekhalot* texts, a symbol for the ascension of the worshipper through the seven 'palaces' to the throne of God, indicated by the mosaic field with the Tora shrine – this was meant to be 'holy ground', as

[58] Hengel, *Judentum*, 275-318; K. Schubert, 'Israel im Altertum', 228-34; K. Schubert – U. Schubert, 'Vertreibung', esp 174-7.

[59] K. Schubert, 'Bedeutung des Bildes', 17-22.

[60] Stemberger, 'Bedeutung'; Hachlili, 'Zodiac'.

[61] Stemberger mentions this and other sites where such mosaic floors have been unearthed ('Bedeutung', 23-25).

[62] Stemberger, 'Bedeutung' deals with this in greater detail.

[63] For transcription and translation see Hüttenmeister-Reeg, *Synagogen*, 167.

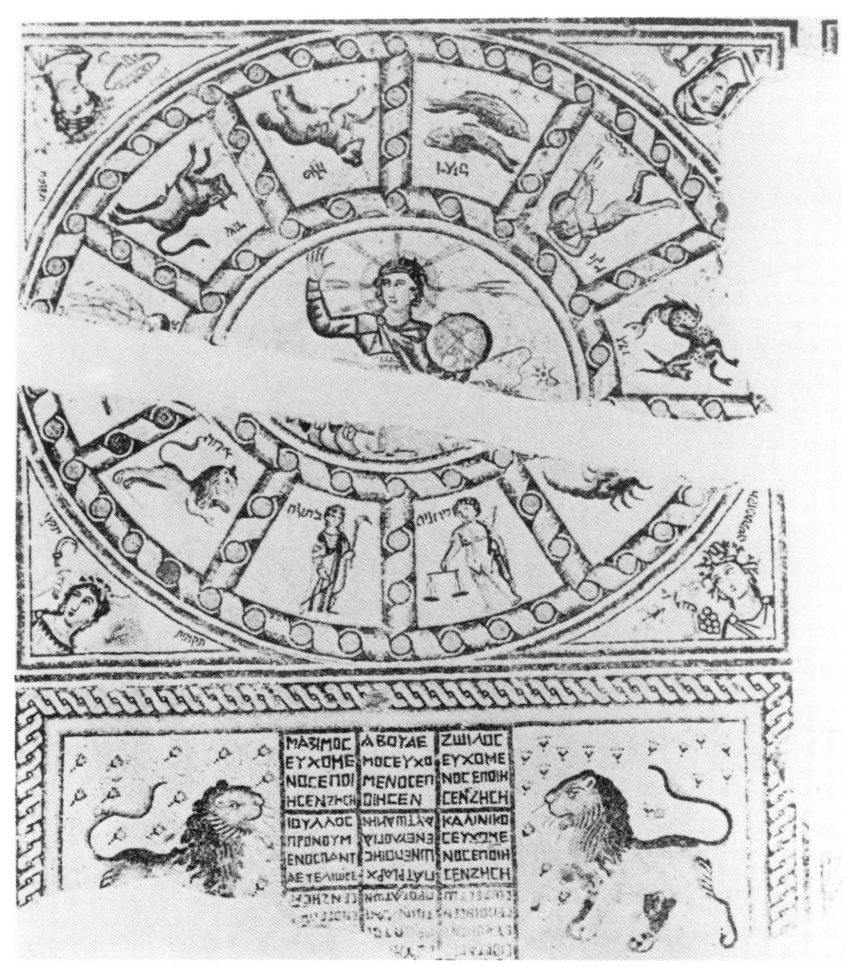

26. Zodiac and votive inscriptions
Mosaic floor, Hammath Tiberias synagogue, 4th cent. (p167)

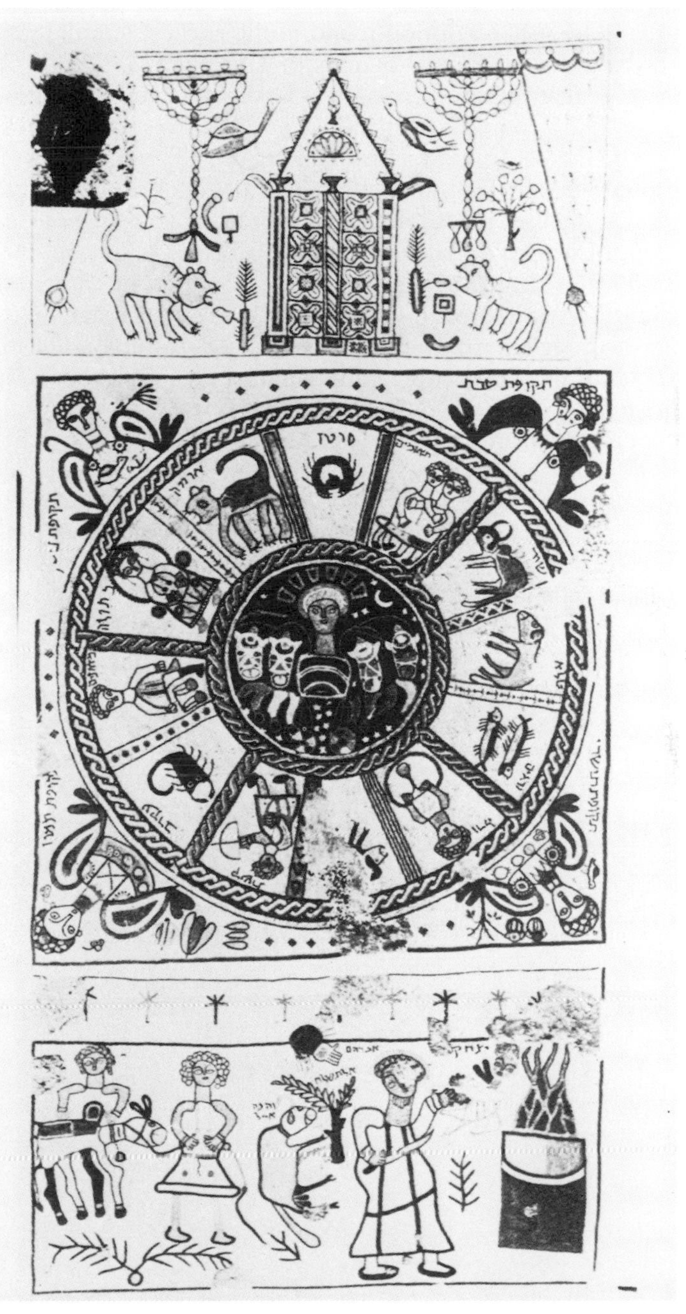

27. Binding of Isaac; Zodiac; Temple implements
Mosaic floor, Beth Alpha synagogue, early 6th cent. (p167)

shown already by the inscription found in the earliest stratum giving this appellation to the synagogue at Hammath Tiberias.[64]

In the mosaic floor of the synagogue at Beth Alpha the conception of the synagogue as 'holy ground' is even more clearly expressed. This mosaic is to be dated in the time of Emperor Justinian I (518-527), about 200 years later than that of Hammath Tiberias. Situated immediately in front of the field with the zodiac signs is a scene depicting Abraham's offering of Isaac. Just as in the Dura Europos synagogue above the Tora scroll niche, this is also meant to indicate Temple Mount symbolism.[65] Whoever entered the synagogue knew this symbolism and understood himself to be standing on 'holy ground', even though there is no extant inscription expressly indicating this. The portrayal of the Tora shrine with menorot etc., which at Beth Alpha follows the field of zodiac signs being situated directly in front of the Tora scroll niche, is similar in type to that at Hammath Tiberias. Yet these two analogous depictions also show significant differences. Two lions, depicted at Beth Alpha beneath the *menorot*, are certainly meant to express messianic hope as the Lions of Judah. It is more important however that on the gable of the Tora shrine, two birds are depicted, one on the right and one on the left – apparently indicating the cherubim in the Temple. This mosaic as well has the sense of expressing the presence of the Shekhina.

[64] Already in the 5-6th cent. synagogue at Naaran, excavated 1919-21, there is a connection between the zodiac signs and the Aramaic description אתרא קדישא, 'holy place'. See Wilnai, *Madrikh*, vol. 'Yerushalayim (etc)', 421f.

[65] Cf above, p166.

Chapter Three

Jewish Programmatic Painting: The Dura Europos Synagogue

It is generally accepted that programmatic painting in the sense of the portrayal of sequences is characteristic first of Jewish art, as we know it, e.g., from the Dura Europos synagogue in the mid-third century, whereas in the Christian context it is not attested until later.[66] We will therefore examine a few examples of such programmatic paintings from Jewish sources before illustrating with examples their impact on Christian iconography.

The archaeological findings are in agreement with the literary sources. One early witness dates to the third century, beginning with the time of Septimius Severus (193-211). It consists of coins from the Asia Minor city of Apamea that depict Noah and his wife in two narrative scenes, first in the ark, and second, in an attitude of prayer after having disembarked **(pl. 28)**.[67] It is entirely possible that the geographical situation of Apamea inspired the Jews of this city to use a depiction of the Flood story in their synagogue.[68]

The most extensive witness is of course the synagogue at Dura Europos on the Euphrates from the middle of the third century. The scene above the Tora scroll niche has already been discussed above. The panel above it was repainted twice in the eleven years in which the synagogue was decorated with frescos (245-256), indicating that those responsible for the content of the paintings were still not satisfied with the identification of the Tree of Life with the Tora alone, but wanted to give the messianic-eschatological theme more expression.

The First Repainting above the Tora Niche **(pl. 29)**

The first repainting shows a ruler dressed in Persian garb seated upon a throne in the crown of the Tree of Life. Before this throne, two figures are depicted in ancient dress, the *chiton* and *himation*. That they stand before and not behind the throne is intended to show that they are members of the royal entourage of a very special kind and rank. Together with the two figures, a striding lion underneath the throne has been added. This suggests

[66] Thus, e.g., Tronzo, *Catacomb*, 76; Weitzmann-Kessler, *Frescos*, 149f.
[67] Effenberger, *Frühchristliche Kunst*, 89; Weitzmann, *Age of Spirituality*, 383f (no. 350).
[68] Effenberger, *Frühchristliche Kunst*.

28. Noah and wife: in the ark, after disembarking
Coin, Apamea, 3rd cent. (p171)

an identification of the lion with the Lion of Judah. The figure on the throne would then be none other than King Messiah, and the two attendant figures could represent the Patriarchs and the Exilarchs. Hence, this is a contemporization and adaptation to the situation of a city on the border between the Roman and Sassanid Empires. The messianic passage in Jacob's blessing of his sons (Gen 49:10) was already interpreted in this sense in a *baraita* in the Babylonian Talmud:

> 'The scepter shall not depart from Judah' – these are the Exilarchs in Babylon who rule Israel with the scepter, 'and the lawgiver between his feet' – these are the heirs of Hillel who teach the Tora in public.[69]

Thus the first repainting depicts both the messianic as well as the contemporary political aspect of Gen 49:10.

The Second Repainting **(pl. 30)**

The messianic-eschatological aspect is expressed even more clearly and distinctly in the third stratum, i.e., in the second repainting. The single panel was now divided into two parts. In the lower panel only the striding lion remained from the second stratum. Jacob's blessing from Gen 49 and Gen 48:13-20 was added at the left and the right (from the viewer's perspective). On the left, above the blessing from Gen 49 concerning the twelve sons of Israel, sits an Orpheus figure, clothed in Persian garments, wearing a Phrygian cap and playing a lyre – which is with certainty to be identified with King David. The lion from the second stratum fits both the Orpheus and the David motif. A similar Orpheus, so indicated by the mosaic adscript 'David', was found in the mosaic pavement of a synagogue in Gaza dated to the very early sixth century.[70] The placement of Orpheus-David directly above Jacob's blessing from Gen 49, is apparently meant to illustrate Jacob's words concerning the tribe of Judah in a messianic sense. However, the depiction (lower right) of Jacob blessing Joseph's sons, Manasseh and Ephraim, had a contemporary historical aspect for third century Judaism. This is probably a reference to the second messianic figure, attested in texts since the second half of the second century, the Messiah from the house of Joseph-Ephraim who was destined to suffer and die.[71] The two aspects of

[69] bSan 5a. Further texts concerning messianic understanding of Gen 49:10 in K. Schubert, 'Bedeutung des Bildes', 18f. Weitzmann-Kessler, *Frescos*, 91f, 165 see in the enthroned figure not the Messiah but David himself, and suggest that the two attendant figures are 'indeed prophets', more specifically, Samuel and Nathan. Kessler however also considers possible the interpretation of the enthroned figure as Messiah (p165). In this case he judges the attendants to be Yoshua b. Yotsadak and Zerubbabel. However an interpretation of the scene consistent with its location and the time of its origin (mid-third century), which, moreover, can be supported by Rabbinic texts, seems to me to be more probable.

[70] Ovadiah, 'Synagogue', pl. on p130; U. Schubert, *Spätantikes Judentum*, 66.

[71] bSuk 52a; TgY Exod 40:11. See Dalman, *Messias*; Klausner, *Ha-raayon ha-meshihi* 2, p215-32; Urbach, *Sages* (Hebr), 618-20.

29. Messianic scene
Fresco, 1st repainting of no. 25, Dura Europos, c. 250 (p171)

30. Jacob's blessing; Orpheus/David; above: messianic scene (?)
Frescos, 2nd repainting of no. 25, Dura Europos, c. 250 (p173)

31. Tabernacle/Temple; elements of the sacrificial cult
Fresco, Dura Europos synagogue, c. 250 (p177)

Jacob's blessing according to Gen 48 and Gen 49 portray then the two aspects of Israel's messianic hope in the third century: the expectation of a Messiah from the house of Joseph and the house of David – doubtless a sequence characteristic of those in the frescos of the synagogue of Dura Europos. This sequence is continued in the upper picture. The enthroned figure is again depicted, this time surrounded by several figures. This portrayal is probably also intended to illustrate the Messianic Age, or perhaps the coming world as well, which, according to Rabbinic understanding, was supposed to follow the Messianic Age.[72] The pictures above the Tora shrine niche in Dura Europos are an impressive witness that the Jews employed an extensive program of figurative representations in the very area in which the tradition arose that determined their future course.

From the remaining abundance of pictures in the Dura Europos synagogue, we will examine only those that, to be understood correctly, presuppose a knowledge of Rabbinic Scripture interpretation. We make no attempt here to interpret the entire program – assuming that a theme sufficiently unifying to encompass all pictorial representations even existed. However, the scenes to the right and left of the Tora shrine niche certainly belong together.

The Temple/Tabernacle (pl. 31)

The scene on the left side shows a wall with three doors behind which is a temple-like building that apparently represents the Tabernacle and the Temple. From the open front of this building there is a clear view into the interior of the Temple enclosure. Inside there is a Tora shrine revealing the Ark of the Covenant. The common appellation ארון for both shrines made a portrayal of this sort possible. Directly before the Ark is a *menora*. Beside this is a priestly figure identified with a Greek adscript as Aaron. To the right of the wall which surrounds the holy area stands a ram with a bullock positioned above him; above these, two men wearing Persian garb and smaller in stature stand beside Aaron while raising trumpets to their mouths. To the the left of the wall stands a reddish brown cow, apparently a reference to the red heifer (Num 19:1-3). A man with an axe holds the cow by the horn, evidently preparing to slaughter it. Above the red cow are two more men in Persian garb also holding trumpets. The four men with horns, to the right and left of Aaron, are probably an allusion to Num 10:2.[73] What we have here is an illustration of the Temple cult.

[72] K. Schubert, 'Bedeutung des Bildes', 21f.
[73] U. Schubert, *Spätantikes Judentum*, 45-47.

The Heavenly Temple **(pl. 32)**

The picture to the right of the Tora shrine niche is devoted to a depiction of the Heavenly Temple, the ascension to which had been the goal of Jewish mystics probably already in the mishnaic period.[74] The entire area is filled out with seven polychrome merloned walls. In the upper half of the picture, over, and spanning, the fourth to the seventh ringwall, is a classic ancient temple. There is a suggestion of fire behind the seventh wall. Apparently, the Temple is supposed to stand inside. This is probably the pictorial representation of the Heavenly Temple as the *Hekhalot* mystics conceived it, and to which they strove to ascend.[75]

The Childhood of Moses **(pl. 33)**

The scenes portraying the childhood of Moses are particularly instructive for our discussion of a comprehensive narrative depiction. From right to left the following scenes are depicted. A wall with tower and opened gate symbolizes Egypt. Before it sits Pharaoh flanked by two court officials, all in Persian dress; one of the officials holds a writing tablet upon which he is writing. Pharoah and the other official hold their right hands up in a speech gesture; before them stand the two Hebrew midwives, likewise with right hands raised in speech gesture. Another female figure, bending in front of the first midwife, is apparently placing the basket containing the baby Moses among the reeds. The left side of the picture is completed by the scene of Moses' discovery by Pharoah's daughter. She is standing naked in the Nile, holding little Moses supported on her left thigh while she points to the scene behind her with her right hand. That she herself is standing in the waters of the Nile is not unexpected since Exod 2:5 states that Pharaoh's daughter came down to the river to bathe. It must be remembered that in the third century CE, in which the frescos in Dura Europos are to be dated, the vocalization of the Bible text was still not fixed. Thus we read in Exodus Rabba[76] that R. Yehuda and R. Nehemya, two scholars from the second half of the second century, disagreed about whether the word in Exod 2:5 was to be read as אמה or אמה. In the one sense the text is to be translated as we know it, 'she sent her handmaid', in the other sense however, 'she stretched forth her hand'. The familiar Targums, Onkelos and Yonatan, adopted the second interpretation. The Rabbinic commentary supplemented this with the reason for her wish to bathe: she was leprous and desired to cool herself. But when she touched the basket containing the baby Moses

[74] Scholem, *Major Trends*, 40-79; id, *Jewish Gnosticism*; Gruenwald, *Apocalyptic*; id, *Apocalypticism*; Schäfer, *Hekhalot-Studien*.
[75] Maier, *Kultus*; U. Schubert, *Spätantikes Judentum*, 47f.
[76] ExodR 1,23 to Exod 2:5 (Mirqin 5, p37); bSot 12b.

32. Heavenly Temple
Fresco, Dura Europos synagogue, c. 250 (p178)

33. Scenes from the childhood
Fresco, Dura Europos synagogue, c. 250 (p178)

34. The return of the ark
Fresco, Dura Europos synagogue, c. 250 (p182)

she was cleansed instantly.[77] According to another explanation, she desired to purify herself from the idol worship of her father's house.[78] At all events, it is not surprising in the Rabbinic discussion that Pharaoh's daughter herself stands naked in the waters of the Nile.

Behind the woman in the water stand three girls clothed in *peplos*-like Greek robes. The items in their hands – wash basin, pitcher, spice chest, and in particular, a large yellow mussel shell – indicate that these women (who according to the biblical text are handmaids to Pharaoh's daughter) are nymphs, in accordance with the ancient notion of the infancy narrative for a ϑεῖος ἀνήρ.[79] The final scene at the left leads us again to the realm of Rabbinic exegesis. A female figure, who has apparently received the baby Moses from Pharaoh's daughter, is handing him over to another woman. According to Exod 2:7-9 these two women are Miriam and Yokheved, the sister and mother of Moses. However, their clothing and appearance here show them to be the two midwives treating with Pharaoh, who, according to Exod 1:15 are called Shifra and Pua. This interpretation is found in Rabbinic exegesis, e.g., in the first half of the third century when Rav interprets the two women in Exod 1:15 to be Yokheved and Miriam.[80] In the depiction of Moses' infancy on the west wall of the Dura Europos synagogue then we find a combination of Rabbinic motifs and motifs specific to Late Antiquity, in particular those characteristic for the Syro-Palestinian area in the Talmudic period.[81]

The Return of the Ark (pl. 34)

A further important picture on the west wall depicts the return of the Ark of the Covenant from the land of the Philistines. Here as well two scenes are combined into one picture. The right side of the panel portrays the destruction brought about by the Ark in the temple of Dagon at Ashdod (1 Sam 5:1-4). The left side portrays 1 Sam 6:7-14, i.e., the return of the Ark to Beth Shemesh. The Philistines were commanded to return the Ark on a wagon drawn by two cows that had never been yoked. The direction chosen by the cows was to be regarded as determined by the will of God. The Ark is depicted as a Tora shrine being drawn by the cows on a two-wheeled wagon leaving the land of the Philistines.[82] The Rabbinic interpretation begins with 1 Sam 6:12, וישׁרנה הפרות, 'Then the cows went straight'. In the Babylonian Talmud this text acquires a very singular reinterpretation. The word וישׁרנה is understood here not as deriving from ישׁר 'to be straight', but

[77] ExodR ib; TgY Exod 2:5.
[78] bSot 12b.
[79] Goodenough, *Symbols* 9, p203-24; 11 pl. 186-9.
[80] bSot 11b; TgY and FrgTg Exod 2:5.
[81] U. Schubert, *Spätantikes Judentum*, 41-43.
[82] Ib 48f.

from שיר 'poem, song':

> Said R. Yohanan in the name of R. Meir: They rendered song.... And what did they sing?... R. Yitshak Nappaha said: [They sang:]
>
> Sing, O sing, acacia tree,
> Ascend in all thy gracefulness,
> With golden weave they cover thee,
> The sanctuary-palace hears thy eulogy,
> With divers jewels art thou adorned.[83]

Here the allusion to the Ark, made of acacia wood, is unmistakeable. R. Yitshak Nappaha lived at approximately the same time in which the Dura Europos synagogue was decorated with pictures. The Ark had somewhat the same function in the Tabernacle and the Temple as the Tora shrine did at this time in the synagogue, which was understood as 'holy ground'. It was therefore not difficult to depict the Ark as a Tora shrine. Given that Tora scrolls were probably brought into the synagogues of the third century in ceremonial procession,[84] the saying related of R. Yitshak Nappaha may well reflect a liturgical formula designed for such a procession. And it may be that the cows drawing the wagon with the Tora shrine itself were also meant to remind the members of the congregation of this connection.[85]

Elijah and The Priests of Baal on Mt. Carmel (pl. 35-36)

On the south wall of the synagogue there is a depiction of the sacrifice of the priests of Baal on Mount Carmel which likewise can only be understood in the light of Rabbinic interpretation. Wood has been piled on an altar and upon the wood lies a bull prepared for sacrifice. The scene **(pl. 35)** depicts the vain attempt of the priests of Baal to induce their god to consume the sacrifice with fire as related in 1 Kgs 15:25-29. According to a Rabbinic tradition, they knew from the very beginning that their goal could only be reached by deceit:

> This teaches us that Hiel built the altar hollow. They [the priests of Baal] put him inside and said to him: When you hear [our] voice light the fire immediately which you have with you and ignite the sacrifice from below. Therefore the Holy One, blessed be He, caused a serpent to come which bit him, and he died.[86]

The God of Israel cannot be deceived! This is exactly what the frescos of

[83] bAZ 24b.
[84] For this problem see Levine, *Synagogue*, 18. A relief was found in Kefar Nahum that apparently portrays a small wagon used for the conveyance of Tora scrolls; Wilnai, *Madrikh*, vol. 'Haifa, (etc)', 285.
[85] Gutmann, 'Programmatic Painting', esp 148f.
[86] YalShim to 1Kgs 18:26 (no. 214).

35. Hollow altar of the Baal priests on Mt. Carmel
Fresco, Dura Europos synagogue, c. 250 (p183)

36. Elijah's sacrifice on Mt. Carmel
Fresco, Dura Europos synagogue, c. 250 (p187)

37. Resurrection scenes from Ezek. 37
Fresco, Dura Europos synagogue, c. 250 (p187)

Dura Europos portray.[87] In narrative-like sequence Elijah's sacrifice follows the unsuccessful attempt at sacrifice by the Baal priests **(pl. 36)**. According to 1 Kgs 18:30-38 his prayer was heard by the God of Israel. The bull burns upon the altar despite everything having been thoroughly soaked with water beforehand.[88]

The Ezekiel Cycle (pl. 37)

On the north wall there is a depiction of the Ezekiel cycle according to Ezek 37. The theme is the resurrection of the dead, a doctrine possessing dogmatic character for Pharisaic and Rabbinic Judaism.[89] Moreover, Ezek 37:1-14 was probably from the very first a symbol for the eschatological restoration of the Jewish people, and had therefore messianic character. God, who speaks to the prophet Ezekiel, is symbolized throughout by a hand which reaches into the picture from the upper border. From left to right, Ezekiel, with raised hand, is thrice depicted in Persian garb as he receives the divine commission. At the prophet's feet lie numerous body parts instead of the bones mentioned by the biblical text. Ezek 37:7 relates that the prophet experienced an earthquake as the bones joined themselves together. The third picture of Ezekiel wearing his Persian clothes is based on this verse. Beside the prophet there is a split mountain with an olive tree on each peak. To the right of the cleft in the mountain there is a fallen house. This as well as the cleft mountain are illustrative of the earthquake, during the course of which the resurrection of the dead occurs. From the mountain itself further body parts appear which – likewise via the earthquake – apparently join themselves together to form three additional human bodies. To the right of the cleft mountain stands the fourth of the Ezekiel figures clothed in Persian garb. His right hand is raised to the hand of God which is stretched out to him. His left hand is pointing to the three reformed, but still lifeless, human bodies. This scene illustrates Ezek 37:9, 'Then he said to me, "Prophesy to the wind, prophesy, son of man, and say to it, These are the words of the Lord God: Come, O wind,[90] come from every quarter and breathe into these slain, that they may come to life.' The continuation in v. 10 states: 'Breath came into them; they came to life and rose to their feet, a mighty host'. Standing beside the top figure of the three reclining reunited corpses is a feminine figure in Greek garb with butterfly

[87] U. Schubert, *Spätantikes Judentum*, 35f. The tradition of Hiel's thwarted deceit was widespread, as in ExodR 15,15 (Mirqin 5, p180).

[88] The interpretation of the scene in the light of this Rabbinic tradition is generally accepted. Thus Weitzmann-Kessler, *Frescos*, 111: 'Kraeling and all scholars describing this secene identified him as Hiel.'

[89] According to mSan 10:1 whoever denied the resurrection of the dead had no part in the world to come (see below).

[90] Hebrew רוח means both 'wind' and 'spirit'.

wings. She probably represents the *pneuma* revivifying the dead, corresponding to the Hebrew word, רוח, 'wind, spirit'. To the right of the pneuma figure stands Ezekiel once again, this time clothed in *chiton* and *himation*, and beckons with his right hand to three *psychai*, who enter as souls into the three reclining bodies thus filling them anew with life. These three *psychai* are similar to the *pneuma* figure, albeit somewhat smaller. As a sign of revivification the large *pneuma* figure touches with both hands the head of the top figure of the three bodies lying before her. The impression gained is that this portrayal stems from the widespread trichotomous anthropology of Late Antiquity.[91] Man consists of soul, spirit (*pneuma*), and body. Thus already in Josephus' *Ant.* 1:34 [1:1,2]: 'God fashioned man by taking dust from the earth and instilled into him spirit (πνεῦμα) and soul (ψυχή).' An analogous conception regarding the expected resurrection is found in the Babylonian Talmud,[92] where it is said that the souls of the righteous dead are found in the Seventh Heaven, along with the dew by means of which God revivifies the dead bodies. 'Souls' can here easily be identified with the *psychai*, and the 'dew' functionally with the pneuma.

To the prophet's right stand ten resurrected men, perhaps as a reference to the full number for a liturgical congregation. Next come more body parts which have not been rejoined, and beside them, once again, an Ezekiel figure dressed in Hellenistic garb, to whom the hand of God is reaching down from above, and at Ezekiel's right, once again a depiction of a mountain. The sequence further to the right is extraordinarily difficult of interpretation and therefore will not be discussed here. The question remains however concerning the meaning of the body parts which have not been rejoined in proximity to the ten resurrected bodies. They probably symbolize those groups of sinners, which according to Rabbinic understanding, have no part in the resurrection. The Rabbinic scholars considered the doctrine of the resurrection compulsory, but there was also the widespread opinion that not all – the exception being the worst sinners – would participate in the resurrection. This differentiation between sinners who will be resurrected to judgement and those who will not be resurrected at all is already found in Mishna Sanhedrin 10:1-3. With clear anti-Sadducee point the Babylonian Talmud comments:[93] 'He denies the resurrection of the dead, therefore he will have no part in the resurrection of the dead, for the Holy One, blessed be He, always metes out measure for measure.'[94]

[91] U. Schubert, 'Vorlage', esp. 3f.; Simon, 'Entstehung'.

[92] bHag 12b.

[93] bSan 90a.

[94] bMeg 14a, cited above n34, also contains a reference to trichotomous anthropology, since God provides the human body with spirit (רוח) and soul (נשמה). Weitzmann-Kessler interpret all four feminine winged figures as *psychai* and also identify them with the wind/spirit of the four winds according to Ezek 37:9. Weitzmann also understands as animation the touching of the head of the topmost of the three dead bodies by the large winged figure; likewise also Weitzmann-Kessler, *Cotton Genesis*, 52 pl. 22-25.

Chapter Four

Jewish Influence on Earliest Christian Painting: The Via Latina Catacomb

Of the hitherto known catacombs, the one on the Via Latina discovered in 1955 is not only richest in pictorial decoration, but for this very reason also the most difficult to explain.[95] Besides a depiction of the seated Christ, with Peter and Paul standing by,[96] an unequivocally Christian motif, the ideologically significant grave decoration of this catacomb includes numerous pagan motifs. For example, Cubiculum N is decorated exclusively with Hercules scenes. However, the overwhelming majority of the pictures stemming from the second till the fourth quarter of the fourth century portray biblical scenes, among which the Old Testament scenes represent a definite majority. Since some of these scenes seem to refer to Jewish exemplars, the discovery of the Via Latina catacomb has re-enlivened the discussion about Jewish antecedents to Christian Bible illustration which has been going on since the beginning of this century.[97] It was justifiably assumed that the exemplars for both the frescos in the Dura Europos synagogue and early Christian painting cycles, the oldest of which are in the Via Latina catacomb, were Jewish picture sequences. However, as happens often when a plausible theory appears to gain consensus, an objection was raised – in this case correctly described as a 'step backwards'.[98] It is therefore necessary to take up the problem anew and put the question whether the search for Jewish exemplars to early Christian art is at all necessary and proper.

The three preceding chapters have demonstrated the existence of a

[95] Ferrua, *Le pitture*; U. Schubert, *Spätikes Judentum*, 11-34; Kötzsche-Breitenbruch, *Neue Katakombe*; Tronzo, *Catacomb*.

[96] Ferrua, *Le pitture*, pl. 108.

[97] See discussion in Fink, *Bildfrömmigkeit*, 51-62esp. 56.

[98] Fink, *Bildfrömmigkeit*, with reference to Brandenburg, 'Überlegungen'. This is valid as well for Strauss, *Kunst der Juden* (cf my review in *Kairos* 16 [1974] 88-93), and Stichel, *Namen* (cf my review in *Jahrbuch der österreichischen Byzantinistik* 29 [1980] 370-2); and id, 'Elemente'. To this cf the position taken by Maser, 'Irrwege', esp. 357f n90. Assumptions like Stichel's are also shared by Gutmann, 'Early Synagogue'; id, 'The Dura Europos Paintings'. For a contraposition see Weitzmann-Kessler, *Frescos*. An international symposium entitled 'Die jüdische Wurzel der frühchristlichen Kunst' sponsored by the Wiener Internationale Hochschulkurse, October 1-5, 1991, attempted to set the necessary accents for a proper understanding of this much discussed question.

widespread Jewish pictorial art, the oldest attestations for which come from the third century CE, but the beginnings of which can with probability be dated in the second century. This art arose in that sphere of Judaism customarily referred to as 'normative Judaism'. Its Greco-Roman elements do not surprise us since similar phenomena were abundantly assimilated into Rabbinical Judaism.[99] With great probability, the synagogue can be seen as a point of dissemination for Jewish art. Our task here is not to determine whether illustrated Bibles, Hebrew or Greek, or perhaps Aramaic paraphrases, or pattern books for the painting of synagogues[100] were the mediators between Jewish and Christian artists, but to conclude – here with emphasis – that it was Rabbinic exegesis, not Alexandrian-Philonic, that influenced both the figurative representations in the Dura Europos synagogue and the Christian painting cycles. If one assumes that illustrated Septuagint manuscripts are the source,[101] which is eminently possible, these must not be connected with Egypt, since the cultural power of Egyptian Judaism was broken after the suppression of the revolt in 115 CE. The illustrations themselves clearly indicate a Syro-Palestinian provenance, i.e., that area in which the Talmudic tradition arose and underwent its full development.

Now if Jewish art possessed a developed picture program already in the third century, i.e., at the time of the timid beginnings of a Christian art, as has been repeatedly emphasized, and such picture programs are also attested in Christian sources from the fourth century on, it is difficult to draw any other conclusion than that Christian artists employed optical Jewish exemplars.[102] It can only be described as astonishing when, in an otherwise excellent study, the question concerning 'Jewish influence in early Christian art' is very earnestly put, yet is followed by the remark that this is 'a question that we still cannot answer'.[103] Here it seems to have been overlooked that concerning the relevant art monuments it is first necessary to ask whether these can be explained from Rabbinic sources, and only afterwards can it be asked whether, and to what extent, the originally Jewish exemplars have undergone Christian reinterpretation.[104] For the answer to the first question the student of Rabbinic literature is responsible,

[99] Cf n6 above.

[100] Kretschmar, 'Beitrag'; cf Gutmann, 'Second Commandment'.

[101] Weitzmann-Kessler, *Frescos* localize the assumed picture exemplars the area of Antioch.

[102] Maser, 'Irrwege'.

[103] Tronzo, *Catacomb*, 76 (cf my review in *Kairos* 30-31 [1988-89] 251-3).

[104] In some motifs, e.g., the Flood scene in the Ashburnham Pentateuch, originally Jewish motifs could have been mediated to Christian painters via the Apocrypha, which were widespread in the Christian realm. Jewish legend motifs may have been known in oral tradition to Church fathers as well, and via the Church fathers, may have served as a foundation for Christian illustrators. If however – as in most cases – we are dealing with statements which have their Sitz im Leben in the Rabbinic world, the Rabbinic material must be considered as exclusively relevant for comparison with picture composition.

and for the answer to the second, the student of Patristic literature. When the pictures in the Via Latina catacomb are examined, it is possible to conclude the probability of Jewish influence in many examples,[105] while in some an additional Christian understanding can be presumed. But for others no 'Sitz im Leben' at all can be found in Christian theology, and they can be explained solely from the Jewish tradition. We select here only a few particularly telling examples, for which the influence of the Rabbinic interpretive tradition may be considered certain.

The Moses Sequence in Cubicula C and O **(pl. 38-41)**

The frescos in the Cubicula C and O can be seen as a handy example of Christian reinterpretation of a larger whole with an originally Jewish sense.[106] In both chambers the right wall carries a depiction of the Israelites crossing the Red Sea (pl. 38, 40) and the left, a scene showing formal similarities with the resurrection of Lazarus (pl. 39, 41); indeed the more recent version from the second half of the fourth century in Cubiculum O (pl. 41) has a Lazarus figure added. Although these two depictions were originally understood as 'Risuscitamento di Lazzaro', this interpretation has been abandoned, at least for Cubiculum C. Since the picture sequence in Cubiculum C is the older, that in O being clearly a variant, it must be attempted first of all to account for the details of these scenes in Rabbinic Scripture interpretation on the basis of C. We are dealing throughout with Moses scenes and a periphrasis of Sinai via Abraham's offering of Isaac.

The Call of Moses (Exod 3:1-15), and the Egyptians pursuing the Israelites to the Red Sea (in which the first Egyptians are sinking), are followed by the further progression of the Israelites. Moses, who is looking back at the Egyptians, holds his staff lowered, that the ford may be reflooded with water. Following this on the right, still before the door, is the water miracle. To the left of the door and on the left wall, the Israelites make further progress. At their head is the same figure with staff, clearly identifiable with Moses on the opposite wall. This figure is no longer holding its staff in a lowered position, but raised and pointing at a temple-like building with gable to which a stairway with seven stairs leads. Directly following this scene is Abraham's offering of Isaac. Above the Israelites, who are following the figure with the staff, is another figure standing on a mountain – obviously Moses on Sinai. In front of the mountain is a pillar, which can only be the pillar of cloud or pillar of fire in Exod 13:21 where it represents the presence of God. Since both figures with staff are with all probability to be identified with Moses, the assumption suggests itself that the figure below the Moses on Sinai is likewise Moses, leading the Israelites to the

[105] U. Schubert, *Spätantikes Judentum*; Stemberger, 'Patriarchenbilder'; Ri, 'Mosesmotive'; Kötzsche-Breitenbruch, 'Neue Katakombe'.
[106] Ri, 'Mosesmotive'; Tronzo, *Catacomb*.

38. Moses lowering his staff at the Red Sea.
Via Latina Catacomb, cubiculum C, 4th cent. (p191)

39. Moses and Israel after crossing the Red Sea towards 'Sinai'
Via Latina Catacomb, cubiculum C, 4th cent. (p191)

40. Moses lowering his staff at the Red Sea
Via Latina Catacomb, cubiculum O, late 4th cent. (p191)

41. Promulgation of Tora on Sinai
Via Latina Catacomb, cubiculum O, late 4th cent. (p191)

Tabernacle,[107] or perhaps Sinai.[108] Iconographically remarkable peculiarities are only found on the left wall. It must here be asked what significance is to be attached to the host following Moses, the tempietto at the far right to which the steps are leading, and the upper Moses scene which depicts Moses on Sinai. Are the two scenes, above and below, merely to be understood as a chronological sequence, or do they make a concrete statement which can be divined from Rabbinic literature?

Following Rabbinic tradition, what we probably have here is a portrayal of Moses leading the Israelites to Sinai, and the temple-like building with the seven stairs is an illustrated periphrasis of Sinai. Genesis Rabba relates a discussion about Jacob's dream at Bethel and the meaning of the ladder which Jacob saw in his dream:[109]

> Bar Kappara (c. 200) taught: There is no dream that does not also have an interpretation: 'Behold a ladder' – this means a staircase; 'set up on the earth' – this is the altar... The Sages however interpret it as Sinai: 'He dreamed and behold a ladder' – this is Sinai [for the numerical value of the one equals the numerical value of the other].[110]

The fire (or cloud) pillar above the tempietto can be explained from the Tanhuma Buber:[111]

> 'And he dreamed and behold, a ladder.' R. Elazar bar Shimon bar Yohai said concerning this: He showed him the altar ... 'and the top of it reached to Heaven' – this is the pillar of cloud.

Also in the name of R. Shimon ben Yohai it is claimed that 'ladder' means 'Sinai', followed by a reference to the identical numerical value. An exposition on Ps 68:9 brings the identification of Sinai with the Temple Mount in Jerusalem still closer:[112]

> Whence came Sinai? R. Yose said: It separated itself from Mount Moriah, as the dough offering from the dough, from the place upon which our father Isaac was bound. For the Holy One, blessed be He, said: Because their father Isaac was bound upon it, it is right for his children to receive the Tora upon it. And how do we know that it will return to its place? It says: 'The mountain of the House of the Lord will be established on the mountaintops' (Isa 2:2).

The identification of Sinai, to which Moses leads the Israelites, with Mount Moriah, is here expressed by the scene of Abraham offering Isaac depicted

[107] Kötzsche-Breitenbruch, 'Neue Katakombe', 80, following to A. Graber and H. Stern.

[108] Tronzo, *Catacomb*, thinks this is not Moses but Joshua, leading the Israelites into the promised land.

[109] GenR 68,12 to Gen 28:12f (p785f– the bracketed gloss is in the *Arukh* version; Mirqin 3, p86f); SifNum, Korach 119 (p143).

[110] *Sulam* סלם: 60 + 30 + 40 = 130; *Sinai* סיני: 60 + 10 + 50 + 10 = 130.

[111] TanB Wayeitsei 7 (75a).

[112] MidrPs 68,9 (159b).

to the right, directly following the tempietto.[113]

Moses receiving the Law on Sinai was several times placed in parallel to the proclamation of the Law in the Tabernacle. Thus we read in the Babylonian Talmud:[114] 'It is taught: R. Yishmael said: The universal was spoken on Sinai and the particular in the Tent of Meeting. R. Akiva said: The universal and the particular were spoken on Sinai and repeated in the Tent of Meeting.' Even more clear is the statement in Leviticus Rabba:[115] 'Although the Tora was given on Sinai for a fence around Israel, they were not punishable for it before it had been repeated to them in the Tent of Meeting.' Likewise, several texts identify the Tent of Meeting with the Temple. Thus we read in the Babylonian Talmud:[116] 'We find that the Tabernacle is also called the Temple, and the Temple also the Tabernacle.'[117]

Therefore, we must presuppose a Jewish exemplar which was twice copied in the Via Latina (the second time, in Cubiculum O, being identified with the resurrection of Lazarus via the addition of a Lazarus figure) and which originally included a complete Moses cycle, extending from the Call of Moses, through the Crossing of the Red Sea and the Water miracle, to the journey of the Israelites to Sinai under Moses' leadership. As is particularly clear in Cubiculum O, the giving of the Law to Moses above the Sinai scene is likewise to be understood against the background of Rabbinic tradition, according to which the giving of the Law at Sinai and its proclamation in the Tabernacle complement each other in content, and therefore belong together. The connection of Sinai/Temple with Mount Moriah was likewise common in Rabbinic tradition, so that the portrayal of Abraham's offering of Isaac (following at the right of the *tempietto* symbolizing Sinai) is the consistent conclusion to the painting sequence of Cubiculum C. This is then a self-contained Jewish figure program that, in all its details, can be explained from Rabbinic tradition!

Nonetheless, it must be assumed throughout that Christians read their own meaning into a figure program elaborated in this way. The addition of the Lazarus figure in Cubiculum O is stringent proof of this. But already Cubiculum C, some fifty years older, and even without an added Lazarus figure, allows the same conclusion. Above all, the Israelites' crossing of the Red Sea with dry feet could be understood as a symbol of Christian baptism,[118] to which, on the other hand, God's presence and his Law as

[113] Even Tronzo, *Catacomb*, 63, who is concerned with minimalizing Jewish influence, draws attention to the fact that the identification of Sinai/Temple with Abraham's offering of Isaac is 'documented only in purely Jewish contexts'.

[114] bHag 6a-b; bSot 37b.

[115] LevR 1,10 to Lev 1:1 (p24f; Mirqin 7, p18); YalShim no. 432.

[116] bEr 2a-b; cf discussion bShevu 16b.

[117] Ri, 'Mosesmotive', 68-71; K. Schubert – U. Schubert, 'Marginalien'.

[118] Dölger, 'Durchzug'; Tronzo, *Catacomb*, 61.

antitype for Christ and the New Testament corresponded.[119] The added Lazarus figure in Cubiculum O was also intended to indicate the certainty of resurrection effected through baptism.[120] Such an additional interpretation of the Jewish exemplar in Cubiculum O is also suggested by the replacement of Abraham's offering of Isaac in Cubiculum C with a painting of Daniel in the lions' den, a further resurrection motif.

From these data it must be concluded that the painters of the Via Latina catacomb drew their inspiration, among other sources, from Jewish biblical illustrations, regardless of their original purpose. Where this was deemed appropriate, their original Jewish meaning was reinterpreted and as far as possible adapted to Christian religious and exegetical views. Four further examples will show that in so doing, pictorial motifs were also adopted which apparently underwent no reinterpretation precisely because their Jewish significance was obscure to the Christian painters.

Abraham and the Three Angels at Mamre **(pl. 42)**

In Cubiculum B there is a portrayal of the three angels with Abraham in Mamre that clearly differs from the story related in Gen 18. In the left foreground a bearded Abraham sits under a tree with his right hand raised in a gesture of speech. Three youthful figures, also with raised hands, are depicted standing somewhat elevated over against him. Abraham and the three youths/angels are dressed in tunic and pallium. Beside Abraham, who is seated on a stone, stands a small calf, apparently a reference to Abraham's hospitality, which in Rabbinic literature is particularly accentuated. Thus we read:[121]

> 'And the Lord appeared unto him in the plains of Mamre; and he sat in the tent door in the heat of the day' (Gen 18:1). What is meant by, 'in the heat of the day'? R. Hama son of R. Hanina said: It was the third day from Abraham's circumcision, and the Holy One, blessed be He, came to enquire after Abraham's health; [moreover,] He drew the sun out of its sheath, so that the righteous man should not be troubled with wayfarers [that as a result of the heat no visitors would come]. He sent Eleazar out [to seek travellers], but he found none. Said he, I do not believe thee. – Hence they say there [in Palestine]: slaves are not to be believed. – So he himself went out, and saw the Holy One, blessed be he, standing at the door; thus it is written, 'Pass not away, I pray thee, from thy servant' (v3). But on seeing him tying and untying [the bandages of his circumcision], He said, It is not well to stand here (לא אורח ארעא למיקם הכא); hence it is written, 'And he lifted up his eyes and looked, and lo, three men stood by him,

[119] Simon, 'Remarques'; Wuest, 'Figure de Moïse', esp. 112-118.
[120] Simon, 'Remarques'.
[121] bBM 86b.

42. Abraham visited by the three angels at Mamre
Via Latina Catacomb, cubiculum B, 4th cent. (p198)

and when he saw them, he ran to meet them' (v2): at first they came and stood over him, but when they saw him in pain, they said, It is not well to stand here.

The motif of Abraham's sitting being connected with his circumcision is even more pronounced in the following:[122]

Come and behold the power of circumcision: before Abraham was circumcised, he bowed down upon the ground, and only then did I speak with him, for it says: 'Then Abraham fell on his face' (Gen 17:3). But now that he is circumcised, he sits and I stand.

And elsewhere, Abraham's hospitality receives the greater emphasis:[123]

Another interpretation. 'He sat before the tent' – Was it then the custom of our father Abraham to sit before his tent? This was related solely to teach you how greatly Abraham valued hospitality. Because he had already been two days without guests, he said: Perhaps they believe they will burden me. Then he immediately rose, went out and sat down in front of the door in order to invite in those who might pass by.

Numerous other Rabbinic texts could be cited that describe in detail how the hospitable Abraham invited the three men/angels into his home, and how due to his circumcision, only three days old, he remained sitting during the visit of the three angels.[124] By contrast the text of Gen 18:2 says expressly: 'He ran from the tent door to meet them, and bowed himself to the earth,' and with a few exceptions,[125] this is followed in Christian iconography. Evidence for Abraham sitting in the presence of the angels is found only in Jewish sources, thus the depiction in the Via Latina can only be satisfactorily explained when one assumes a Jewish exemplar.[126] In no wise can the inspiration have come from a literary source here, since it is certain that no Christian artist can have been concerned with emphasizing Abraham's circumcision. It must therefore be assumed that the painter who adopted the Jewish exemplar for the Via Latina catacomb in the fourth century did not understand the original, Jewish sense of the representation.

Whereas since the Middle Ages the scenes of greeting and entertainment were often depicted in Jewish illustrations to Gen 18:1-2,[127] the Rabbis of the Talmudic Period were preoccupied with the question of how the angels' consumption of food could in any way be compatible with their celestial nature. Thus, for example:

R. Tanhum b. Hanilai said: One should never deviate from [local]

[122] PdRE 29 (Luria 64b; Friedlander p205).
[123] MidrGad Gen 18:1 (p290).
[124] Stemberger, 'Patriarchenbilder', 21-33.
[125] Kötzsche-Breitenbruch, *Neue Katakombe*, 57, and pl. 6b-d.
[126] U. Schubert, *Spätantikes Judentum*, 18f; Kötzsche-Breitenbruch, *Neue Katakombe*, 56-60.
[127] K. Schubert, 'Einfluß', esp. 111 (fol 17f).

> custom. For behold, Moses ascended on High and ate no bread, whereas the Ministering Angels descended below and ate bread. 'And ate' – can you really think so? But say: appeared to eat and drink.[128]

It may be that the small calf beside Abraham in the left foreground represents his hospitality, while at the same time thereby avoiding an explicit meal scene.

Jacob's Dream at Bethel (pl. 43)

This depiction is likewise found in Cubiculum B, below 'Abraham and the three angels at Mamre'. Jacob, clothed in tunic and pallium, reclines upon three stones which form a single block. At his left is the heavenly ladder, on which are two male figures dressed as the angels in the Mamre scene, obviously the angels who, according to Gen 28:12, ascend and descend upon the ladder. The upper angel stretches his right hand heavenwards, the lower angel, looking towards the earth, points with his right hand, apparently indicating Jacob.

The portrayal of Jacob reclining upon three stones so much resembles a picture on the north wall in the synagogue at Dura Europos, that a common model is likely.[129] However, the state of preservation of the fresco in the synagogue at Dura Europos precludes a judgement whether Jacob is still sleeping or has already awakened. In the Via Latina he has his eyes opened and is thus already awake. These details correspond with Rabbinic exegesis of Gen 28:11 and 18.

Gen 28:11 states: 'And he took of the *stones* of the place, laid them as a pillow for his head and slept in that place', but in v. 18 it says: 'And Jacob rose early in the morning, took the *stone* that he had laid under his head, set it up for a pillar and anointed it with oil.' This contradiction occasions a discussion between R. Yehuda (bar Ilai), R. Nehemya and the Sages in Genesis Rabba.[130] While R. Yehuda speaks of twelve stones which joined themselves, referring to the twelve tribes that were to issue from Jacob, and the Sages think there were only two stones whose joining signified that Jacob would have only worthy descendants in contrast to Abraham and Isaac, R. Nehemya has his explanation:

> He took three stones and said: The Holy One, blessed be He, joined His name with Abraham, also with Isaac did the Holy One, blessed be He, join His name. And what of me? If the three stones join themselves one with the other, then I will know that the Holy One, blessed be He, also will join His name with me. When they joined them-

[128] bBM 86b. Likewise also in Josephus, Philo and some Church fathers. See Ginzberg, *Haggada*, 108.

[129] U. Schubert, *Spätantikes Judentum*, 24.

[130] GenR 68,11 to Gen 28:11 (p782f; Mirqin 3, p83f); MidrPs 91,6 (200a).

43. Jacob's dream at Bethel
Via Latina Catacomb, cubiculum B, 4th cent. (p201)

> selves, he knew that the Holy One, blessed be He, joined His name with him.[131]

A similar tale is related in the Tanhuma:[132]

> R. Abbahu said in the name of R. Shimon ben Lakish: When the stones that served for his pillow saw the glory of God, they all became soft and became one stone. Whence? Before he had gone to sleep it says: 'He took from the stones of that place,' that is, several stones; but when he woke, it says: 'He took the stone,' that is, only one stone.

The motif of Jacob resting on three stones become one is therefore demonstrably Jewish. Its 'Sitz im Leben' is in the Rabbinic exegesis of Gen 28:11 in comparison with Gen 28:18.

The extraordinary size of Jacob in this picture might also be explained from Rabbinic exegesis. That his figure fills approximately half of the picture can be traced either to his being the main character of the depicted event, or to his being the outsized Jacob who was also the product of Rabbinic tradition. In one exposition, God rolled up the entire land of Israel and placed it under Jacob.[133]

The concrete depiction of the angels on the heavenly ladder corresponds to Rabbinic Scripture interpretation. It has already been mentioned that the upper angel stretches his right hand heavenwards. According to Targums Neophyti and Yerushalmi to Gen 28:12, these are the two angels who had accompanied Jacob, and who afterwards entreated their fellow angels in Heaven to come and see the just man, Jacob, whose face was engraved in the throne of God. Targum Yerushalmi elaborately describes these angels as ascending rather than descending:

> 'He dreamed and behold, a ladder set up on the earth, and the top of it reached to Heaven.' Behold, two angels, who went to Sodom, were cast out of their [heavenly] place because they had betrayed the secrets of the Lord of the world. They were cast out and wandered until the time when Jacob left his father's house; they accompanied him in friendship to Bethel and ascended on this day into Heaven. They spoke and said: Come and behold the just man, Jacob, whose image is engraved in the throne of glory, which you long to look upon. At this the other angels of the Lord descended that they might behold him.

The figurative rendition of this scene in Dura Europos and the attitude of

[131] TgY to Gen 28:11 offers a further variant with reference to the number of stones used by Jacob for his pillow: 'And he prayed at the place of the sanctuary and spent the night there, because the sun had already set; and he took of the four stones of that holy place and laid them under his head and slept in that place.' TgY to 28:10 mentions five miracles which Jacob experienced after he had departed Beer Sheba. Of the second miracle it is related: 'The four stones which he laid for his head, were found in the morning to be a single stone.'

[132] Tanh, Wayeitsei 1 (38a).

[133] R. Yitshak, bHul 91b.

44. The infant Moses discovered by Pharaoh's daughter
Via Latina Catacomb, cubiculum B, 4th cent. (p205)

the upper angel in the Via Latina, show these angels to be ascending, not descending. Even though the lower angel in the Via Latina is pointing earthwards with his right hand, his foot position permits the conclusion that he is ascending. While the upper angel speaks to his fellow angels in Heaven, the lower angel indicates Jacob, whom they have already desired greatly to see. Thus, this also is an unequivocal Jewish depiction motif.[134]

Infant Moses and Pharaoh's Daughter (pl. 44)

This scene is also found in Cubiculum B. In the foreground, the clearly recognizable infant Moses floats in his basket in the Nile. On the bank directly opposite stands Pharaoh's daughter with her hands stretched out towards him. On her right two handmaids look on passively. The outsized figure in the reeds on the left must be identified with Miriam, Moses' sister. The attitude of Pharaoh's daughter, whose hands are stretched out towards Moses, is striking. It can be explained neither by the conventional understanding of Exod 2:5, in which she sends a handmaid to fetch Moses from the water, nor from Josephus' account in *Ant.* 2:224 [9,5], in which she sent 'some swimmers'. Again Rabbinic tradition provides the explanation. We have already seen above that the Rabbinic Sages understood the words of Exod 2:5, ותשלח את אמתה, otherwise than the commonly accepted interpretations today, by reading אמתה 'her hand' instead of אמתה 'her handmaid', and thus translated, 'she stretched forth her hand' (see above p178). Even though the portrayal on the west wall of the synagogue at Dura Europos betrays an entirely different model, it seems that a Jewish exemplar must be assumed for the rendition of this scene in the Via Latina.

The outsized Miriam, sitting in the reeds, also finds a satisfactory explanation in Jewish sources. She is similarly depicted in the fourteenth century Spanish Pesah Haggadot.[135] This emphasizes Miriam's gift of prophecy, which is hinted at already in Exod 15:20. It is explicit in early Rabbinic works:

> Of Miriam it is said: 'Then Miriam, *the prophetess*, the sister of Aaron, took' (Exod 15:20). Why not the sister of Moses? R. Nahman said in Rav's name: She prophesied when Aaron was her only brother, and said: My mother will bear a son who will save Israel. When he was born, the whole house was filled with light. Then her father rose and kissed her on the head. He said to her: My daughter, your prophecy has been fulfilled. But when she put him in the Nile, her father rose and struck her on the head. He said to her: My daughter,

[134] Stemberger, 'Patriarchenbilder', 33-42; U. Schubert, *Spätantikes Judentum*, 18f; Kötsche-Breitenbruch, *Neue Katakombe*, 69f; Nordström, *Castilian Bible*, 63-66.
[135] London, British Library: Add 27210, 9r.; Or 2884, 12r.; Budapest, Akademie der Wissenschaft, A 422, p10.

45. Zimri and Cozbi impaled on Phinehas' lance
Via Latina Catacomb, cubiculum B, 4th cent. (p207)

> what is become of your prophecy? This is what is written: 'And his sister stood at a distance, to know what would be done' (Exod 2:4), to know what would become of her prophecy.[136]

Both the particular kind of the depiction of Pharaoh's daughter (with outstretched hand), as well as the outsized Miriam accentuate details amply attested in Rabbinic literature. This scene as well, therefore, must be denoted as proof of Jewish influence on early Christian figurative art.

Zimri and Cozbi Impaled on Phinehas' Lance (pl. 45)

This badly preserved scene is also found in Cubiculum B. Phinehas the priest, having caught Zimri and Cozbi in unlawful sexual intercourse, has driven his spear through both of them in order to turn away the wrath of God (Num 25:8). The barely recognizable spear rests on Phinehas' left shoulder. The two victims are in a stable position; they are not sliding down the shaft. This corresponds with a widespread legend concerning Phinehas' miraculous spear.[137]

The legend relates six, and in another version twelve, miracles concerning the spear with which Phinehas' spitted Zimri and Cozbi. The simpler version is found in the Talmud:[138]

> 'And Phinehas, the son of Eleazar ... saw it' (Num 25:7). Now, what did he see? Rav said: He saw what was happening and remembered the *halakha*, and said to him, O great-uncle [Moses]! did you not teach us this on your descent from Mount Sinai: 'He who cohabits with a heathen woman is punished by zealots'?[139] He replied, 'He who makes a proposal should also carry it out.'[140] Shmuel said: he saw that 'No wisdom, no understanding, no counsel can avail against the Lord' (Prov. 21:30)[141] – whenever the Divine Name is being profaned, honour must not be paid to one's teacher.[142] R. Yitshak said in R. Eleazar's name: He saw the angel wreaking destruction amongst the people.
>
> 'And he rose up out of the midst of the congregation, and took a spear in his hand' (Num 25:7) – Hence one may not enter the house of learning with weapons – he removed its point and placed it in his undergarment, and went along as though leaning on his stick. As soon

[136] bMeg 14a; bSot 12b-13a. Among the variants, see particularly Mekh dRY, Shira 10 (p151; Lauterbach 2, p81). In mSot 1:9 the opinion is expressed that it was necessary for Miriam to wait only one hour, i.e., for Moses' rescue.

[137] Nordström, *Castilian Bible*, 112-119; U. Schubert, *Spätantikes Judentum*, 32f.

[138] bSan 82a-b. See also ySan 10, 28d-29a.

[139] mSan 9:6.

[140] An Aramaic proverb, literally: 'The reader of the letter is also its executor.'

[141] In the sense of, 'Against a law of God, there is no argument.'

[142] I.e., one acts without waiting for a decision from a teacher.

> as he reached the tribe of Simeon, he exclaimed, Where do we find that the tribe of Levi is greater than that of Simeon? Thereupon they said, Let him pass too, for he enters to satisfy his lust; these abstainers (פרושים) have now declared the matter permissible!
> R. Yohanan said: Six miracles were wrought for Phinehas: (1) Zimri could have withdrawn but did not; (2) he could have cried for help but did not; (3) [Phinehas] struck both the man's male parts and the female parts of the woman; (4) they did not slip off the spear; (5) an angel came and lifted up the lintel [that Phinehas with the spitted pair on his shoulder could pass under it]; (6) an angel came and wrought destruction amongst the people.[143]

The longer version with twelve miracles is attested in several texts. After a slightly different introduction, it is related:[144]

> He followed the Israelites into the brothel (Num 25:8). He drove his spear through both of them, one on top of the other, through the midst of their sexual organs, so that the Israelites might not say: He committed no sexual act. Because he was zealous for the Name of the Holy One, blessed be He, He worked twelve miracles for him: (1) Ordinarily they separate [in such a situation], but the angel held them together. (2) The angel stopped their mouths, that they might not cry out. (3) He directed his spear at her pudenda in order that [Zimri's] member might be seen to be inside her, that the grumblers might not say: [Phinehas] went in and satisfied his lust. (4) He lengthened the spear shaft, that both might be impaled together. (5) He strengthened his arm, that he might lift them both. (6) The spear shaft did not break. (7) They did not slide from the spear, but held fast in place. (8) The angel reversed them on the point of the spear,[145] that their sin might be visible to all. (9) They did not bleed, that Phinehas might not be made unclean. (10) The Holy One, blessed be He, kept them alive, that he might not be made unclean through their death. (11) The angel raised the lintel, that he might carry them through raised up [impaled] before the eyes of all. (12) When he came out, he was set upon by his compatriots. Then the angel descended and smote them. When Phinehas saw that the angel intended to destroy them, he threw them down, rose up and prayed, and caused the angel to depart.

Undoubtedly, therefore, our motif has its origin in Rabbinic tradition.[146] Apart from the effect of this motif on Christian manuscript illumination, which is not the object of this study, it is found in a manuscript *Seder Tikkune Shabbat*, Vienna 1738.[147] While there is no question of dependence

[143] So that the people would not rebel against Phinehas.
[144] NumR 20,25 to Num 25:7 (Mirqin 10, p274f). See also SifNum, Balak 131 (p172f); TgY Num 25:8; Tanh, Balak 21 (89a-b); and cf TanB, Balak 30 (74b-75a).
[145] Tanh ib: 'The angel raised them to the point of the spear.'
[146] Kötzsche-Breitenbruch, *Neue Katakombe*, 85-87; Nordström, *Castilian Bible*.

here, still, this illustration in a Hebrew manuscript is a convincing proof for the Jewish character of the portrayal itself.

There are still other motifs in the Via Latina catacomb that can be traced to the influences of Rabbinic tradition.[148] The above examples, which without doubt appear to stem from Jewish figurative exemplars, must suffice to demonstrate that Jewish figurative art was one of the sources from which early Christian painting benefitted.

[147] Nordström, *Castilian Bible*, 118 pl. 63.

46. Adam and Eve driven from paradise
Vienna Genesis p. 2, Syria, 6th cent. (p211)

Chapter Five

Jewish Traditions in Christian Painting Cycles: The Vienna Genesis and the Ashburnham Pentateuch

Influence from Jewish painting exemplars of Late Antiquity can also be traced in larger Christian painting cycles.[149] A clear example is the 'Vienna Genesis',[150] a manuscript probably of sixth century Syrian provenance,[151] whose Jewish exemplars must be assumed to be significantly older.[152] In the following section we examine only a selection of examples that show a demonstrable influence of Rabbinic iconography.

The Vienna Genesis

ADAM AND EVE DRIVEN FROM PARADISE **(pl. 46)**

Page 2 shows a picture that with great probability was influenced by Rabbinic Scripture interpretation.[153] In the upper part of the picture, in a segment of blue sky, the hand of God points at Adam and Eve leaving Paradise, and at the serpent wound about the Tree of Life. In the middle of the picture, in front of the gate to Paradise (also in the blue sky segment) is a wheel of fire, beside which an angel stands. At the right, Adam and Eve once again, are accompanied by an apparently feminine figure clothed in red, blue and yellow. Only at the right of the picture does Jewish iconography seem to be demonstrable. The wheel of fire, beside which the angel stands, is probably both the constantly turning flaming sword of Gen 3:24, and the representation of the divine Presence as expressed in Ezek 1.[154] The *Merkava* scene described in Ezek 1 is a depiction of the epiphany of God on his throne, and therefore eminently suited for a periphrasis of the *Shekhina*,

[148] U. Schubert, *Spätantikes Judentum*.
[149] The following is largely oriented on K. Schubert, 'Illustrationen', which includes discussion with Gerstinger, *Wiener Genesis*, and Buberl, *Byzantinische Handschriften*.
[150] Mazal, *Kommentar*.
[151] Fillitz, 'Wiener Genesis', esp. 44-46.
[152] According to Otto Pächt, already in the second century BCE; cf Fillitz, 'Wiener Genesis', 45.
[153] Mazal, *Kommentar*, 129-31.
[154] U. Schubert, 'Jüdische Darstellungsweise'; id, 'Einleitung' to K. Schubert, *Bilder-Pentateuch*, esp. 25f.

47. Noah's drunkenness and the curse of Ham/Canaan
Vienna Genesis p. 6, Syria, 6th cent. (p213)

the divine Presence, which according to the Targum tradition was localized before the gate to Paradise after Adam and Eve had been driven out.[155]

In Targum Neophyti to Gen 3:24 we read: 'And he cast forth the man and made the Glory of his Shekhina to dwell from the beginning to the east of the garden of Eden between the Two Cherubim.' Following this is the reference to the Tora being created before the world, a conception drawn from Prov 8:22f, and widespread in Judaism of the Greco-Roman age.[156] The Garden of Eden was created for the righteous, who will then eat the fruits of the Tree of Life. This is their reward for having obeyed the Law of the Tora in this world. The flaming sword is then understood to be a symbol of hell. In the Targum Neophyti, a second emphasizing of the analogous function of the Tora and the Tree of Life follows. He who obeys the Tora is as one who eats the fruits of the Tree of Life: 'The Law is good for those who serve it in this world like the fruits of the Tree of Life.'[157] The wheel of fire has therefore a double function, representing both the divine Presence and the flaming sword, which according to a literal understanding of Gen 3:24 is independent of the cherubim and not held in the hand of a cherub. The angel standing by is an illustration then of the cherubim themselves.

The interpretation of the feminine figure escorting Adam and Eve on their way out of Paradise remains open. She has been identified with the divine Wisdom,[158] and this in turn with the Tora, the divine Law of the world, and rightly so.[159] Thus, this scene illustrates a Targum tradition according to which the Tora functioned as the Tree of Life after the banishment from Paradise. It can therefore be concluded that the right half of the picture, from the wheel of fire to the right border, is based on the scriptural interpretation that has been preserved in the Targums.

THE CURSE OF HAM/CANAAN (pl. 47)

Rabbinic influence can also be determined on page 6.[160] However the motif concerned is also attested in Syrian Church fathers, and it could be mediated to the Vienna Genesis via Syrian Christianity. The miniature portrays Gen 9:20-27 and proceeds from right to left, which accords both with Hebrew and Syriac writing. In the right part of the picture, Noah's drunkenness is depicted, and at the left, his curse and blessing.

According to Gen 9:25 it is not Ham, the guilty one (Gen 9:22) who is cursed, but his son Canaan; thus, Ham is shown holding little Canaan by the hand. Rabbinic tradition attempted to clarify this peculiar situation by

[155] K. Schubert – U. Schubert, 'Vertreibung aus dem Paradies'.
[156] Hengel, *Judentum*; K. Schubert, 'Israel im Altertum'.
[157] Similarly also in TgY and FragTg to Gen 3:24.
[158] Gerstinger, *Wiener Genesis*, 71.
[159] Hengel, *Judentum*, 275-318.
[160] Ginzberg, *Haggada*, 86f; Levene, *Syrian Fathers*, 52, 84.

48. Abraham's victory; Abraham and Melchizedek
Vienna Genesis p. 7, Syria, 6th cent. (p215)

making Canaan the actual sinner. Thus, for example, in Genesis Rabba it says:[161] 'Ham sinned and Canaan was cursed. Why?' A dispute follows between two Palestine scholars from the second half of the second century CE, R. Yehuda and R. Nehemya. R. Yehuda answers exegetically with a reference to Gen 9:1, but R. Nehemya considers Canaan to be the guilty one: 'Canaan saw [Noah] and told them, therefore the curse falls on him who did what was damnable.' In the continuation, the midrash relates Noah's wish for a fourth son, a wish rendered impossible through Ham's sin, so that Noah's curse was visited on Canaan, the fourth son of Ham (Gen 10:6). This is made explicit in a discussion between Rav and Shmuel, two Babylonian scholars from the first half of the third century CE:[162]

> The one said that he castrated him, and the other that he lay with him. The one who spoke of castration said: Because he made a fourth son impossible for him, he cursed him through his fourth son.

Thus the Rabbis emphasized either that Canaan was the actual guilty one or, more frequently, that Ham had castrated Noah, thereby making it impossible for him to father a fourth son.[163] Therefore the portrayal of Ham holding little Canaan by the hand can be accounted for in Rabbinic exegesis, and a Jewish exemplar is probable, although the possibility of Syrian Christian mediation cannot be excluded.

ABRAHAM'S RETURN FROM BATTLE (pl. 48)

The next page may also be traceable to a Jewish exemplar. In the upper right of page 7, Gen 14:7 is portrayed: Abraham and Bera, the king of Sodom. At the upper left is the group of liberated captives: Lot and his family, consisting of three women and three men. Lot's wife, riding ahead, holds a golden bowl in a bulge of her dress.

The accentuation of this bowl is apparently referable to a highly individual Rabbinic exegesis of Gen 14:6:[164]

> 'Then he brought back all the goods, and also brought back his kinsman Lot with his goods, and the women and the people.' Why does it say, 'and also'? – to include all utensils, even those worth no more than a *peruta*.

Such a minute detail can hardly be otherwise explained than that it was copied from a Jewish model.

The miniature in the lower right portrays Abraham's meeting with Melchizedek (Gen 14:18-20). The altar with ciborium behind Melchizedek leaves an impression of Christian origin, and indeed this Genesis text was

[161] GenR 36,7 to Gen 9:25 (p340f; Mirqin 2, p69f). See Revel, 'Contribution', esp. 119.
[162] bSan 70a.
[163] Parallels and variants in Tanh, Noah 15 (17b); TanB, Noah 21 (25a); NumR 10,2 (Mirqin 9, p240); MidrGad Gen 9:25 (p190).
[164] Tanh, Lekh lekha 13 (22b).

49. Abraham informed of Rebecca's birth
Vienna Genesis p. 11, Syria, 6th cent. (p217)

often interpreted in the sense of the Christian Eucharist. However, given the Jewish character of the upper half of the picture, it is not improbable that the lower half is to be understood in an originally Jewish sense. The altar ciborium can only refer to Melchizedek as the 'priest of God Most High'. The words, '[Melchizedek] brought bread and wine' (Gen 14:18), interpreted by Christians as referring to the Eucharist, were understood in a purely inner-Jewish sense in Genesis Rabba:[165] 'R. Shmuel b. Nahman said: He gave [Abraham] the laws of the High Priesthood. "Bread" – this is the showbread, "and wine" – this is the libation offering.' Bread and wine then can be understood here in a purely Jewish context.

The altar with ciborium fits well the assumption that Melchizedek passed on the laws of the High Priesthood to Abraham. Melchizedek wears the same royal robes as King Bera of Sodom, pictured above him. The picture then emphasizes at once Melchizedek's priestly and kingly character.[166] This depiction also exemplifies how an illustration reflecting Jewish exegesis could be reinterpreted in a Christian sense.

ABRAHAM INFORMED OF REBECCA'S BIRTH **(pl. 49)**

Rabbinic influence may also be visible in the miniature on page 11.[167] In the upper left an angel confirms the promises to Abraham (Gen 22:15-18). To the right, Abraham returns to his servants (Gen 22:19). Below, Abraham sits meditating in front of his tent, next to a well – an allusion to Beersheba. Two servants are hurrying towards him, one of them obviously bringing a message.

Genesis Rabba comments on this passage:[168] 'While [Abraham] was still on Mount Moriah he received the message that the [future] wife of his son had been born, for it says: Behold Milcah also has borne (Gen 22:20).' According to Gen 22:23 Bethuel, son of Abraham's brother Nahor and of Milcah, fathered Rebecca who was later to become the wife of Isaac. Thus Abraham learned of the birth of his son Isaac's future spouse immediately after the promise of descendants. In Yalkut Shimoni (Genesis, no. 102) this scene is expanded somewhat. According to this version, Abraham pondered over the woman to whom he should marry his miraculously redeemed son, and considered the daughters of Aner, Eshkol, and Mamre. 'Then the Holy One, blessed be He, spoke to him: There is no need, for the [future] wife of Isaac, your son, is already born.'

Abraham's reflective attitude before his tent could be expressing his deliberations concerning his son's future wife, although here it is his servant

[165] GenR 43,6 to Gen 14:18 (p420f; Mirqin 2, p135). In bNed 32b it is pointed out that the descendants of Melchizedek were no longer priests.

[166] Cf the discussion concerning his priestly character in NumR 4,8 (Mirqin 9, p72).

[167] Revel, 'Contribution', 120f; Mazal, *Kommentar*, 139f.

[168] GenR 57,1 to Gen 22:20f (p612; Mirqin 2, p279).

50. Eliezer and Rebecca
Vienna Genesis p. 14, Syria, 6th cent. (p220)

51. Jacob and the 'messengers'
Vienna Genesis p. 21, Syria, 6th cent. (p220)

instead of God who brings him the joyous news. In contrast to this miniature, the Rabbis emphasize that Abraham learns of Rebecca's birth while he is still standing on Mount Moriah; while according to the biblical text he did not learn of the birth of Nahor's and Milcah's descendant until after he had returned to Beersheba.

ELIEZER AND REBECCA (pl. 50)

P. 14 contains a highly individual iconography that is also probably derived from a Jewish background. The upper part depicts the meeting between Eliezer, Abraham's servant, and Rebecca at the well (Gen 24). Below right, Rebecca tells 'her mother's household' of the meeting (Gen 24:28). Laban then went out to Eliezer at the well (Gen 24:29) and invited him into the house (Gen 24:31). But here, Rebecca's mother stands before Eliezer who is sitting on a large rock, and speaks to him.

This scene may well be an illustration of the Rabbinic interpretation of Gen 24:55. According to Targum Yonatan to Gen 24:33,[169] Bethuel wanted to poison Eliezer, but, in accordance with the paraphrase to Gen 24:55, ate of the poisoned food himself and died. Thereupon, the brother and the mother bade Eliezer to remain during the period of mourning for the deceased father. The picture here apparently depicts this conversation between Rebecca's mother and Eliezer.

JACOB AND THE 'MESSENGERS' (pl. 51)

P. 21 depicts Gen 32:6-13. In the upper part Jacob is standing before two angels who are addressing him. This is probably not meant to illustrate Gen 32:2,[170] but rather Gen 32:4 and 7. At all events, the מלאכים named here are intended as messengers and not angels.

However, there is a Rabbinic discussion concerning this in Genesis Rabba:[171] 'מלאכים – These were but messengers of flesh and blood. The Sages said, These were real angels.' Thereupon follows the further proof that real angels having appeared to Hagar, Eliezer, and Joseph, 'how much more' must they have appeared to Jacob.[172] The interpretation of Jacob's messengers as angels then, is likewise traceable to a Jewish exemplar.

[169] See also GenR 60,12 (p652; Mirqin 2, p312); YalShim Gen no. 109; MidrGad Gen 24:55 (p407).

[170] Thus Gerstinger, *Wiener Genesis*, 93.

[171] GenR 75,4 to Gen 32:4 (p881; Mirqin 3, p166). See Revel, 'Contribution', 122f.

[172] Somewhat more abbreviated, but similar in content, is the tradition in YalShim Gen no. 130. Moreover in TanB, Wayishlah 3 (82a) there is a reference to Ps 91:11, in support of the argument that the messengers who had sent Jacob forth were angels.

JOSEPH'S DREAM (pl. 52)

Umambiguous Rabbinic influence is found again on page 29, an illustration of Gen 37:9-14. The miniature in the upper left reveals Joseph's dream, according to which the sun, moon and eleven stars bow down before him. To the right of this there is an illustration of Gen 37:10: 'But when he told it to his father and to his brothers, his father rebuked him, and said to him, ... Shall I and your mother and your brothers indeed come to bow ourselves to the ground before you?' However, according to the biblical story, Rachel, Jacob's mother, was already dead. Who is the woman beside Jacob and what does 'I and your mother' mean?

According to Rabbinic tradition, the woman beside Jacob is Bilhah, who raised Jacob. Thus we find in Genesis Rabba:[173]

> R. Levi, in the name of R. Hama bar Hanina, said: [Our father] Jacob believed that the resurrection of the dead would occur yet in his days, for it says, 'Shall I and your mother and your brothers indeed come?' (Gen 37:10) – 'shall I and your brothers indeed come', would be understandable! But what is meant by, 'I and your mother?!' The mother was indeed already dead; yet it says, 'I and your mother and your brothers'. However [Jacob] our father did not know that this referred to Bilhah, the handmaid of Rachel, who raised him [Joseph] as a mother.[174]

Bilhah is dressed here exactly as the figure standing behind Jacob in the picture on page 30, upper left.[175] The woman beside Jacob then, can be none other than Joseph's foster mother, Bilhah.

In this and in the following pictures of the story of Joseph, Rabbinic influence becomes particularly clear-cut, such that without it many details could not be explained at all.

JOSEPH'S FAREWELL TO BENJAMIN (pl. 53)

P. 30 shows both elements that can be explained from Rabbinic literature, and those that cannot, at least not from the common Rabbinic sources. Primary among these is Joseph's farewell to Benjamin, perhaps because he, as Rachel's son, was likewise raised by Bilhah. Benjamin, still weeping, watches his brother Joseph, who is walking away and meeting an angel. This is an illustration of Gen 37:15, which says: 'And a man found him wandering in the fields; and the man asked him, What are you seeking?'

Targum Yonatan interprets, 'And a man met him' in the sense of 'Gabriel met him in the form of a man'. Targum Neophyti to this text reads: 'An

[173] GenR 84,11 to Gen 37:10 (p1014; Mirqin 4, p19).

[174] YalShim Gen no. 141.

[175] For the identification of the woman behind Bilhah, see Levin, 'Some Jewish Sources', esp. 242; likewise, Mazal, *Kommentar*, 150.

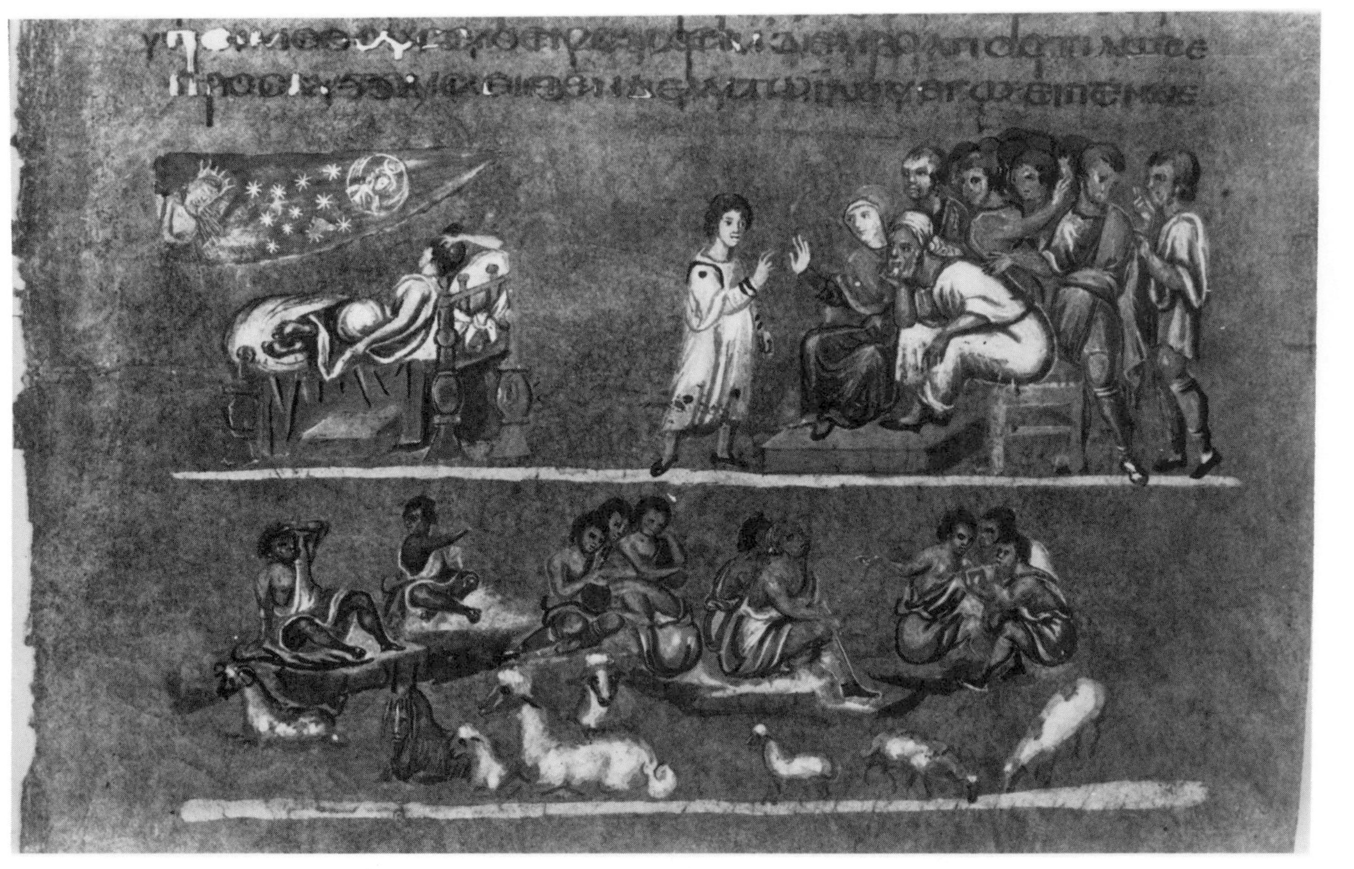

52. Joseph, 'master of dreams' (Gen 37:19)
Vienna Genesis p. 29, Syria, 6th cent. (p221)

53. Joseph parting from Benjamin and meeting with his other brothers
Vienna Genesis p. 30, Syria, 6th cent. (p221)

54. Joseph, Potiphar's wife and Asenath
Vienna Genesis p. 31, Syria, 6th cent. (p225)

angel met him in the form of a man'. A further variant is found in Pirkei de Rabbi Eliezer:[176] 'The boy went out and strayed from the way. And the angel Gabriel met him .... He said to him: What do you seek? He answered him: I seek my brothers... Then he led him to his brothers.' The interpretation of the man whom Joseph met on his way to find his brothers in the sense of an angel, was then the common explanation in Rabbinic tradition.[177]

In the lower left panel a man who directs Joseph on the way to his brothers is once again portrayed. The biblical wording, which speaks only of 'a man', is probably taken up here again.[178] The painter of the scene from Gen 37:15 in the 'Vienna Genesis' then, used an exemplar in which the angel Gabriel accompanied Joseph in the sense of the Jewish tradition, and moreover, as איש 'man', apparently also showed him the way to his brothers.

The right half of the picture shows Joseph's brothers at the moment of his arrival. The brothers are apparently in disagreement about what to do with Joseph (Gen 37:20f). As he arrives, Joseph is sniffed by a dog. This probably corresponds to the Rabbinic tradition according to which Joseph's brothers set the dogs on him,[179] as we find it in Genesis Rabba:[180] 'They said: [Come,] let us kill him, let us set the dogs on him.'[181] In this sense, the sniffing dog is an additional detail that makes a Jewish exemplar probable.

JOSEPH AND ASENATH (pl. 54)

Before the attempt had been made to understand the miniatures of the 'Vienna Genesis' via the Rabbinic sources, those of page 31 presented significant difficulties: they were described as 'delightful genre scenes' or 'novelistic ingredients'.[182]Not until the search had led to exemplars inspired by Rabbinic tradition was the right track discovered.[183]

Several Rabbinic texts are relevant for our sequence. Here we learn that Asenath, the daughter of Shechem and Dinah (and thus granddaughter to Jacob and niece to Joseph), was a foster daughter in the house of Potiphar. According to Gen 41:45, Joseph married 'Asenath, the daughter of Potiph-

[176] PdRE 38 (Luria 89a; Friedlander p292).

[177] Tanh, Wayeshev 2 (45a); YalShim Gen no. 141; MidrGad Gen 37:15-16 (p634). And see Nordström, 'Jewish Legends', esp. 489; Levin, 'Some Jewish Sources', 241; Gutmann, 'Joseph Legends', esp. 182; Pächt, 'Ephraimillustration', esp. 252; Mazal, *Kommentar*, 150.

[178] Pächt, 'Ephraimillustration', 253 and Mazal, *Kommentar*, 150 consider this also to be the angel from the upper right panel.

[179] So rightly, Mazal, *Kommentar*, 151.

[180] GenR 84,14 to Gen 37:18 (p1017; Mirqin 4, p21).

[181] YalShim, Gen no. 141; MidrGad Gen 37:18 (p634).

[182] Gerstinger, *Wiener Genesis*, 102; Buberl, *Byzantinische Handschriften*, 114.

[183] Levin, 'Some Jewish Sources', 242f; Gutmann, 'Joseph Legends', 182f; Revel, 'Contribution', 124-6; Mazal, *Kommentar*, 151-3.

era', who was identified with the Potiphar in whose house Joseph had served. This Asenath bore to Joseph two sons, Ephraim and Manasseh, and through them Potiphar's barren wife got grandchildren.

Thus, in Genesis Rabba,[184] after Shmuel bar Nahmani compared the behavior of Tamar with that of Potiphar's wife, it is said:

> As the one was motivated by good intentions, so also was the other. For R. Yoshua b. Levi said: She learned through her astrologer that she would get a son by [Joseph]. But she knew not whether her own or by her daughter.

That Asenath was the daughter of Shechem, borne to him by Dinah after he had raped her, is richly attested in Rabbinic literature, e.g., in Targum Yonatan to Gen 41:45: 'And [Pharaoh] gave to him Asenath for his wife, her whom Dinah bore to Shechem, and whom the wife of Potiphar, potentate of Tanis, had raised.' This motif is expanded even further in Pirkei de-R. Eliezer.[185] It is first mentioned that Shechem, by deception, robbed and then raped Dinah. She became pregnant and bore Asenath. Being the issue of a rape, the child was sent away by Jacob, but protected by '...a golden disk [diadem] inscribed with the שם המפורש [i.e., the name of God], which he fastened about her throat.... Then the angel Michael descended from Heaven and led her to Egypt to the house of Potiphera, for Asenath was designated to be the wife of Joseph.' Potiphar's wife, being barren, raised her as her own daughter. According to another version, it was also Asenath who prevented Potiphar from killing Joseph, 'for she came secretly to Potiphera and told him the truth under oath'.[186]

There is then a thoroughly satisfactory explanation for the above sequence. At the left, Joseph flees, having left his garment behind. To the right of this scene, he stands once again before a door, looking back at it. At the far right stands the star gazer – clearly identifiable by her robe, decorated with stars, and her headband, decorated with sun and moon symbols; by the spindle in her hand she is also characterized as a Greek goddess of fate.[187] Consequently, the woman in red with the mirror is Potiphar's wife. The naked infant lying in a cradle before her, by virtue of the golden diadem on its head, can be none other than Asenath.[189] The lower half of the picture could thus depict the content of the star gazer's vision. Here as well, the spinning woman could be understood as a goddess of fate,[189] or as Potiphar's wife.[190] But the obviously male child who stands before her can by

[184] GenR 85,2 to Gen 38:1 (p1081; Mirqin 4, p32).
[185] PdRE 38 (Luria 87b-88a; Friedlander p287f).
[186] YalShim Gen no. 146.
[187] Levin, 'Some Jewish Sources', 242-4; Mazal, *Kommentar*, 151.
[188] Thus already Levin, 'Some Jewish Sources', and Mazal, *Kommentar*.
[189] Levin, 'Some Jewish Sources'.
[190] Revel, 'Contribution', 126; Mazal, *Kommentar*, 152.

no means be identified with Asenath. Rather, Asenath must be the naked baby, who embraces the woman in green holding her.[191]

JOSEPH AND POTIPHAR'S WIFE (pl. 55)

Page 32 continues the story of Joseph and Potiphar's wife. In the upper half, at the far right, Potiphar's wife sits on a folding stool with a handmaid clothed in blue standing behind her. Three men, recognizable by their dress as court officials,[192] stand before Potiphar's wife, whose right hand is raised in a gesture of speech. A fourth man, likewise dressed as a court official, is hurrying towards the scene from outside. A servant directs him with his right hand towards the open door. The lower half shows Potiphar's wife once again, and beside her the handmaid in blue. The handmaid presents, as *corpus delicti*, the garment that Joseph left behind when he fled from Potiphar's wife. Three men and a woman stand before these two women. Two of these men are dressed as the court officials in the upper half, the third is portrayed without such tokens of honor. The two women are denouncing Joseph to the court official standing directly before them, who may be Potiphar himself.[193] This would suggest the plainly dressed man standing behind him to be Joseph. At the far left, a court official and a woman are pointing either at this figure, or at Joseph's garment.

The interpretation of the illustration on page 32 must be consistent with the seduction scene on page 31. There, Potiphar's wife is reclining in bed, her characteristic pose in Jewish iconography.[194] She holds in her hands the garment of the fleeing Joseph. The continuation of the scene is provided by the illustration on page 32 – the return of Potiphar and his wife's conversation with the court officials.

Rabbinic interpretation emphasizes that the entire household had gone to a Nile feast. Potiphar's wife exploited this opportunity to catch Joseph alone in the house. She could only achieve this, however, by pretending to keep her bed because of sickness. Accordingly, the Talmud relates:[195]

[191] Mazal, *Kommentar* sees Asenath in the woman in green, even though she is fondling a child. He thinks the boys below are perhaps Ephraim and Manasseh, and believes that the entire scene could be a vision of Joseph. Weitzmann, *Illustrations* (Addenda), 255 sees in the two trees (below right) a reference to a Nile festival mentioned in Rabbinic tradition, which, with the exception of his wife, the entire house of Potiphar celebrated. However, the influence of this tradition is not found until the next page (32).

[192] Already Gerstinger, *Wiener Genesis*, 103 identified the three men in the upper field as 'chamberlains in the uniform of Byzantine court officials'. It is thus the more astonishing that he identifies the three figures at the lower left as 'three of the servants involved in a lively discussion about what has occured'.

[193] Buberl, *Byzantinische Handschriften*, 114f; Pächt, 'Ephraimillustration', 253.

[194] London, British Library Add 27210, 6v.; Or 2884, 7r.

[195] bSot 36b. Cf YalShim Gen no. 146; Tanh, Wayeshev 9 (48a); GenR 87,7 (p1071f; Mirqin 4, p61); CantR 1 (beginning); PesR 6 (23a).

55. Potiphar's wife accuses Joseph
Vienna Genesis p. 32, Syria, 6th cent. (p227)

56. Jacob blesses Ephraim and Manasseh
Vienna Genesis p. 45, Syria, 6th cent. (p230)

> 'And there was none of the men of the house' etc. – is it possible that there was no man in a huge house like that of this wicked [Potiphar]!? It was taught in the School of R. Yishmael: That day was their feast-day, and they had all gone to their idolatrous temple; but she had pretended to be ill because she thought, I shall not have an opportunity like today for Joseph to associate with me.

The upper half on page 32 is clarified by the following midrash tradition:[196] 'When they all returned from their idol worship, including the women, they came to visit her.' In our depiction, three court officials, having already arrived, wait on Potiphar's wife, who speaks to them, while Potiphar himself is hurrying towards them from outside.[197] The identification of the hurrying figure with Potiphar is suggested by the midrash, according to which the entire household was at the Nile feast.

An explanation for the lower half is provided by the continuation of the midrash. Having returned from their idol worship, the wives of the dignitaries ask Potiphar's wife:

> Why are you so distressed? Indeed, have you perhaps made eyes at this servant?... Then they said to her: You have no other recourse but to tell your lord to have him locked up in prison. Then she said to them: If I complain of him to my husband, he will not believe me. But if you will all tell your husbands that Joseph tried to force you, then I will also tell my husband and he will have him imprisoned.[198]

The lower picture column on page 32 actually appears to be a pictorial translation of this tradition. At the far right, Potiphar's wife is bringing her charge against Joseph, whereby the handmaid is presenting Joseph's abandoned garment as proof. Behind Potiphar stands a man, who is distinguished by his dress from all other men in this picture. This is either Joseph – albeit otherwise attired than on the preceding pages – or someone who is also hearing the charge against Joseph. Behind this figure stands an Egyptian couple, supporting the charge against Joseph by indicating with their hands the damning garment.

JACOB BLESSING EPHRAIM AND MANASSEH (pl. 56)

Not until the miniature depicting Jacob's blessing upon Ephraim and Manasseh on page 45 can the influence of Jewish iconography again be detected with a high degree of probability. Of course, Jacob's crossed hands could also have a Christian reference, being understood both as the cross of Jesus, and as the subordination of Judaism to the Christian Church.[199]

In Jewish tradition the crossed hands receive several interpretations.

[196] MidrGad Gen 39:14 (p669).
[197] For the identification of this last figure with Potiphar see Pächt, 'Ephraimillustration', 253.
[198] MidrGad ib.
[199] Stechow, 'Jacob', esp. 261-4.

Thus the Rabbis understood them in the sense that Jacob thereby showed his preference for Ephraim. This came about, according to the Rabbis, because Ephraim disregarded himself and thus showed himself to be humble,[200] as we read in Genesis Rabba:

> 'And Israel stretched out his right hand and laid it upon the head of Ephraim, who was the younger' (Gen 48:14). R. Hun[i]a said: Do we not already know from the geneology that he was the younger? Why then does it say, 'He was the younger'? He had no thought for himself. What was his reward? He attained the birthright.[201]

Standing to the left of Joseph, who has brought his sons before his father, is a woman not mentioned in the biblical account, who can doubtless be identified with Asenath.[202] According to a widespread Rabbinic tradition, Jacob at first had doubts about blessing the sons of Joseph and Asenath, because of fears that they might have been the issue of an illegitimate marriage. The Rabbinic exegesis of Gen 48:9, 'These are my sons, whom God has given me 'by this' (בזה)' addresses this point. The Rabbis refer the phrase בזה to the marriage contract, which Joseph is said to have produced for his father, and only then was Jacob prepared to bless his grandsons. Targum Yonatan to Gen 48:9 relates: 'And Joseph said to his father: These are my sons, whom God has given me. This is the marriage contract by which I have taken to wife Asenath, daughter of Dinah, your daughter.' Even more clear-cut is the explanation in Pesikta Rabbati:[203]

> Joseph began to plead and said to him: Father, my sons are righteous even as I am. These are my sons, whom God has given me 'by this'. What does 'by this' mean? He brought Asenath, their mother, to his father and said to him: Father, I pray thee for the sake of this righteous woman.

The motif of Jacob's doubts being dispelled by his introduction to Asenath and the producing of the marriage contract is also emphasized in other midrashim.[204] The later midrash tradition concentrated increasingly on Asenath's significance and added further legendary aspects. Hence, it is said that immediately after Jacob's arrival in Egypt she tended him as his nurse. When he became ill, she told her husband so that he might ask his father to bless his sons while there was yet time.[205] According to the Jewish tradition then, Asenath's participation in Jacob's blessing upon Ephraim and Manasseh was a necessity. It follows therefore, that Jacob's crossed

[200] The Rabbinic sources are listed by Stemberger, 'Patriarchenbilder', 45f.
[201] GenR 6,4 to Gen 1:16 (p43f; Mirqin 1, p40f); GenR 37,7 (p349f; Mirqin 2, p76); PesR 3 (12b).
[202] Gerstinger, *Wiener Genesis*, 109; Buberl, *Byzantinische Handschriften*, 125; Mazal, *Kommentar*, 158; Philonenko, *Joseph et Aséneth*, 129.
[203] PesR 3 (12a). See Gutmann, 'Joseph Legends', 183.
[204] E.g., MidrGad Gen 48:9 (p821).
[205] Jellinek, *Bet ha-Midrasch* 6, p83.

hands – given the exemplar for the 'Vienna Genesis' – are rather to be understood in the Jewish than the Christian context.

JACOB'S BLESSING AND BURIAL (pl. 57-58)

The miniature on page 47 portrays the story in Gen 49:28-33, where Jacob instructs his sons to bury him with his fathers in the cave of Machpelah.[206] The aged patriarch, Jacob, sits in the middle, flanked right and left by his descendants. There appear to be ten persons on the right (including the heads visible in the background), while at the left, four of his descendants stand beside the patriarch. Thus, there are fourteen persons who, after receiving their blessings from Jacob, have been commissioned to bury him in the cave at Machpelah.

This peculiar arrangement has a satisfactory explanation in Rabbinic literature: the four figures at the left are Joseph with his two sons, Ephraim and Manasseh, and behind them, Joseph's brother, Benjamin. At the right stand the ten remaining sons of Jacob. According to Rabbinic exegesis, Jacob at first had doubts about including Joseph's sons in the blessings, because the original promise to him spoke only of twelve sons. The account in Pesikta Rabbati relates:[207]

> If I bless them [Joseph's sons], I will not fulfill the word of the Holy One, blessed be He, who said to me: Twelve tribes will I bring forth from you. But if I do not bless them, it will be bad for you [Joseph]. Therefore I will bless them.

The picture may portray the group following Jacob's blessing in the sense of the Rabbinic understanding, i.e., besides Jacob, fourteen persons.

Joseph is portrayed in this picture, as in the two preceding pages, dressed in the garb of an Egyptian court official. This accords with the Jewish tradition according to which Jacob desired to pay honor to the Egyptian kingdom in the person of Joseph. Hence it was necessary to characterize Joseph, through his raiment, as an Egyptian noble. The biblical basis for this is Gen 48:2, where Jacob/Israel 'summoned his strength, and sat up in bed'. Genesis Rabba, e.g.,[208] relates that he did this 'in order to pay honor to the [Egyptian] kingdom'.[209]

The last picture on page 48 shows the burial of Jacob in the cave of Machpelah. The magnificent bed on which the dead Jacob is lying is striking and reminds of the bed depicted in the Ashburnham Pentateuch, fol. 50r.[210] It also corresponds to a Rabbinic tradition reflected in the Targums to Gen

[206] Gerstinger, *Wiener Genesis*, 110; Buberl, *Byzantinische Handschriften*, 127; Mazal, *Kommentar*, 159.
[207] PesR 3 (11a).
[208] The motif is already found in Mekh dRY, Pisha 13 (Lauterbach 1, p101).
[209] GenR 97,2 to Gen 48:2 (p1242; Mirqin 4, p294).
[210] See below, p242.

57. Jacob's blessing
Vienna Genesis p. 47, Syria, 6th cent. (p232)

58. Jacob's death bed and burial
Vienna Genesis p. 48, Syria, 6th cent. (p232)

50:1. Already in Tg. Neophyti it is related that, 'Joseph laid his father on a bed of ivory, overlaid with gold and set with pearls, and strengthened with precious stone, byssus and purple.' The accentuation of Jacob's magnificent bed could be a further indication that the miniaturist of the 'Vienna Genesis' had at his disposal an exemplar of Jewish origin.

The above examples have in essence confirmed the thesis of a Jewish background for the pictures in the 'Vienna Genesis'. Our examination of the Rabbinic material allows no conclusion whether the miniaturist(s) also used non-Jewish exemplars in addition to his Jewish sources. The majority of pictures can be explained from the biblical text. Where there are extra-biblical elements, most of these can be clarified by Rabbinic sources, which certainly allows the assumption of a Jewish model behind the 'Vienna Genesis'. In addition, picture traditions also found in medieval Hebrew illuminated manuscripts occur here and there.[211] This of course raises the question how such traditions could survive from antiquity into the Middle Ages, since there is no attestation for Jewish figurative art from the seventh to the twelfth century. On the other hand, we must reckon with the transmission of motifs by Syrian Christians who lived in the same area as the Rabbinic scholars, and, like the near-Eastern Jews, spoke Aramaic as the language of commerce. Scholarship is left here with open questions, but the probability of the use of picture exemplars of Jewish origin cannot be dismissed.

The Ashburnham Pentateuch

The iconography of the Ashburnham or Tours Pentateuch, a late seventh century Latin Vulgate manuscript, again requires the assumption of Jewish exemplars.[212] However, no firm conclusion is possible concerning the extent of these exemplars. Many Rabbinic texts which might be consulted regarding the interpretation have a parallel either in the Apocrypha or in Patristic literature. Since the Apocrypha were preserved by the early Christians rather than their Jewish contemporaries, they could have inspired Christian artists directly; the conclusion of an intermediate Jewish exemplar would thus be unnecessary. That such a conclusion is nonetheless possible is proved by the numerous Rabbinic texts that suggest themselves for the explanation of the illustrations which go beyond the biblical text. Likewise, motifs that can be understood both from the Rabbinic and the Patristic texts could just as easily have been mediated from the Jewish as the Christian side. Certainty in the question cannot be attained. Methodologically therefore, we must distinguish picture elements that reveal Jewish iconography with near-certainty from those that recall not only Rabbinic,

[211] Cf n194 above.
[212] The following is largely oriented on K. Schubert, 'Miniaturen'.

59. Jacob fleeing Laban and preparing to meet Esau
Ashburnham Pentateuch fol. 30r, late 7th cent. (p237)

but also apocryphal and Patristic texts. The pictures of the Ashburnham Pentateuch comprehend several scenes per page, not all of which permit the presupposition of a Jewish model. Yet we will not neglect these completely, because they sometimes are a necessary complement to those depictions comprehensible only from Rabbinic texts.[213] Therefore, we will first treat those folios where the influence of Rabbinic iconography is particularly clear, and only then those where it is merely possible.

LABAN'S PURSUIT OF JACOB (pl. 59)

Relatively solid ground with regard to Jewish iconography, albeit in one small detail, is not reached until fol. 30r. It concerns an illustration of Gen 31:22-32:4 – Laban's pursuit of Jacob, the settling of a peace covenant between Laban and Jacob, the parting of the two families, and Jacob's sending of messengers to his brother, Esau. In the upper half of the picture Laban searches Jacob's tents for the teraphim stolen by Rebecca. In the lower half, upper left, the conclusion of the peace pact between Laban and Jacob is depicted. The left picture shows Jacob, Laban and the latter's two sons, sharing a meal at the stone circle or heap that was built as a witness to the covenant (31:46). To the right of this, the agreement between Laban and Jacob is depicted, according to which the stone circle and מצבה (monument) mark the boundary between the territories of the two treaty partners (31:51f). At the lower left, Laban and his two sons depart on camels, while Jacob and his tribe are shown travelling on from the center of the picture towards the right (32:1f). At the far right, center, are two young men with outstretched hands, obviously Jacob's messengers to Esau (32:4).

Although the biblical narrative is illustrated here without midrashic ornament, the stone circle surrounding the מצבה corresponds with the literal understanding of the Hebrew word גל (31:51f; cf. the root גלל, 'to roll' and גלגל 'wheel'). This word is translated in the LXX with βούνος (hill,

[213] In 'Miniaturen', I differed with exaggerations such as by Gutmann, 'Jewish Origin'; Hempel, 'Problem'; id, 'Jüdische Traditionen'. The opposite assumption however, that there were no Jewish or Rabbinic models for the Ashburnham Pentateuch, is absolutely groundless. One often has the impression that massive prejudices are being grounded with scholarly ornamentation. A true example is Rickert, *Studien*, who p25-27 formulates his biased starting point: 'Based on typological aspects, the investigation should show the impact of Christian theology on the formation of the pictures'. No attempt is made to do justice to the Ashburnham Pentateuch as a whole; only the title page and the Noah story are treated, with the following justification: 'Two of the illustrations, the title page and depiction of the Flood, are considered the chief arguments for the influence of Jewish models on the Ashburnham Pentateuch, and thus on Christian book illumination as a whole, and this still in the most recent scholarly literature on this subject.' But these very folios are among those for which no certainty in either direction can be attained (see my 'Miniaturen', 193, 198f). On the other hand, really typical examples found elsewhere are ignored. This Bonn dissertation shows that the Christian archaeologist is overtaxed when it comes to judging the relevance of Rabbinic texts for understanding early Christian book illumination.

60. Joseph receives and sups with his brothers
Ashburnham Pentateuch fol. 44r, late 7th cent. (p239)

mound) and in the Vulgate, which text is illustrated here, with *tumulus* (hill, mound). The clear portrayal of a stone circle surrounding the מצבה as Jacob takes his leave from Laban, is an unambiguous indication for a Jewish exemplar, since the depiction can only have been prompted by the Hebrew text itself, not from the Greek or Latin translations.

JOSEPH SUPS WITH HIS BROTHERS **(pl. 60)**

Fol. 44r also contains elements that can only be satisfactorily explained if one assumes Jewish influence on the content of the portrayal. At the upper left, the second arrival of Israel's sons – this time including Benjamin – at Joseph's house in Egypt is shown (Gen 43:26-29). The picture follows the biblical text exactly. Joseph is sitting on a chair with young Benjamin standing before him. Joseph's brothers kneel before him and offer him gifts. The following scene is below this, directly in the center of the picture (43:30). The adscript reads: *Joseph ubi plaget.*

The scenes in the middle and lower left are referable to a Jewish background. Two tables are depicted at which a banquet is being held. Below this are found kitchen and cellar scenes. At the upper table, the twelve brothers are seated together, while young Benjamin sits on a folding stool at Joseph's side. In a seating order alternating between black and white, the Egyptians sit at the lower table, apart from the brothers. The separation between the Israelites and the Egyptians, who take their food at a second table, corresponds exactly with the text of Gen 43:32. However, Joseph's eating at his brothers' table with Benjamin sitting beside him diverges from the text. Gen 43:32 relates: 'They served [Joseph] by himself, and them by themselves, and the Egyptians who ate with him by themselves'. It is then said in Gen 43:33 that his brothers 'sat before him', and in 43:34: 'Portions were taken to them from Joseph's table'. In our picture however all the brothers, including Joseph, sit around a circular table reaching together toward the viands in the middle of the table. Here only two tables are pictured, whereas according to the biblical text three were required: one table for Joseph, one for his brothers and a third for the Egyptians. The two tables, however, are sufficiently accounted for by Rabbinic tradition,[214] which, despite some variation in the seating order of the other brothers, invariably and unanimously declared that the two sons of Rachel, Joseph and Benjamin, sat beside each other. Thus, e.g., Genesis Rabba:[215]

> [Joseph] took the cup and pretended to prophesy with it. He said: Judah, who is king, shall sit at the head. Ruben, who is the first-born, shall sit beside him as his second. [And thus he did with all (his other

[214] Gutmann, 'Jewish Origin', 341; Hempel, 'Jüdische Traditionen', 351.
[215] GenR 92,5 to Gen 43:30-33 (p1142f; Mirqin 4, p119).

61. Jacob's blessing and burial at paradisal Machpelah
Ashburnham Pentateuch fol. 50r, late 7th cent. (p241)

brothers).] He said: I have no mother and this youth has no mother, for his mother died at his birth, and thus he must sit beside me.[216]

At the lower right, Gen 44:1-12 is depicted. The cup is found in Benjamin's pack, whereby Jacob's sons are forced to return to Joseph. Directly above this, is the illustration of the brothers maintaining their innocence (Gen 44:14-17).

Fol. 44r seems to have been influenced by the Jewish tradition of Scripture interpretation. Joseph sitting with Benjamin and his other brothers around the same table is sufficient proof. Since this legend was also known to the Eastern Church fathers, Ephraim and Basil,[217] it is certainly possible that the pictorial arrangement may have originated with a Christian artist acquainted with a legend of this sort. But this supposition is less probable since at one point even the Latin adscript has the flavor of a Hebrew translation.[218]

JACOB BLESSING EPHRAIM AND MANASSEH AND HIS BURIAL (pl. 61)

Fol. 50r may also be dependent on a Jewish exemplar. This leaf is among the most interesting and informative of the entire Ashburnham Pentateuch. In the center left, Jacob's blessing upon Ephraim and Manasseh is depicted (Gen 48:8-22). Exactly as emphasized by v. 14, Jacob crosses his hands, laying his right hand on Ephraim's and his left on Manasseh's head. As in the synagogue at Dura Europos, Joseph is pictured bringing his two sons before his aged father.[219] Jacob's crossed hands are also found (but without Joseph) in a scene of Jacob's blessing of Ephraim and Manasseh in the Via Latina catacomb.[220] As in the Via Latina, Ephraim is not only the younger, but also the smaller. This fits perfectly with the Rabbinic interpretation of the text which emphasizes that Ephraim was preferred because he had 'lowered himself', i.e., he was modest and unpretentious.[221] Jacob's remaining eleven sons, who are waiting to be blessed also (Gen 49), stand behind his bed at the right. The combination in one picture of Jacob's two blessings – one upon Ephraim and Manasseh and the other upon the patriarchs of the twelve tribes of Israel – is found not only here, but also in the Dura Europos synagogue.[222]

In the upper left Gen 50:1-6 is portrayed: following Jacob's embalming

[216] See also GenR 93,7 to Gen 44:18 (p1165; Mirqin 4, p139f); Tanh, Wayigash 4 (53a-b); TgY Gen 43:33.
[217] Gutmann, 'Jewish Origin', 341, n62.
[218] U. Schubert has pointed out that *pigella* corresponds to the Hebrew פיגול, "the eating of forbidden meat".
[219] Weitzmann-Kessler, *Frescos*, 21-24.
[220] See Schubert, 'Miniaturen'.
[221] See above p231.
[222] Weitzmann-Kessler, *Frescos*, 24-26.

and period of mourning, Joseph goes to the 'household of Pharaoh' with the request to bury his father in Canaan. Pharaoh, depicted making a speech gesture, grants Joseph his request. He is sitting on a folding stool with his feet propped on a footrest. Before Pharaoh stand two servants, apparently awaiting his orders. Joseph is approaching Pharaoh from the right. He is bowing with his hands stretched out in a gesture of supplication. Behind Pharaoh at the left, looking out the window, Pharaoh's wife appears, although she is not mentioned in the biblical account in Gen 50:1-5. The adscript *regina*, 'queen', places her identification beyond doubt.[223] To the immediate right of this scene is an illustration of Gen 50:15. The adscript describes this scene sufficiently: *Hic filii iacob post defuncto patre rogant ioseph fratrem suum ne reddat eis malum pro malo*, 'The sons of Jacob, after their father's death, ask Joseph, their brother, not to return evil upon them for evil'; and: *ioseph loquitur leniter fratribus*, 'Joseph speaks gently to his brothers'. At Joseph's right, his wife can be recognized in a window frame, probably as a parallel to the depiction of Pharaoh's wife looking out the window.[224]

The scene at the center right leads us once again to Rabbinic tradition. Jacob is being buried by his sons in the cave at Machpelah. Above the gravesite there is the adscript, *spelunca duplex* (double cave). At the left, a framed picture showing a Paradise landscape can be seen. Underneath this picture stands a group of fifteen men. Joseph can be recognized in the right foreground. The man at the front left of the group has white hair and beard.[225] Apart from the group of fifteen, two additional men carry the mummified body of Jacob into the grave. The first man, standing in the grave, is taking the body by the head and shoulder while the second supports it under the rump. In front of the grave stands an elaborately finished bier, which looks rather like a bed.[226] Below this, filling the entire lower section, are horse-drawn wagons and Egyptian servants, the latter recognizable by their black skin.

Rabbinic Scripture interpretation, which may be accepted with the greatest probability as the background for the motifs of this depiction, allows the presumption that the bearded old man standing at Joseph's left is the Patriarch, Judah. Thus, in Targum Neophyti to Gen 50:1:

> And Joseph fell upon the face of his father and wept over him and kissed him. And Joseph laid his father on a [bier] of ivory, overlaid with gold and set with pearls, and strengthened with precious stone, byssus and purple. And there were poured out there wines and perfumes; there were burnt there precious aromas. There stood there

[223] Hempel, 'Problem', 106 also sees here an influence of Rabbinic tradition, but this is rather improbable. Cf K. Schubert, 'Miniaturen', 206f.
[224] In this connection, Hempel's supposition of a Jewish exemplar ('Problem') is unconvincing.
[225] Von Gebhardt, *Miniatures*, 19 considers this to be one of the elders mentioned in Gen 50:7.
[226] Cf above p232.

> kingdoms and rulers from the sons of Ishmael; there stood there rulers from the sons of Esau; there stood there rulers from the sons of Keturah; there stood Judah, the lion; men of his brothers. Judah answered and said to his brothers:Come, let us plant for our father a tall cedar, its top reaching unto the heavens...[227]

The elaborately finished bier, upon which Jacob was carried to the cave at Machpelah, can easily be identified with the bier or bed described here. That a total of not twelve, but seventeen men appear, also fits well with the Targum tradition according to which others besides the sons of Israel were present at Jacob's burial. According to the tradition, the white-haired, bearded figure is Judah, who speaks of the tall cedar to be planted in honor of his deceased father. The Paradise landscape above is perhaps intended to express this.

A further possible meaning for this Paradise landscape is the characterization of the cave of Machpelah as the burial site for the imperishable, and therefore fragrant, bodies of Adam and Eve. A tradition attributed to R. Banaa (first half of the third century CE), a burial cave surveyor, relates:[228]

> R. Banaa used to mark out caves [where there were dead bodies]. When he came to the cave of Abraham, he found Eliezer the servant of Abraham standing at the entrance: He said to him: What is Abraham doing? He replied: He is sleeping in the arms of Sarah, and she is looking fondly at his head. He said: Go and tell him that Banaa is standing at the entrance [with the task of surveying the cave]. Said Abraham to him: Let him enter; it is well known that there is no passion in this world. So he went in, surveyed the cave, and came out again. When [in his surveying] he came to the cave of Adam, a voice came forth from heaven saying, Thou hast beholden the likeness of my image, my likeness itself thou mayest not behold. But [he said] I want to mark out the cave.

It can be clearly seen from this text that Adam's body still retains paradisal qualities. In this connection there is yet another tradition of interest, according to which both Adam and the Temple in Jerusalem are the work of God's hands in a special way;[229] Temple and Paradise conceptually belong together in Jewish tradition.[230]

This is combined with the three angels' visit to Abraham in Pirkei de-R. Eliezer.[231] When the three angels appeared to Abraham, he first thought they were guests from among the people of the land. He desired to prepare a good meal for them and gave Sarah the directions. As Sarah prepared the dough for the meal she became aware that she was menstruating. Thereby

[227] Similarly TgY to Gen 50:1.
[228] bBB 58a.
[229] ARNa 1 (Schechter 4b).
[230] Maier, *Kultus*.
[231] PdRE 36 (Luria 84b; Friedlander p275); MidrGad Gen 23:9 (p384).

62. The Egyptian slavery of the Israelites
Ashburnham Pentateuch fol. 56r, late 7th cent. (p245)

the food which she had prepared became unclean, and thus Abraham was no longer able to set it before his guests. He decided then to slaughter a calf from his herd for his guests. The calf however ran away and fled into the cave of Machpelah. Following him, Abraham 'found there Adam and Eve lying asleep upon their bier. Lights burned above them and a fragrance like perfume exuded from them. For this reason he desired to be buried in the cave at Machpelah'.

On the one hand, the Paradise landscape beside the cave probably serves to characterize this cave as a gravesite of imperishable and fragrant bodies, and on the other, it could illustrate Judah's words about the tall cedar to be planted in honor of their deceased father.

THE EGYPTIAN SLAVERY **(pl. 62)**

The extraordinarily richly illustrated fol. 56r also shows definite connections to Rabbinic tradition.[232] In the upper field, Pharaoh is twice depicted. At the left, he gives his servants the order (according to the adscript) to oppress the sons of Israel that they might not continue to proliferate. At the upper right, Pharaoh sits in speech gesture and accuses the two midwives standing before him of not following his orders (Exod 1:18f). Behind Pharaoh's two servants at the upper left, three men are standing who are again pictured at the right, standing behind the two midwives. Two of them are black, one white. These are probably Pharaoh's counselors, who in Rabbinic tradition are connected with the subject of the Israelites' oppression in Egypt. In Rabbinic tradition Pharaoh's words, 'Come, let us deal shrewdly with them' (Exod 1:10), were interpreted as his taking counsel with these three advisors. Targum Neophyti to this text reads: 'Come, let us take evil counsel concerning them. We will make laws to reduce their numbers before they multiply even further'.[233] Rabbinic tradition here mentions three advisors to Pharaoh, just as here three men are depicted standing behind Pharaoh's servants. In this vein the Talmud first states to Exod 1:10 that they took counsel whether Israel should be exterminated with fire, sword or water, and then goes on to relate:[234]

> R. Hiyya b. Abba said in the name of R. Simai [first half, third century]: There were three in that plan, viz. Balaam, Job and Jethro. Balaam who devised it was slain; Job who silently acquiesced was

[232] Hempel's assumption ('Problem', 106) that an illustrated Pesah haggada served as the model for this folio is pure speculation. Illustrated haggadot are unknown before the thirteenth century.

[233] Likewise, TgY to Exod 1:10.

[234] bSot 11a. Cf ExodR 1,9 (Mirqin 5, p19f). The traditionist here is not R. Simai, but R. Simon (c. 300 CE).

63. Tora given at Sinai and in the Tabernacle
Ashburnham Pentateuch fol. 76r, late 7th cent. (p247)

afflicted with sufferings; Jethro, who fled, merited that his descendants should sit in the Chamber of Hewn Stone.[235]

The portrayal of Pharaoh with three counselors then accords superbly with the Rabbinic understanding of Exod 1:10.[236]

At center left and lower left the Egyptian slavery is depicted, which acquired numerous embellishments in Rabbinic interpretation. The pictures however follow the biblical text, revealing no specific Rabbinic motifs. In the lower right corner, the baby Moses is discovered in the Nile and rescued by Pharaoh's daughter. Neither do we find here references to Rabbinic legends.

Above this scene, the argument between the two Israelites which Moses arbitrates, and the murder of the Egyptian by Moses are shown. To the right of this, Moses is already in Midian (Exod 2:16f). Moses dips water from a well for Jethro's daughter. Further to the right are several sheep. Two of these are drinking from a trough, while a third approaches the trough from the left. The blue band, leading from the direction of the well towards the trough, and surrounding it, is striking. Apparently, this is meant to depict the abundance of water flowing into the trough. This curious representation is very well accounted for by the following Rabbinic interpretation: 'Moses dipped but once, and watered thereby the entire herd. Thus were the waters blessed by him'.[237] The clear-cut accentuation of the water from which the sheep are drinking could also be understood as a reference to a possible Jewish exemplar. To the right of this scene, Moses can be seen standing before the burning bush.

THE LAW ON SINAI AND IN THE TABERNACLE (pl. 63)

A Rabbinic background can first be surmised again at fol. 76r.[238] The upper half of the leaf depicts Exod 24:1-8, and the lower half, v. 9-18. On the peak of Sinai, God in the form of a human head appears in flames in a shining circle of clouds. Moses, Aaron, Nadab, and Abihu are also on the mountain, while the elders of Israel stand at the foot. Beside them Moses stands with the tablets of the Law befor an altar, to which young men of Israel are carrying their sacrifices. At Moses' left are male and female Israelites, who according to the adscript are saying: *Omnia quae precepit deus faciemus*, 'All that the Lord has spoken we will do' (v. 7). The lower half of the leaf shows the Tabernacle or Tent of Meeting, into which Moses and Joshua are

[235] לשכת הגזית 'hewn chamber', describes the seat of Sanhedrin in the Temple area. Cf Schürer, *Geschichte* 2, p264f; Klausner, *Historia* 3, p95; Hoenig, *Great Sanhedrin*; Mantel, *Studies*, 82f.

[236] Pharaoh's three counselors remained a permanent topos of the illustration to Exod 1:10; see, e.g., Brit. Libr. Add 27210, 10v; K. Schubert, *Bilderpentateuch*, fol. 71.

[237] ExodR 1,32 (Mirqin 5, p51).

[238] K. Schubert – U. Schubert, 'Marginalien'.

entering from one side, while Aaron, Nadab, and Abihu enter from the other. V. 9 relates another ascent of Sinai, with Moses this time accompanied by Aaron, Nadab, and Abihu; in v. 13 his escort is Joshua. The very men enter the Tabernacle then who according to v. 9-18 climb Mount Sinai. The representation of the Tabernacle at the foot of Sinai recalls the fresco in the Via Latina catacomb where below the scene of Moses receiving the Law on Sinai is a portrayal of Moses leading the Israelites to a temple sanctuary.

It is almost certain that this temple sanctuary is to be understood from the Rabbinic interpretation which takes Isa 2:2 as a cipher for Mount Sinai.[239] Temple and Tabernacle or Tent of Meeting are interchangeable concepts in Rabbinic tradition, as in the following tradition:

> We find that the Tabernacle (משכן) was called Sanctuary (מקדש) and that the Sanctuary was called Tabernacle.... we find that the Sanctuary was called Tabernacle and that the Tabernacle was called Sanctuary. One may well agree that the Sanctuary was called Tabernacle since it is written in Scripture, 'And I will set my Tabernacle (משכני) among you' (Lev 26:11). Whence, however, do we infer that the Tabernacle was called Sanctuary? If it be suggested: From the Scriptural text, 'And the Kohathites the bearers of the Sanctuary set forward, that the Tabernacle might be set up against their coming' Num 10:21), that [surely] was written in respect of the [holy] ark. – Rather it is from the following text [that the inference was made:], 'And let them make Me a Sanctuary, that I may dwell (ושכנתי) among them' (Exod 25:8).[240]

In the lower part of the picture then, those five persons enter the Tent of Meeting who had experienced the epiphany on Mount Sinai according to Exod 24:9-18.

Still further elements of Rabbinic exegesis can shed light on the combination in one picture of Sinai and Tabernacle. The Tora was not binding until it had been repeated in the Tent of Meeting:

> It is taught that R. Yishmael [early second century CE] said: The universal was spoken on Sinai and the specific in the Tent of Meeting (אוהל מועד). R. Akiva [early second century CE] said: Both the universal and the specific were spoken on Sinai and repeated in the Tent of Meeting. It was repeated a third time on the plains of Moab.[241]

Accordingly, as we have seen already, the Israelites become punishable for the Tora only after its repetition in the Tabernacle.[242] A different juxtaposition of Sinai and Tent of Meeting is found in the following:[243]

[239] See p196f.
[240] bEr 2a-b. Cf bShev 16b; NumR 12,3 to Num 10:1 (Mirqin 10, p11-15).
[241] bHag 6a-b; bSot 37b.
[242] See above n115.
[243] LevR 20,10 (p468; Mirqin 8, p20).

> 'On the day of his wedding, on the day of the gladness of his heart' (Cant 3:11) – 'On the day of his wedding', is Sinai. 'And on the day of the gladness of his heart', is the Tent of Meeting.

Whether one understands the Tabernacle at the foot of Sinai to be a periphrasis for Sinai itself, or a sign that the Tora was not binding until it had been proclaimed in the Tent of Meeting, the 'Sitz im Leben' for such an understanding is in Rabbinic Judaism. Rather than oral tradition taken over by Christians, this can only have come from a Jewish pictorial exemplar, the symbolic significance of which could no longer be understood by Christians. The emphasis on the problem concerning when the Tora became effective was irrelevant for Christians.[244]

As stated above, we must also consider those folios of the Ashburnham Pentateuch whose illustrations can be understood not only from a picture exemplar, but also from oral or literary traditions shared by Christians. Foremost here are Jewish legends and interpretations found reflected also in Patristic literature. Motifs transmitted in the Jewish Apocrypha found an echo in the Christian sphere where Hebrew and Aramaic texts were known in Greek and other common language translations in antiquity. When such motifs are also found in Rabbinic texts, it must remain open from where the Christian illustrators of the Ashburnham Pentateuch and other Byzantine or early medieval manuscripts drew their inspiration.[245]

CAIN AND ABEL (pl. 64)

The first to be considered is fol. 6r. It contains individual pictures from Gen 3:21-4:9. The first picture, upper left, shows Adam and Eve grieving under a bower. Beside this, likewise under a bower, Eve is suckling her two sons. Here one can refer to the apocryphal book, *The Life of Adam and Eve*, which begins with the words: 'When they were driven out of Paradise they made for themselves a [hut] and mourned for seven days, weeping in great sorrow. But after seven days they began to hunger and sought food to eat, but found none.'[246] The picture at the far right, which represents Cain and Abel with their sacrifices, recalls a similar iconography in the Via Latina catacomb. Moving from right to left, the next scene shows God's acceptance of Abel's sacrifice. Cain drops his head and hands in despair.

In the center and lower picture strips, on green and violet backgrounds, the story of Cain and Abel is taken up once again. The depicted sequence however does not accord with the biblical account. In the middle strip, on a

[244] Hence the impossibility of apodictic conjectures such as expressed by Brenk, *Mosaiken*, 128: therefore 'ist es durchaus möglich, daß eine Illustration überhaupt erst durch Christen erfolgte'.

[245] This is also valid for the Cotton Genesis rescension; cf Weitzmann-Kessler, *Cotton Genesis*.

[246] Cf Gutmann, 'Jewish Origin', 338.

64. Cain and Abel
Ashburnham Pentateuch fol. 6r, late 7th cent. (p249)

green background, Eve is first of all pictured in a bower holding the naked baby Cain. To the right of this, Adam is pictured as a tiller of the ground, and at the far right Cain is undergoing interrogation by God concerning his brother's whereabouts. In the lower picture strip, on a violet background, Abel is seen tending his flock at the left, and Cain is tilling the ground at the right. Below this Cain slays Abel, whom he is holding by the hair. The representation of two large rams, one brown and the other white, running towards each other in the uppermost part of the lower picture strip, is striking. The white ram is clearly proceeding from Cain's area, and the brown ram is running towards him. This recalls a Rabbinic tradition according to which the fratricide was brought about by an animal straying from Abel's flocks and causing damage to Cain's fields.[247] The motif of conflict between Cain and Abel is well-attested in Rabbinic tradition. Genesis Rabba relates that at the distribution of goods, Cain received the earth and soil, while Abel was given the moveable goods. The midrash continues: 'One said: The earth upon which you stand belongs to me! The other said: What you see belongs to me! One said: Leave! The other said: Get out!'[248] Elsewhere we read, with explicit reference to Abel's flocks:[249]

> Cain said to Abel: Let us divide the world! He answered him: Yes. Then Abel took his flocks, and Cain went to till the soil. They agreed not to meddle in each other's affairs. When Abel took his herd, he began to pasture it, but Cain pursued him from the mountain to the plain and from the plain to the mountain, until they came to blows. Abel defeated Cain and he fell under him. When Cain saw that he was beaten, he began to cry out: Abel, my brother, do no evil unto me! Abel showed mercy to him and left him alone. But Cain rose up and slew him, for it says, 'Cain rose up' (Gen 4:8), because he had fallen before.

The lower strip, on violet background, could fit the above mentioned Rabbinic tradition. The exact division of the areas, Abel's to the left and Cain's to the right, connected with the scene of the murder, is striking. This fits superbly the Rabbinic tradition in which the fratricide was brought about by a conflict over these two spheres of life. Moreover, that the individual Cain scenes are distributed over all three portrayals, supports taking the lower picture strip as a unity meant to show Cain's fratricide and its causes. But the mixture of apocryphal and Rabbinic motifs on this page, and the fact that Christians might also have adopted legends about Cain and Abel via oral tradition, prohibit the certain conclusion in favor of a Jewish picture exemplar here.

[247] Hempel, 'Problem', 105; id, 'Jüdische Traditionen', 350.
[248] GenR 22,7 to Gen 4:8 (p213; Mirqin 1, p170).
[249] Tanh, Bereshit 9 (9b); cf MidrGad Gen 4:8 (p118f).

65. Giants drowned under Noah's ark
Ashburnham Pentateuch fol. 9r, late 7th cent. (p253)

THE GIANTS IN THE FLOOD **(pl. 65)**

Fol. 9r is a representation of the Flood. Beneath the ark, not only men and animals are perishing but also giants. This motif suggest a Jewish background.[250] The giants are not mentioned in the account of Gen 7:21, where it is said that all men and animals died in the Flood, although they do appear in Gen 6:4 prior to the Flood story. But in *1 Enoch* 15 and 16 these giants are called spoilers of mankind, as, e.g., in 15:8: 'But now the giants who are born from the (union of) the spirits and the flesh shall be called evil spirits upon the earth, because their dwelling shall be upon the earth'. A similar idea deriving from Gen 6:1-4 is found in *Jub.* 5. The motif of giants as the offspring of fallen angels was also known to the Latin West, as can be seen from Augustine's polemic against this notion in *Civ. Dei* 15:23. The Giant motif appears in Rabbinic tradition in several ways. Their punishment in the waters of the Flood, as portrayed in the Ashburnham Pentateuch is also known. Trusting in their great height, they blasphemed against God, reasoning that no flood waters could be deep enough to overwhelm them. This tale is fully developed in Pirkei de-R. Eliezer,[251] where the Giants are reported to have said:

> If [God] brings floodwaters against us, [these can do us no harm] for we are tall and the waters will not reach our throats. And if he causes the waters of the deep to rise up against us, [these can do us no harm] for the soles of our feet are large enough to cover the founts [from which the waters] of the deep [spring forth].... What did the Holy One, blessed be He, do? He heated the waters of the deep until they burned them, so that their skin sloughed off.

According to Genesis Rabba,[252] R. Yohanan bar Nappaha (second half, third century) said: 'Every single drop which the Holy One, blessed be He, caused to fall upon them, he first heated in Gehenna, and then let it fall upon them.'[253] The idea that the Giants were punished with hot water was also connected with their sexual transgression. Rav Hisda, who taught around the turn of third-fourth century, is reported to have said: 'With hot passion [i.e., with hot semen] they sinned, and by hot water they were punished.'[254]

The clear-cut emphasis on the Giants' punishment by the Flood waters in relatively early Rabbinic traditions makes a Jewish picture exemplar very possible. On the other hand, the motif is well-attested in the Apocrypha and was even known to Church fathers. Hence, neither does this picture

[250] Gutmann, 'Jewish Origin', 338f; Hempel, 'Jüdische Traditionen', 350.
[251] PdRE 22 (Luria 51b; Friedlander p162).
[252] GenR 28,9 to Gen 6:7 (p267; Mirqin 1, p208f).
[253] Cf LevR 7,6 (p161; Mirqin 7, p84).
[254] bSan 108b; bRH 12b.

66. Isaac and Ishmael
Ashburnham Pentateuch fol. 18r, late 7th cent. (p255)

permit a conclusion on whether a Jewish or a Christian model served for the precise iconographic figuration.[255]

ISAAC AND ISHMAEL (pl. 66)

Rabbinic influence could possibly be responsible for the scenes of the story of Abraham depicted on fol. 18r. The picture at center right shows Sarah and Hagar with their sons standing before Abraham. Abraham's sons Isaac and Ishmael scuffle with one another, with Ishmael grasping Isaac by the hair while holding him fast with the other hand. This representation corresponds exactly with the Rabbinic interpretation of מצחק, 'jesting, sporting, playing', in Gen 21:9, which is translated in the Vulgate with *ludentum*, 'playing, sporting', in the LXX with παίζοντα, 'playing, sporting', and in the Syrian Vulgate with *megachek*.

Among other interpretations there is a widespread understanding of מצחק as 'striving, fighting', as in Tosefta Sota 6:6, 'R. Yishmael [early second century] said מצחק means one who sheds blood, for it says, '[Let the young men arise and play before us].... And each caught his opponent by the head' (2 Sam 2:14-16).' According to Genesis Rabba,[256] R. Elazar, son of R. Yose the Galilean (second half, second century CE), taught that מצחק meant 'shedding of blood'.[257] This interpretation is also found in the Syrian Church fathers:[258] 'Where it says "laughed": He laughed at him and made fun of Isaac, as one who was envious of him and jealous. Or: He struck him, as certain people teach; for example: 'Let the young men arise and play before us' (2 Sam 2:14), means "let them fight".'

Both Rabbinic exegesis and that of the Syrian Church fathers knew the appeal to 2 Sam 2:14 in order to understand the word 'playing' in the sense of 'fighting'. Moreover, the motif of strife between Ishmael and Isaac is very ancient in Jewish Scripture interpretation, since it is already presupposed in Gal. 4:29. Hence, this leaf also forbids a certain conclusion on whether the model was Jewish or Christian.

REBECCA AND SHEM/MELCHIZEDEK (pl. 67)

Fol. 22v presents an illustration to Gen 25:21-23: After being barren, Rebecca finally becomes pregnant in consequence of Isaac's prayer. But

[255] Concerning the great discrepancy in size of the flood victims, Rickert, *Studien*, 171-80 (in general rejecting Jewish picture models) considers the smaller bodies to have been 'reduced for the sake of perspective'. He even believes it possible that the outspread arms of the giants' bodies are connected with a depiction from a Dionysian sarcophagus of a 'satyr with reversed arm position' (p178)!

[256] GenR 53,11 to Gen 21:10 according to most mss (p568; Mirqin 2, p245).

[257] See also TanB, Shemot 24 (8a); PdRE 30 (Luria 66b; Friedlander p215f).

[258] Levene, *Syrian Fathers*, 41, 93, 277f.

67. Rebecca and Shem/Melchizedek
Ashburnham Pentateuch fol. 22v, late 7th cent. (p255)

the two babies, later Jacob and Esau, strove with each other already in her womb: 'So she went to inquire of the Lord. And the Lord said to her, Two nations are in your womb, and two peoples, born of you, shall be divided; the one shall be stronger than the other, the elder shall serve the younger.'

The representation of this scene recalls Rabbinic tradition.[259] In the right part of the picture Rebecca is kneeling in a temple-like building. Behind her stand two women, apparently her handmaids; before her is an altar table, from which the hand of God points at her. In the left part of the upper picture, an old man sits on a folding chair with his right hand raised in a speech gesture. Before him stands a male figure who is pointing to the scene where Rebecca is kneeling.

According to Rabbinic tradition, the temple-like building in which Rebecca apparently brings her request before God is the study house of Shem, as in Targum Neophyti to Gen 25:22: 'And she went to the school of Shem the Great to beseech mercy from before the Lord.'[260] Already in the early tradition of Scripture interpretation Shem was understood to be a Priest, justifying the depiction of his study house as temple. For example, the Targums all equate Shem with Melchizedek.[261] This tradition must have been widespread, as is shown e.g. by the Babylonian Talmud, Ned 32b, where it is said in the name of R. Yishmael (early second century CE): 'The Holy One, blessed be He, intended to bring forth the priesthood from Shem, as it is written, "And [Melchizedek] was the priest of the most high God" (Gen 14:18); in the event however God brought it forth from Abraham. There are yet other traditions that understand Shem as priest. According to other traditions, he offered the sacrifice following Noah's disembarkment from the Ark,[262] and Noah gave him the priestly vestments he had inherited from Adam.[263] Hence, the scene to Rebecca's left could depict Shem/Melchizedek, who learns from a servant that Rebecca has come and offered a prayer.

The Shem-Rebecca legend however was also known to the Church fathers, particularly the Syrian fathers,[264] as in the Syrian *Treasure Cave* 31:5f: 'When Isaac became sixty years old, Rebecca became pregnant with Jacob and Esau. In her birth pains, she went to Melchizedek, and he prayed over her...'. A similar Syrian text relates:

[259] Gutmann, 'Jewish Origin', 339f; Hempel, 'Problem', 105; idem, 'Jüdische Traditionen', 351.

[260] See also TgY and FrgTg to Gen 25:22; GenR 63,6 (p682f; Mirqin 3, p13); MidrGad Gen 25:22 (p435); MidrPs 9,7 (42b). In bMak 23b R. Eleazar (ben Pedat, 2nd half, 3d century) says that the Holy Spirit appeared in the judgement court of Shem.

[261] TgNeoph, TgY and FrgTg to Gen 14:18.

[262] GenR 30,6 to Gen 6:9 (p272; Mirqin 2, p11).

[263] NumR 4,8 (Mirqin 9, p72).

[264] Gutmann, 'Jewish Origin', 340; Ginzberg, *Haggada*, 118 cites among the Eastern Church fathers, Ephraim and Theodoret, and among the Western fathers, Jerome.

> 'So she went to inquire of the Lord' (Gen 25:22)... For this reason she went to a special place that had been set aside by them for the worship service. It seems that she inquired of a priest like Melchizedek, or another. There are those who say that she went to him [himself] for he was [yet] alive at that time. Rabban said there was another priest in Melchizedek's place and she inquired of him.[265]

Two possibilities confront us then: the model for the upper half of fol. 22v was either directly influenced from Rabbinic biblical interpretation and traditional legend, or it received its promptings indirectly via the Church fathers. Hence, this folio also allows no firm conclusion on whether its model arose in the Jewish or the Christian sphere.

These selected examples from the Ashburnham Pentateuch should demonstrate that for some depictions a very high degree of probability exists in favor of a Jewish picture model, whereas for others the evidence is inconclusive. Jews and Christians lived together in the geograpically constricted Syro-Babylonian region; thus, motifs which did not depict specifically Jewish themes may also have been known to Christians in oral tradition. But the possibility of such a transmission does not allow us to conclude that it actually occurred, not even in the case of thematic portrayals whose 'Sitz im Leben' is clearly Jewish-Rabbinic.

Concluding Remarks

In the first decades following the Second World War, art historians, cooperating with Rabbinic scholars or using midrashic texts in translation, discovered that illustrations in early Christian Bible manuscripts represent not only the biblical text, but also an interpretive tradition attested in Talmud and Midrash. The discoveries of mosaic pavements in Israel with figurative motifs, and above all, the frescos of the mid-third century synagogue at Dura Europos on the Euphrates, at first led to the conclusion that the early Christian illustrators used Jewish picture models, which, although no longer extant, could be reconstructed from iconographic peculiarities of early Christian and Byzantine book illumination.[266]

Initially, an illustrated Septuagint suggested itself as the most likely candidate, since it seemed the only credible source for influences on Byzantine book illumination. Support was sought in a fresco from Pompeii which supposedly represented the Judgement of Solomon.[267] Indeed, if it really is

[265] Levene, *Syrian Fathers*, 38, 96, 299f.

[266] Weitzmann, 'The Illustration'; id, 'Question'; Nordström, *Castilian Bible*; id, *Miniatures*; id, 'Temple Miniatures'; id, 'Water Miracles'; Pächt, 'Ephraimillustration'; Hempel, 'Problem'; Kraeling, *Synagogue*; Narkiss, *Golden Haggadah*; Revel-Neher, 'Présence juive'; id, 'Hashpaot yehudiot'; id, 'Codex amiatinus'; Sed Rajna, *Einleitung*.

[267] Narkiss, 'Elements', esp. 187f, correctly points out here that two assistant judges, in accordance with Rabbinic legal procedure, sit in attendance beside Solomon.

the Judgement of Solomon, this scene presupposes figurative depiction of biblical motifs at a very early period, already in the early first century CE if not earlier. This thesis met with contradiction. It was pointed out that the frescos in the synagogue at Dura Europos do not reflect the Alexandrian but the Palestinian tradition of biblical interpretation,[268] and that the cultural viability of Alexandrian Judaism was broken after the revolt of 115 CE.[269] The figurative depictions in the early Christian and Byzantine context also show indications of Rabbinic rather than Alexandrian exegesis.[270] It was further pointed out that motifs which are well-attested in the formation of Rabbinic tradition were also known in the Christian and Islamic spheres, and that such motifs need not necessarily have originated with a Jewish picture model, since their transmission might have been accomplished orally. A classic example is the motif of Abraham in Nimrod's furnace.[271]

Indeed, a countercurrent developed against the hypothesis of a widespread Jewish figurative art and in particular against an illustrated Septuagint originating in the Jewish sphere, whose motifs derived not from the Alexandrian, but from the Syro-Palestinian tradition of Scripture interpretation. It was maintained that Jewish picture models played virtually no role at all and that oral tradition alone can be considered.[272] The frescos of the mid-third century CE synagogue at Dura Europos and the numerous similarities between iconographic peculiarities in Dura Europos and the later Byzantine book illumination were not thought to be decisive.[273] This theory, even though it still continues to be vigorously defended,[274] lacks a persuasive foundation in the available material.[275] Of course, all motifs known both to the Rabbis and the Church fathers must not necessarily derive from Jewish picture models.[276] However, it has been demonstrated in the preceding chapters that motifs also exist whose 'Sitz im Leben' is exlusively in Rabbinic exegesis, and thus were not adopted from the Patristic tradition. When such motifs can be established either in the Via Latina Catacomb or in early Christian manuscript illuminations, the conclusion seems unavoidable that Christians adopted these from Jewish picture models because of their visual appeal, and that they no longer understood the

[268] Gutmann, 'Early Synagogue'.

[269] K. Schubert, 'Problem', esp. 13.

[270] U. Schubert, *Spätantikes Judentum*.

[271] Gutmann, 'Abraham'.

[272] Strauss, *Kunst der Juden*; Stichel, *Namen*; Brandenburg, 'Überlegungen'; Brenk, *Mosaiken*; Gutmann, 'Early Synagogue'; Rickert, *Studien*. Tronzo, *Catacomb* is somewhat more careful in this regard.

[273] See latest comments by Weitzmann-Kessler, *Frescos*.

[274] Gutmann, 'Early Synagogue'; id, 'Dura Europos Synagogue Paintings'.

[275] Cf my reviews to Strauss and Stichel, above n98.

[276] For motifs attested not only in Rabbinic literature but also in Church Fathers and OT Apocrypha, we have on principle reckoned with the possibility of oral mediation, even though this is not very probable, given the abundance of Rabbinic material.

original Jewish sense of the pictures. At the latest then, we must reckon with Jewish picture models of whatever type from the beginning of the third century CE, which could have then influenced Christian illustrators. This does not exclude the possibility, however, that the odd Jewish motif owed its use in the Christian context to an oral tradition.

In summation, it can be stated that: 1) Rabbinic motifs that contradict Christian theology cannot have been transmitted orally. 2) Motifs in Christian manuscripts, whose iconographic peculiarities are traceable to the models in the frescos of Dura Europos – models which do not come from Alexandria, but from the region between Antioch on the Orontes and Seleucia-Ctesiphon – originate in Jewish picture models.[277]

[277] Weitzmann-Kessler, *Frescos*.

Abbreviations

Abbreviations of Rabbinic and other sources are given at the beginning of the source indexes.

ABull	The Art Bulletin
ALGHJ	Arbeiten zur Literatur und Geschichte des hellenistischen Judentums
ANRW	Aufstieg und Niedergang der römischen Welt, eds W. Haase – H. Temporini
AuC	Antike und Christentum
AusBR	Australian Biblical Review
BA	Bibliothèque de l'Arsenal, Paris
BASOR	Bulletin of the American Schools of Oriental Research
BJRL	Bulletin of the John Rylands Library
BM	British Museum, London
BN	Bibliothèque Nationale, Paris
BR	Bibliothèque Royale, Brussels
BuL	Bibel und Liturgie
ByZ	Byzantinische Zeitschrift
CCL	Corpus Christianorum, Series latina
CF	Classical Folia (New York)
CII	Frey, Corpus Inscriptionum Iudaicarum
ClassQ	Classical Quarterly
Compendia	Compendia rerum judaicarum ad Novum Testamentum, Section I, vols 1-2; Section II, vols 1-3; Section III, vol 1-
CrSt	Cristianesimo nella storia
CSEL	Corpus scriptorum ecclesiasticorum latinorum
EJ	Encyclopaedia Judaica
ET	English translation
EvTh	Evangelische Theologie
FS	Festschrift
GLAJJ	Stern, Greek and Latin Authors on Jews and Judaism
Hell	Hellenika (Thessalonike)
HistTheor	History and Theory

HTR	Harvard Theological Review
HUCA	Hebrew Union College Annual
IEJ	Israel Exploration Journal
ISSQ	Indiana Social Studies Quarterly
JANES	Journal of the Near Eastern Society
JAuC	Jahrbuch für Antike und Christentum
JAOS	Journal of the American Oriental Society
JEH	Journal of Ecclesiastical History
JJA	Journal of Jewish Art
JJS	Journal of Jewish Studies
JQR	Jewish Quarterly Review
JSHRZ	Jüdische Schriften aus hellenistisch-römischer Zeit
JSNT	Journal for the Study of the New Testament
JSemS	Journal of Semitic Studies
LQR	Law Quarterly Review
MMW	Museum Meermanno-Westreenianum, the Hague
NTS	New Testament Studies
OLZ	Orientalische Literaturzeitung
ÖN	Österreichische Nationalbibliothek
OTP	Charlesworth, Old Testament Pseudepigra
PAAJR	Proceedings of the American Academy for Jewish Research
PEQ	Palestine Exploration Quarterly
PG	J.P. Migne, Patrologia graeca
PIASH	Proceedings, Israel Academy of Sciences and Humanities
PL	J.P. Migne, Patrologia latina
PW	Pauly-Wissowa, Realencyklopädie der classischen Altertumswissenschaft
PWCJS	Proceedings of the World Congress of Jewish Studies (Jerusalem)
RA	Revue archéologique
RB	Revue biblique
RBen	Revue bénédictine
RBPh	Revue belge de philologie et d'histoire
REG	Revue des études grècques
RHE	Revue d'histoire ecclésiastique
RIL	Rendiconti dell'Istituto Lombardo, Classe di Lettere, Scienze morali e storiche
RM	Revue Mabillon
RSC	Rivista di studi classici
RSR	Revue des sciences religieuses
SB	Staatsbibliothek
SBB	Studies in Bibliography and Booklore

SC	Sources chrétiennes
TDNT	Kittel-Friedrich, Theological Dictionary of the New Testament
ThViat	Theologia viatorum
TLZ	Theologische Literaturzeitung
TQS	Theologische Quartalschrift
TRE	Theologische Realenzyklopädie
TSK	Theologische Studien und Kritiken
TWNT	Theologisches Wörterbuch zum Neuen Testament (eds Kittel-Friedrich)
ZKG	Zeitschrift für Kunstgeschichte
ZNW	Zeitschrift für die neutestamentliche Wissenschaft und die Kunde der älteren Kirche
ZRRG	Zeitschrift für Religions- und Geistesgeschichte
ZWT	Zeitschrift für wissenschaftliche Theologie

Cumulative Bibliography

Works by the same author(s) are arranged alphabetically by first noun. If involved in various functions, a person's name appears in the following order: single author, co-author, editor, co-editor. Greek and Hebrew types in titles of books and articles are transliterated.

ALLEN, P. 'An Early Epitomator of Josephus, Eustathius of Epiphaneia'. *ByZ* 81 (1988) 1-11

ALTANER, B. 'Augustinus und die griechische Patristik'. *RBen* 62 (1952) 201-215

AMARU, B.H. 'Land Theology in Josephus' Jewish Antiquities'. *JQR* 71 (1981) 201-29

AMIR, Y. 'Die Begegnung des biblischen und des philosophischen Monotheismus als Grundthema des jüdischen Hellenismus'. *EvTh* 38 (1979) 2-19

– 'Monotheistische Korrekturen heidnischer Texte', in Koch-Lichtenberger, *Begegnung*

– '*Theokratia* as a Concept of Political Philosophy', in *Scripta classica israelitica* 8-9 (1989) 83-105

ARING, P.G. *Christen und Juden heute – und die 'Judenmission'. Geschichte und Theologie der protestantischen Judenmission in Deutschland*. Frankfurt 1987

ARMSTRONG, A.H. 'The Self-Definition of Christianity in Relation to Later Platonism', in Sanders, *Self-Definition* 1, 74-99

ARTZ, F.B. *The Mind of the Middle Ages. A.D. 200-1500. An Historical Survey*. Chicago 1980

ATTRIDGE, H.W. 'Josephus and His Works', in *Compendia* II/2, 185-232

BAILEY, J.L. 'Josephus' Portrayal of the Matriarchs', in Feldman-Hata, *Josephus*, 154-79

BARAS, Z. 'The "Testimonium Flavianum" and the Martyrdom of James', in Feldman-Hata, *Josephus*, 338-48

BARDENHEWER, O. *Geschichte der altkirchlichen Literatur* 1-5. Freiburg 1913-32

BARDY, G. 'Le souvenir de Josèphe chez les Pères'. *RHE* 43 (1948) 179-91

BARNES, T.D. *Constantine and Eusebius*. Cambridge (Mass) 1981

BARNETT, P.W. 'The Jewish Sign Prophets – A.D. 40-70 – Their Intentions and Origins'. *NTS* 27 (1981) 679-97

BASNAGE, J. *La Republique des Hébreux*. Amsterdam 1713

BASSER, H. 'Josephus as Exegete'. *JAOS* 107 (1987) 21-30

BAUER, W. *Griechisch-deutsches Wörterbuch zu den Schriften des Neuen Testaments und der frühchristlichen Literatur*. Berlin 1988

BAUMBACH, G. 'Bemerkungen zum Freiheitsverständnis der zelotischen Bewegung'. *TLZ* 92 (1967) 257-258

– *Jesus von Nazareth im Lichte der jüdischen Gruppenbildung*. Berlin 1971

– 'Das Sadduzäerverständnis bei Josephus Flavius und im Neuen Testament'. *Kairos* 13 (1971) 17-37

– '"Volk Gottes" im Frühjudentum'. *Kairos* 21 (1979) 30-47

BAUMGARTEN, A.I. 'Josephus and Hippolytus on the Pharisees'. *HUCA* 55 (1984) 1-25

BECKER, A. *Franks Casket. Zu den Bildern und Inschriften des Runenkästchens von Auzon*. Frankfurt 1973

BEDJAN, P. (ed) *Homiliae selectae Mar-Jacobi Sarugensis* 1-5. Paris/Leipzig 1905-10

BEIN, A. *Die Judenfrage. Biographie eines Weltproblems* 1-2. Stuttgart 1980

BELL, A.A. *An Historiographical Analysis of the "De excidio Hierosolymitano" of Pseudo-Hegesippus* (diss Univ of N. Carolina at Chapel Hill) 1977

– 'Classical and Christian Traditions in the Work of Pseudo-Hegesippus'. *ISSQ* 33 (1980) 60-64

– 'Josephus and Pseudo-Hegesippus', in Feldman-Hata, *Josephus*, 349-61

BELSER, 'Lukas und Josephus'. *TQS* 77 (1895) 634-62; 78 (1896) 1-78

BERGER, K. 'Hellenistisch-heidnische Prodigien und die Vorzeichen in der jüdischen und christlichen Apokalyptik', in *ANRW* II/23.2, 1428-1469

BERGGREN, J. *Bibel und Josephus über Jerusalem und das Heilige Grab*. Lund 1862

BERNARDI, J. 'De quelques sémitismes de Flavius Josèphe'. *REG* 100 (1987) 18-29

BIENERT, W.A. 'Das Zeugnis des Josephus', in W. Schneemelcher, *Neutestamentliche Apokryphen* 1: *Evangelien*. 5th ed Tübingen 1987, 387-9

BILDE, P. *Flavius Josephus between Jerusalem and Rome. His Life, His Works and Their Importance*. Sheffield 1988

BIRDSALL, J.N. 'The Continuing Enigma of Josephus's Testimony about Jesus'. *BJRL* 67 (1985) 609-22

BJERKELUND, C. *PARAKALÔ. Form, Funktion und Sinn der parakalô-Sätze in den paulinischen Briefen*. Oslo 1967

BLATT, F. (ed) *The Latin Josephus* 1: *Introduction and Text. The Antiquities: Books I-V*. Aarhus 1958

BLAU, L. 'Early Christian Archaeology from the Jewish Point of View'. *HUCA* 3 (1926) 157-214

BLUMENKRANZ, B. *Juden und Judentum in der mittelalterlichen Kunst*. Stuttgart 1965

BOLGAR, R.R. (ed) *Classical Influences on European Culture A.D. 500-1500. Proceedings of an International Conference Held at King's College, Cambridge, April 1969*. Cambridge 1971-76

BOMSTAD, R.G. *Governing Ideas of the Jewish War of Flavius Josephus* (diss Yale Univ) New Haven 1979

BOWMAN, S. 'Josephus in Byzantium', in Feldman-Hata, *Josephus*, 362-85

BOYSEN, C. (ed) *Flavii Josephi opera ex versione latina antiqua* 6: *De Judaeorum vetustate sive contra Apionem libri II* (CSEL 37) Vienna 1898

BRANDENBURG, H. 'Überlegungen zum Ursprung der frühchristlichen Bildkunst', in *Atti del IX Congresso Internazionale di Archaeologia Christiana, Roma 1975* 1. Citta del Vaticano 1978, 331-

BRENK, B. *Die frühchristlichen Mosaiken in S. Maria Maggiore in Rom*. Wiesbaden 1975

BRUCE, F.F. 'Tacitus on Jewish History'. *JJS* 29 (1984) 33-44

BUBERL, P. *Die byzantinischen Handschriften: Der Wiener Dioskurides und die Wiener Genesis*. Leipzig 1937

– *Die illuminierten Handschriften in Steiermark* 1: *Die Stiftsbibliothek zu Admont und Vorau*. Leipzig 1911

BURCHARD, C. 'Die Essener bei Hippolyt. Hippolyt, Ref. IX 18, 2-28, 2 und Josephus, Bell. 2, 119-161'. *JSemS* 8 (1977) 1-41

BUTCHER, S.H. (ed) *Demosthenes orationes* 1. Oxford 1955

BYATT, A. 'Josephus and Population Numbers in First Century Palestine'. *PEQ* 105 (1973) 51-60

BYVANCK, S.W. *La miniature dans les Pays-Bas septentrionaux*. Paris 1937

CALLU, J.P. 'Le De Bello Judaico du Pseudo-Hégésippe. Essai de datation', in J. Straub (ed) *Bonner Historia-Augusta- Colloquium 1984/1985*. Bonn 1987, 111-142

CAMPENHAUSEN, H. von, 'Die Entstehung der Heilsgeschichte. Der Aufbau des christlichen Geschichtsbildes in der Theologie des ersten und zweiten Jahrhunderts'. *Saeculum* 21 (1970) 189-212

CASSIDY, R.J. *Society and Politics in the Acts of the Apostles*. New York 1987

CASTELLIO, S. (ed) *Biblia sacra... et inde ad Christum ex Josepho... eiusdem delineatio reipublicae Judaicae ex Josepho*. Basle 1556

CATALOGUS *Noordnederlandse Miniaturen*. Catalogue, Brussels 1971

CERIANI, A.M. (ed) *Translatio Syra Pescitto Veteris Testamenti* 1-2. Milan 1876-83

CHAPEAUROUGE, D. de, *Einführung in die Geschichte der christlichen Symbole*. Darmstadt 1987

CHARLESWORTH, J.H. (ed) *The Old Testament Pseudepigrapha* 1-2. London 1983-85

COHEN, S.J.D. *From the Maccabees to the Mishnah*. Philadelphia 1987

– 'History and Historiography in the "Against Apion" of Josephus', in *Essays in Jewish Historiography* (HistTheor Supp 27) Middletown (Conn) 1988, 1-11

– *Josephus in Galilee and Rome. His Vita and His Development as a Historian*. Leiden 1979

– 'Josephus, Jeremiah, and Polybius'. *HistTheor* 21 (1982) 366-81

– 'Parallel Historical Tradition in Josephus and Rabbinic Literature'. *PWCJS* 9, B/1 (1986) 7-14

CONZELMANN, H. *Die Mitte der Zeit. Studien zur Theologie des Lukas*. Tübingen 1964

– *Heiden – Juden – Christen. Auseinandersetzungen in der Literatur der hellenistisch-römischen Zeit*. Tübingen 1981

CORNFELD, G. *Daniel to Paul*. Tel Aviv 1962

COWLEY, A. *Aramaic Papyri of the Fifth Century B.C.* Oxford 1923

DALMAN, G. *Der leidende und sterbende Messias der Synagoge im ersten nachchristlichen Jahrtausend*. Berlin 1888

DANBY, H. *The Mishnah. Translated from the Hebrew, etc*. Oxford 1933, repr 1967

DAMMERTZ, D.V. *et al.*, *Benedictus. Eine Kulturgeschichte des Abendlandes*. Geneva 1980

DANIEL, J.L. *Apologetics in Josephus* (diss Rutgers Univ) New Brunswick 1981.

DAUBE, D. 'Three Legal Notes on Josephus After his Surrender'. *LQR* 93 (1977) 191-194

DELLING, G. 'Zum Corpus Hellenisticum Novi Testamenti'. *ZNW* 54 (1963) 1-15

– 'Josephus und die heidnischen Religionen'. *Klio* 43-45 (1965) 263-9

DEUTSCH, G.N. *Iconographie de l'illustration de Flavius Josèphe au temps de Jean Fouquet* (ALGHJ 12) Leiden 1986

– 'The Illustration of Josephus' Manuscripts', in Feldman-Hata, *Josephus*, 398-410

– 'The Myth of Maria Of Azov'. *Zemanim* 4 (1984) 21-28 (Hebr)

– 'Un portrait de Josèphe dans un manuscrit occidental du IXe siécle'. *Revue de l'art* 53 (1981) 53-55

DEXINGER, F. 'Ein "messianisches Szenarium" als Gemeingut des Judentums in nachherodianischer Zeit?' *Kairos* 17 (1975) 249-78

DIETZFELBINGER, C. (ed) *Pseudo-Philo; Antiquitates biblice* (JSHRZ II/2) Tübingen 1975

DÖLGER, F. 'Der Durchzug durch das Rote Meer als Sinnbild der christlichen Taufe'. *AuC* 2 (1930) 63-

DOWNING, F.G. 'Common Ground with Paganism in Luke and Josephus'. *NTS* 28 (1982) 546-59

– 'Redaction Criticism: Josephus' Antiquities and the Synoptic Gospels'. *JSNT* 8 (1980) 46-65; 9 (1980) 29-48

DUBY, G. *Die Kunst des Mittelalters* 1. *Das Europa der Mönche und Ritter 980-1140*. Stuttgart 1984

DURLIAT, M. *Romanische Kunst*. Freiburg 1983

EEFFENBERGER, A. *Frühchristliche Kunst und Kultur; von den Anfängen bis zum 7. Jahrhundert*. Leipzig, 1986

EHRENSTEIN, T. *Das Alte Testament im Bilde*. Vienna 1923

EISLER, R. *Iêsous basileus ou basileusas* 1-2. Heidelberg 1929-30

EPSTEIN, I. (ed, trans) *The Babylonian Talmud* 1-18. London 1952-61

FAIDER, P. 'Un manuscrit de la versio antiqua de Flavius Josèphe conservé à la bibliothèque de Mons'. *RBPh* 7 (1928) 141-4

FELDMAN, L.H. 'Flavius Josephus Revisited: the Man, his Writings, and his Significance', in *ANRW* II/21.2, 763-862

– 'Hellenizations in Josephus' "Jewish Antiquities": The Portrait of Abraham', in Feldman-Hata, *Josephus*, 133-53
– *Josephus and Modern Scholarship (1937-1980)*. Berlin 1984
– *Josephus. A Supplementary Bibliography*. New York 1986
– 'Josephus' Portrait of Noah and its Parallels in Philo, Pseudophilo's "Biblical Antiquities", and Rabbinic Midrashim'. *PAAJR* 55 (1988) 31-57
– 'Postscript to: Josephus and Modern Scholarship (1937-1980)', in *ANRW* II/20.2, 1298-1304
– *Studies in Judaica. Scholarship on Philo and Josephus (1937-62)*. New York 1963
– 'Use, Authority and Exegesis of Mikra in the Writings of Josephus', in *Compendia* II/1, 455-518
FELDMAN, L.H. (ed, trans) *Josephus* 9: *Antiquities. Books XVIII-XX*. Cambridge (Mass) 1965
FELDMAN, L.H. – HATA, G. (eds) *Josephus, Judaism, and Christianity*. Detroit 1987
FERGUSON, C. *et al.*, *Medieval and Renaissance Miniatures from the National Gallery of Art* [exhibit catalogue]. Ed by G. Vikan. Washington (DC) 1975
FERRUA, A. *Le pitture della nuova catacomba di Via Latina*. Citta del Vaticano 1960
FILLITZ, H. 'Die Wiener Genesis – Resumé der Diskussion', in *Beiträge zur Kunstgeschichte und Archäologie des Frühmittelalters – Akten zum VII. internationalen Kongreß für Frühmittelalterforschung, Sept. 1958*. Graz/Köln 1962, 44-48
FINK, J. *Bildfrömmigkeit und Bekenntnis*. Köln 1978
FLEISCHER, E. *Eretz-Israel Prayer and Prayer Rituals as Portrayed in the Geniza Documents*. Jerusalem 1988 (Hebr)
– *On the Antiquity of the Qedusha: a Publication of a Pre-Yannaic Poetic Cycle* (Hasifrut) Tel Aviv 1970
FLUSSER, D. 'Der Bericht des Josephus über Jesus', in id, *Entdeckungen im Neuen Testament* 1. Neukirchen 1987, 216-26
– *The Josippon [Josephus Gorionides]; Edited with an Introduction, Commentary and Notes* 1-2. Jerusalem 1978-80
– 'Josippon, a Medieval Hebrew version of Josephus', in Feldman-Hata, *Josephus*, 386-97
– *Judaism and the Origins of Christianity*. Jerusalem 1988
– 'Der lateinische Josephus und der hebräische Josippon', in *Josephus-Studien* (FS O. Michel) Göttingen 1974, 122-32
FORESTI, F. 'Gesù e i Galilei. Focalizzazione di alcune caratteristiche del giudaismo galilaico'. *Teresianum* 36 (1985) 485-96
FORNARO, P. 'Il cristianesimo oggetto di polemica indiretta in Flavio Giuseppe (Ant. Jud. IV, 326)'. *RSC* 27 (1979) 431-46
FREY, J.B. 'Les juifs à Pompei'. *RB* 42 (1933) 365-83
– *Corpus Inscriptionum Judaicarum* 1. Citta del Vaticano 1936
GADAMER, H.-G. *Gesammelte Werke*. Tübingen 1986-
– *Kleine Schriften* 1-4. Tübingen 1967-77
– *Wahrheit und Methode*. Tübingen 1986
GASPAR, C. – LYNA, F. *Les principaux manuscrits à peinture de la Bibliothèque Royale de Belgique* 1-2. Brussels 1984
GEBHARDT, O. von, *The Miniatures of the Ashburnham Pentateuch*. London 1883.
GERSTINGER, H. *Die Wiener Genesis*. Vienna 1931
GIBLIN, C.H. *The Destruction of Jerusalem According to Luke's Gospel: A Historical-Typological Moral*. Rome 1985
GIDAL, N.T. *Die Juden in Deutschland*. Gütersloh 1988
GIET, S. 'La "Guerre des Juifs" de Flavius Josèphe et quelques énigmes de l'Apocalypse'. *RSR* 26 (1952) 1-29
– 'Les épisodes de la Guerre Juive et l'Apocalypse'. *RSR* 26 (1952) 325-62
GINZBERG, L. *Die Haggada bei den Kirchenvätern*. Berlin 1900
– *The Legends of the Jews* 1-7. Philadelphia 1910-38
GÖDEKE, M. *Geschichte als Mythos. Eusebs Kirchengeschichte*. Frankfurt 1987

GOFF, F.R. 'Antoine Vérard and his Woodcut of Jerusalem', in *Gutenberg-Jahrbuch* 1973, 344-50
GOLDENBERG, D. *The Halakhah in Josephus and in Tannaitic Literature. A Comparative Study* (diss Dropsie Univ) Philadelphia 1978
GOLDBERG, A. *Untersuchungen über die Vorstellung von der Schekhina in der frühen rabbinischen Literatur*. Berlin 1969
GOODENOUGH, E.R. *An Introduction to Philo Judaeus*. Oxford 1962
– *Jewish Symbols in the Greco-Roman Period* 1-13. New York 1953-68
GOSSMANN, H.-C. 'Die Möglichkeit der literarischen Abhängigkeit des Josephus von Ovid. Dargestellt am Beispiel der Sintfluterzählung'. *ZRGG* 41 (1989) 83-86
GRANT, M. *Morgen des Mittelalters*. Bergisch-Gladbach 1982
GRANT, R.M. *Eusebius as Church Historian*. Oxford 1980
GREEN, R. *et al.* (eds) *Herrad of Hohenbourg. Hortus deliciarum* 1-2. Leiden 1979
GRIMM, W. [Review to] 'M. Bachmann, Jerusalem und der Tempel', *TLZ* 107 (1982) 275-7
GRINFIELD, E. *Scholia hellenistica in Novum Testamentum Philone et Josepho patribus apostolicis aliisque ecclesiae antiquae scriptoribus necnon libris apocryphis maxime deprompta* 1-2. London 1848
GRUENWALD, I. *Apocalyptic and Merkavah Mysticism*. Leiden 1980
– *From Apocalypticism to Gnosticism*. Frankfurt/M 1988
GUEVARA, H. *La resistencia judía contra Roma en la epoca de Jesús* (diss Rome) Meitingen 1981
GUTBROD, J. *Die Initiale in Handschriften des achten bis dreizehnten Jahrhunderts*. Stuttgart 1965
GUTMANN, J. 'Abraham in the Fire of the Chaldaeans: a Jewish Legend in Jewish, Christian and Islamic Art'. *Frühmittelalterliche Studien* 7 (1973) 342-52
– 'The Dura Europos Paintings: The State of Research', in Levine, *Synagogue*, 61-72
– 'The Dura Europos Synagogue Paintings and their Influence on Later Christian and Jewish Art'. *Artibus et Historiae* 17 (1988) 25-29
– 'Early Synagogue and Jewish Catacomb Art and its Relation to Christian Arts', in *ANRW* II/21.2, 1313-42
– 'The Jewish Origin of the Ashburnham Pentateuch Miniatures', in Gutmann, *No Graven Images*, 329-46
– 'Joseph Legends in the Vienna Genesis'. *PWCJS* 5/4 (1973) 181-4
– 'Josephus' Jewish Antiquities in Twelfth-Century Art: Renovatio or Creatio?' *ZKG* 48 (1985) 434-41
– 'Programmatic Painting in the Dura Synagogue', in id (ed) *The Dura Europos Synagogue: A Re-evaluation (1932-1972)*. Missoula 1973, 137-54
– 'The Second Commandment and the Image'. *HUCA* 32 (1961) 161-74 (repr in id, *No Graven images*)
– 'Was There a Biblical Art at Pompeji?' *Antike Kunst* 15 (1972) 122-4
GUTMANN, J. (ed) *No Graven Images*. New York 1971
– *The Synagogue. Studies in Origin, Archaeology and Architecture*. New York 1975
HAASE, W. (ed) *Hellenistisches Judentum in römischer Zeit: Philon und Josephus* (ANRW II/21.1) Berlin 1984
HACHLILI, R. 'The Zodiac in Ancient Jewish Art: Representation and Significance'. *BASOR* 228 (1977) 61-77
HARDWICK, M.E. *Josephus as a Historical Source in Patristic Literature through Eusebius* (diss Hebrew Union Coll) Cincinnati 1987.
HARNACK, A. *Geschichte der altchristlichen Literatur* 1-3. Leipzig 1893-1904
HARTER, W.H. *The Causes and the Course of the Jewish Revolt Against Rome, 66-74 C.E., in Recent Scholarship* (diss Union Theol Sem) New York 1982
HATA, G. 'Is the Greek Version of Josephus' "Jewish War" a Translation or a Rewriting of the First Version?' *JQR* 66 (1975) 89-108

HAUSSHERR, R. 'Templum Salomonis und Ecclesia Christi. Zu einem Bildervergleich der Bible moralisée'. *ZKG* 31 (1968) 101-121

HEINEMANN, I. 'Die Allegoristik der hellenistischen Juden außer Philon'. *Mnemosyne* 5 (1952) 130-38

– 'Josephus' Method in the Presentation of Jewish Antiquities'. *Zion* 5 (1940) 180-203

– *Philons griechische und jüdische Bildung*. Breslau 1932

HEINEMANN, J. *Studies in Jewish Liturgy*. Jerusalem 1981 (Hebr)

HEINISCH, P. *Der Einfluß Philos auf die älteste christliche Exegese*. Münster 1908

HELM, R. (ed) *Fulgentius Fabius Planciades. De aetatibus mundi et hominis*. Leipzig 1898

HEMPEL, H. 'Jüdische Traditionen in früchristlichen Miniaturen', in Gutmann, *No Graven Images*, 347-61

– 'Zum Problem der Anfänge der AT Illustration', in Gutmann, *No Graven Images*, 81-113

HENGEL, M. 'Die Hellenisierung des antiken Judentums als *praeparatio evangelica*'. *Humanistische Bildung* 4 (1981) 1-30

– *Judentum und Hellenismus*. 3rd ed Tübingen 1988

– 'Proseuche und Synagoge', in Gutmann, *Synagogue*, 27-54

– 'Die Synagogeninschrift von Stobi', in Gutmann, *Synagogue*, 110-48

– *Zur urchristlichen Geschichtsschreibung*. Stuttgart 1984 (ET, J. Bowden, *Acts and the History of Earliest Christianity*, Philadelphia 1980)

– *The Zealots. Investigations into the Jewish Freedom Movement in the Period from Herod I until 70 A.D.* Edinburgh 1989

HÉRENGER, A. 'Flavius Josèphe et la littérature évangélique'. *Revue juive de Genève* 2 (1934) 321-30

HOBSON, A. *Große Bibliotheken der Alten und der Neuen Welt*. München 1970

HOENIG, S.B. *The Great Sanhedrin*. Philadelphia 1953

HOFFMANN, K. *Die Ethik des jüdischen Geschichtsschreibers Flavius Josephus* (diss) Erlangen 1920

HÖLSCHER, G. 'Josephus', in *PW* 9 (1916) 1934-2000

HOMBURGER, O. *Die illustrierten Handschriften*. Bern 1962

HÜTTENMEISTER, F. – REEG, G. *Die antiken Synagogen in Israel*.Wiesbaden 1977

ISAAC, E. (trans.) '1 (Ethiopic Apocalypse of) Enoch', in Charlesworth, *OTP* 1, 5-89

JELLINEK, A. (ed) *Bet ha-Midrasch. Sammlung kleiner Midraschim und vermischter Abhandlungen aus der ältern jüdischen Literatur*. 3rd ed Jerusalem 1967

JOHNSON, M. 'Life of Adam and Eve', in Charlesworth (ed) *OTP* 2, 249-95

KAHLE, P. *The Cairo Geniza*. 2nd ed Oxford 1959

KALLANDER, D.C. *The Defense of Jerusalem in the Roman Siege of 70 C.E.: A Study of First Century Apocalyptic Ideas* (diss Miami Univ) 1980

KASTING, H. *Die Anfänge der urchristlichen Mission. Eine historische Untersuchung*. München 1969

KAUFMANN, C.M. *Romanesque Manuscripts 1066-1190*. London 1975

KEIL, H. (ed) *Grammatici Latini* 1-6. Leipzig 1855-74

KEIM, T. *Aus dem Urchristenthum*. Zürich 1878 [1-27: 'Josephus im Neuen Testament']

KELLER, H.L. *Reclams Lexikon der Heiligen und der biblischen Gestalten. Legende und Darstellung in der bildenden Kunst*. Stuttgart 1984

KITTEL, G. – FRIEDRICH, G. (eds) *Theologisches Wörterbuch zum Neuen Testament*. Stuttgart 1933-73

KLAUSNER, J. *Historia shel ha-bayit ha-sheni* 3. Jerusalem 1950

– *Ha-raayon ha-meshihi be-Yisrael*. Tel Aviv 1956

KLOTZ, A. (ed) *C. Iulii Caesaris Commentarii. Vol. 2. Commentarii Belli civilis*. Leipzig 1926

KNOPF, R. *et al.*, *Einführung in das Neue Testament*. Berlin 1949

KOCH, H. *Die Abfassungszeit des lukanischen Geschichtswerkes. Eine historisch-kritische und exegetische Untersuchung*. Leipzig 1911

KOCH, D.-A. – LICHTENBERGER, H. (eds) *Begegnung zwischen Christentum und Judentum in Antike und Mittelalter* (FS H. Schreckenberg) Göttingen 1991

KOELLNER, H. *Die illuminierten Handschriften der Hessischen Landesbibliothek Fulda* 1: *Handschriften des 6. bis 13. Jahrhunderts*. Stuttgart 1976

KOPIDAKES, M.Z. 'Josepos homerizôn'. *Hell* 37 (1986) 3-25

KORNFELD, W. *Onomastica Arameica aus Ägypten* (Österr. Akad. d. Wissenschaft. Phil. hist. Kl., Sitzungsberichte, Bd. 333) Vienna 1978

KÖTZSCHE-BREITENBRUCH, L. *Die neue Katakombe an der Via Latina in Rom*, in *JAuC* Suppl 4. Münster 1977

KRAABEL, A.T. 'The Diaspora Synagogue', in *ANRW* II/19.1, 477-510

KRAELING, C. *The Synagogue (The Excavations at Dura Europos, Final Report)* VIII, pt. I. New Haven 1956

KRENKEL, M. *Josephus und Lukas. Der schriftstellerische Einfluß des jüdischen Geschichtschreibers auf den christlichen nachgewiesen*. Leipzig 1894

KRETSCHMAR, G. 'Ein Beitrag zur Frage nach dem Verhältnis zwischen jüdischer und christlicher Kunst in der Antike', in *Abraham unser Vater* (FS O. Michel) Leiden 1963, 295-319

KUNZE, H. *Geschichte der Buchillustration in Deutschland. Das 15. Jahrhundert*. Stuttgart 1976

LADOUCEUR, D. *Studies in the Language and Historiography of Flavius Josephus* (diss Brown Univ) 1977

LAMPE, P. *Die stadtrömischen Christen in den ersten beiden Jahrhunderten. Untersuchungen zur Sozialgeschichte*. Tübingen 1987

LAQUEUR, R. *Der jüdische Historiker Flavius Josehus. Ein biographischer Versuch auf neuer quellenkritischer Grundlage*. Gießen 1920

LAUER, P. *Les enluminures romanes de la Bibliothèque Nationale*. Paris 1927

LEANY, A.R.C. *The Rule of Qumran and Its Meaning*. London 1966

LEGNER, G. *Deutsche Kunst der Romanik*. München 1982

LEIDINGER, G. *Minaturen aus Handschriften der Bayerischen Staatsbibliothek in München*. Heft 1: *Das sogenannte Evangeliarum Kaiser Otto III*. München 1912

LEUSDEN, J. *Philologus hebraeo-mixtus*. Utrecht 1682

LEVENE, A. *The Early Syrian Fathers on Genesis – from a Syrian Ms. on the Pentateuch in the Mingana Collection*. London 1951

LEVIN, M. 'Some Jewish Sources for the Vienna Genesis'. *ABull* 54 (1972) 241-4

LEVINE, L.I. (ed) *Ancient Synagogues Revealed*. Jerusalem 1981

– *The Synagogue in Late Antiquity*. Philadelphia, 1987

LEWIS, S. 'Tractatus adversus Judaeos in the Gulbenkian Apocalypse'. *ABull* 68 (1986) 543-66

LEWY, H. 'Josephus the Physician, a Medieval Legend of the Destruction of Jerusalem', in *Journal of the Warburg Institute* 1 (1937) 221-42

LICHTENBERGER, H. 'Paulus und Josephus in Rom', in Koch-Lichtenberger, *Begegnung*

LIEBERMAN, S. *Hellenism in Jewish Palestine*. New York 1962

LINDER, A. *The Jews in Roman Imperial Legislation*. Detroit 1987

LINDESKOG, G. *Das jüdisch-christliche Problem. Randglossen zu einer Forschungsepoche*. Uppsala 1986

MAIER, J. *Vom Kultus zur Gnosis – Bundeslade, Gottesthron und Merkabha*. Salzburg 1964

MALACHI, Z. *Studies in Medieval Hebrew Literature*. Tel Aviv 1971 (Hebr)

MANITIUS, M. *Handschriften antiker Autoren in mittelalterlichen Bibliothekskatalogen*. Leipzig 1935

MANTEL, H. *Studies in the History of the Sanhedrin*. Cambridge (Mass) 1961

MARCOVICH, M. (ed) *Hippolytus: Refutatio omnium haeresium*. Berlin 1986

MARTIN, H. *Le Boccace de Jean sans peur de cas des nobles hommes et femmes*. Brussels 1911

MARTIN, L.H. 'Josephus' Use of Heimarmene in the Jewish Antiquities XIII, 171-3'. *Numen* 28 (1981) 127-37

MASER, P. 'Irrwege ikonologischer Deutung? Zur Diskussion um die spätantik-jüdische Kunst'. *Rivista di Archaeologia Christiana* 56 (1980) 331-367

MASON, S.N. 'Was Josephus a Pharisee? A Re-examination of Life 10-12'. *JJS* 40 (1989) 31-45

MAYER, G. 'Josephus Flavius', in *TRE* 17, 258-64
MAZAL, O. *Buchkunst der Gotik*. Graz 1975
– *Buchkunst der Romanik*. Graz 1978
– *Kommentar zur Wiener Genesis, Faksimile Ausgabe des Codex theol.gr.31 der Österreichischen Nationalbibliothek in Wien*. Frankfurt a.M. 1980
MAZAR, B. 'The Tobiads'. *IEJ* 7 (1957) 137-45; 229-38
McCOWN, C. 'The Araq el-Emir and the Tobiads'. *BA* 20 (1957) 63-76
McNEILE, A. *An Introduction to the Study of the New Testament*. Oxford 1953
MEIER, J.P. 'Jesus in Josephus: A Modest Proposal'. *CBQ* 52 (1990) 76-103
MELLINKOFF, R. *The Horned Moses in Medieval Art and Thought*. Berkeley 1970
MELMOTH, W. (ed, trans) *Pliny. Letters* 1-2. London 1953
MENSINGA, J.A.M. 'Eine Eigenthümlichkeit des Marcusevangeliums'. *ZWT* (1889) 385-393
MEURGEY, J. *Les principaux manuscrits à peintures du Musée Condé à Chantilly*. Paris 1930
MICHAELSON, S. – MORTON, A.Q. 'The New Stylometrie: A One-Word Test of Authorship for Greek Writers'. *ClassQ* 22 (1972) 89-102
MICHEL, O. 'Die Rettung Israels und die Rolle Roms nach den Reden im "Bellum Judaicum"', in *ANRW* II/21.2, 949-76
– 'Spätjüdisches Prophetentum', in *Neutestamentliche Studien für Rudolf Bultmann*. Berlin 1954, 60-66
MICHEL, O. – BAUERNFEIND, O. (ed, trans) *Flavius Josephus, De Bello Judaico* 1-3. Darmstadt 1959-69
MIZUGAKI, W. 'Origen and Josephus', in Feldman-Hata, *Josephus*, 325-37
MOMIGLIANO, A. *Die Juden in der Alten Welt*. Berlin 1988
MUNDO, A. '"Bibliotheca". Bible et lecture du Carême d'après saint Benoît'. *RBen* 60 (1950) 65-92
MYNORS, R.A.B. (ed) *Cassiodori senatoris Institutiones*. Oxford 1961
NABER, S.A. (ed) *Flavii Josephi opera omnia* 1-6. Leipzig 1888-96
NARKISS, B. *The Golden Haggadah*. London 1970
– 'Pagan, Christian and Jewish Elements in the Art of Ancient Synagogues', in Levine, *Synagogue*, 183-8
NEUBAUER, A. *Medieval Jewish Chronicles*. Oxford 1887-95, repr Jerusalem 1967
NEUSNER, J. *A Life of Rabban Yohanan Ben Zakkai, Ca. 1-80 C.E.* Leiden (1962) 1970
– 'Rabbis and Community in Third Century Babylonia', in id (ed) *Religions in Antiquity; Essays in Memory of E.R. Goodenough*. Leiden 1968, 438-59
NICKELSBURG, G.W.E. 'Revealed Wisdom as a Criterion for Inclusion and Exclusion: From Jewish Sectarianism to Early Christianity', in J. Neusner et al. (eds) *To See Ourselves as Others See Us*. Chico 1985, 73-91
NIESE, B. (ed) *Flavii Josephi Antiquitatum Judaicarum Epitoma*. Berlin 1896
– (ed) *Flavii Josephi opera* [editio major] 1-7. Berlin 1885-95
– (ed) *Flavii Josephi opera recognovit* [editio minor] 1-6. Berlin 1888-95
NIKIPROWETZKY, V. 'La mort d'Éleazar fils de Jaïre et les courants apologétiques dans le "De Bello Judaico" de Flavius Josèphe', in *Hommages à André Dupont-Sommer*, Paris 1971, 461-90
NODET, E. 'Jesus et Jean-Baptiste selon Josèphe'. *RB* 92 (1985) 321-384; 497-525
NORDEN, E. *Agnostos Theos. Untersuchungen zur Formgeschichte religiöser Rede*. Darmstadt 1956.
– *Die antike Kunstprosa*. Darmstadt 1958
NORDSTRÖM, B.C. *The Duke of Alba's Castilian Bible*. Uppsala 1967
– 'Some Jewish Legends in Byzantine Art'. *Byzantion* 35-37 (1955-57) 487-508
– *Some Miniatures in the Hebrew Bible* (Synthronon) Paris 1968
– 'The Temple Miniatures in the Peter Comesta Manuscript at Madrid', in Gutmann, *No Graven Images*, 39-74
– 'The Water Miracles of Moses in Jewish Legend and Byzantine Art', in Gutmann, *No Graven Images*, 277-308

Omont, H. *Antiquités et Guerre des Juifs de Josèphe*. Paris 1906
O'Neill, J.C. 'The Silence of Jesus'. *NTS* 15 (1969) 153-67
Oepke, A. *Das neue Gottesvolk*. Gütersloh 1950
Ovadiah, A. 'The Synagogue at Gaza', in Levine, *Ancient Synagogues*, 129-32
Pächt, O. 'Ephraimillustration, Haggadah und Wiener Genesis', in Gutmann, *No Graven Images*, 249-60
Parente, F. 'Flavius Josephus' Account of the Anti-Roman Riots Preceding the 66-70 War, and its Relevance for the Reconstruction of Jewish Eschatology during the First Century A.D.' *JANES* 16-17 (1984-5 [1987]) 183-205
– 'L'episodio dell'Egiziano in Acta 21.38. Qualche osservazione sulla possibile dipendenza degl' Atti Apostoli da Flavio Giuseppe'. *RIL* 112 (1978) 360-76
Paton, W. *et al.* (eds) *Plutarch. Moralia* 3. Leipzig 1929
Paul, A. 'Flavius Josephus' Antiquities of the Jews – An Anti-Christian Manifesto'. *NTS* 31 (1985) 473-80
Pelletier, A. *Flavius Josèphe, adaptateur de la Lettre à Aristée. Une réaction atticisante contre la Koinè*. Paris 1962
– (ed, trans) *Flavius Josèphe, Autobiographie*. Paris 1959
– (ed, trans) *Josèphe, Guerre des Juifs* 1-3. Paris 1975-82
Philonenko, M. *Joseph et Aséneth*. Leiden 1968
Pines, S. *An Arabic Version of the Testimonium Flavianum and Its Implications* (PIASH) Jerusalem 1971
Plümacher, E. 'Bibliothekswesen'. *TRE* 6 (1980) 413-426
– 'Lukas als griechischer Historiker', in *PW* Suppl. 14, 235-64
– *Lukas als hellenistischer Schriftsteller. Studien zur Apostelgeschichte*. Göttingen 1972
– 'Neues Testament und hellenistische Form. Zur literarischen Gattung der lukanischen Schriften'. *ThViat* 14 (1977-8) 109-123
Pohlmann, K.-F. *Studien zum dritten Esra. Ein Beitrag zur Frage nach dem ursprünglichen Schluß des chronistischen Geschichtswerkes*. Göttingen 1970.
Porcher, J. *Französische Buchmalerei*. Recklinghausen 1959
Poetscher, W. 'Josephus Flavius, Antiquitates 18,63f.', in id, *Hellas und Rom*, Hildesheim 1988, 360-77
Pratscher, W. *Der Herrenbruder Jakobus und die Jakobustradition*. Göttingen 1987
Price, J.J. *Jerusalem Under Siege. An Internal History of the City During the Jewish Revolt, 66-70 C.E.* (diss Princeton Univ) Princeton 1987
Rajak, T. 'Josephus and the "Archaeology" of the Jews'. *JJS* 33 (1982) 465-477
– *Josephus. The Historian and His Society*. London 1983
Rappaport, S. *Agada und Exegese bei Flavius Josephus*. Vienna 1930
Reinach, T. *Textes d'auteurs grecs et romains relatifs au judaïsme* (repr) Hildesheim 1963
Reinach, T. et al. (eds, trans) *Oeuvres complètes de Flavius Josèphe* 1-7. Paris 1900-32
Renan, E. 'Les mosaïques de Hamman-Lif'. *RA* III/3 (1884) 273-5
Rengstorf, K.H. (ed) *A Complete Concordance to Flavius Josephus* 1-4. Leiden 1973-83
Revel, E. 'La contribution des textes rabbiniques à l'étude de la Genèse de Vienne'. *Byzantion* 42 (1972) 115-130
Revel-Neher, E. 'Du Codex amiatinus et ses rapports avec les plans du tabernacle dans l'art juif et dans l'art byzantin'. *JJA* 9 (1982) 6-17
– 'La présence juive dans l'iconographie paléo-chrétienne'. *L'arche* (1972) 51-55
– 'Hashpaot yehudiot ba-ikonografia ha-bizantit'. *Rimmonim* (1983) 44-51
Rhoads, D. *Some Jewish Revolutionaries in Palestine from 6 A.D. to 63 A.D. According to Josephus* (diss Duke Univ) Durham 1973
Ri, Su-Min (Andreas), 'Mosesmotive in den Fresken der Katakombe der Via Latina im Lichte der rabbinischen Tradition'. *Kairos* 17 (1975) 57-80
Richter, C.H. (ed) *Josephus Flavius, opera omnia* 1-6 (Bibliotheca Sacra Patrum Ecclesiae Graecorum. Pars I) Leipzig 1826-27

Rickert, F. *Studien zum Asburnham Pentateuch (Paris, Bibl. Nat. 2334)* (diss) Bonn 1986
Ring, G. *A Century of French Painting, 1400-1500*. London 1949
Rivkin, E. 'Defining the Pharisees: The Tannaitic Sources'. *HUCA* 40-41 (1969-70) 205-249
Robb, D.M. *The Art of the Illuminated Manuscript*. London 1973
Robert, L. *Nouvelles inscriptions de Sardes*. Paris 1964
Roos, A.G. 'Lesefrüchte'. *Mnemosyne* 2 (1935) 233-44
Roper, C.D. *Factors Contributing to the Origin and Success of the Pre-Christian Jewish Missionary Movement* (diss Univ of Michigan) 1988
Rowland, C. *Christian Origins. An Account of the Setting and Character of the Most Important Messianic Sect of Judaism*. London 1985
Sachau, E. *Aramäische Papyrus und Ostraka aus einer jüdischen Militärkolonie zu Elephantine*. Leipzig 1911
Sanders, E.P. (ed) *Jewish and Christian Self-Definition* 1-3. London 1980-82
Saulnier, C. 'Lois romaines sur les Juifs selon Flavius Josèphe'. *RB* 88 (1981) 161-98
Schäfer, P. *Der Bar Kokhba-Aufstand*. Tübingen 1981
– 'Die Flucht Jochanan b. Zakkais aus Jerusalem und die Gründung des "Lehrhauses" in Jabne', in *ANRW* II/19.2, 43-101
– *Hekhalot-Studien*. Tübingen 1988
Schalit, A. 'Die Erhebung Vespasians nach Flavius Josephus, Talmud und Midrasch. Zur Geschichte einer messianischen Prophetie', in *ANRW* II/2, 207-327
Schäublin, C. 'Josephus und die Griechen'. *Hermes* 110 (1982) 316-41
Schenk, W. 'Gefangenschaft und Tod des Täufers. Erwägungen zur Chronologie und ihren Konsequenzen'. *NTS* 29 (1983) 453-83
Schiller, G. *Ikonographie der christlichen Kunst* 1-4. Gütersloh 1966-80
Schlatter, A. *Das Evangelium des Lukas. Aus seinen Quellen erklärt*. Stuttgart 1960
– *Der Evangelist Johannes. Wie er spricht, denkt und glaubt. Ein Kommentar zum vierten Evangelium*. Stuttgart 1930
– *Der Evangelist Matthäus*. Stuttgart 1948
– *Der Glaube im Neuen Testament* (Stuttgart 1927) repr Darmstadt 1963
– *Wie sprach Josephus von Gott?* Gütersloh 1910
Scholem, G. *Jewish Gnosticism, Merkabah Mysticism and Talmudic Tradition*. New York 1960
– *Major Trends in Jewish Mysticism*. New York 1941
Schrage, W. 'Synagoge', in *TWNT* 7, 806-50
Schreckenberg, H. *Ananke. Untersuchungen zur Geschichte des Wortgebrauchs*. München 1964
– *Bibliographie zu Flavius Josephus*. Leiden 1968
– *Die christlichen Adversus-Judaeos-Texte und ihr literarisches und historisches Umfeld (1.-11. Jh.)* [1] Frankfurt 1982;
– *Die christlichen Adversus-Judaeos-Texte (11.-13. Jh.)* [2] Frankfurt 1988
– *Die Flavius-Josephus-Tradition in Antike und Mittelalter*. Leiden 1972.
– 'Die patristische Adversus-Judaeos-Thematik im Spiegel der karolingischen Kunst'. *Bijdragen* 49 (1988) 119-138
– 'Flavius Josephus und die lukanischen Schriften', in W. Haubeck – M. Bachmann (eds) *Wort in der Zeit* (FS K.H. Rengstorf) Leiden 1980, 179-209
– 'Josephus und die christliche Wirkungsgeschichte seines "Bellum Judaicum"', in *ANRW* II/21.2, 1106-1217
– 'Neue Beiträge zur Kritik des Josephustextes'. *Theokratia* 2 (1970-72) 81-106
– [Review of] 'Feldman, Josephus and Modern Scholarship'. *Gnomon* 57 (1985) 408-15
– *Rezeptionsgeschichtliche und textkritische Untersuchungen zu Flavius Josephus*. Leiden 1977
– *Supplementband mit Gesamtregister* to: *Bibliographie zu Flavius Josephus*. Leiden 1979
– 'The Works of Josephus and the Early Christian Church', in Feldman-Hata, *Josephus*, 315-24

– 'Vernunftlose Wesen? Zum Judenbild frühscholastischer Apologeten des 12. Jahrhunderts und zum Christentumsbild zeitgenössischer jüdischer Autoren', in P. Freimark – H. Richtering (eds) *Gedenkschrift B. Brilling*. Hamburg 1988, 14-74

SCHUBERT, K. 'Die Bedeutung des Bildes für die Ausstattung spätantiker Synagogen – dargestellt am Beispiel der Toraschreinnische der Synagoge von Dura Europos'. *Kairos* 17 (1975) 11-23

– 'Der Einfluß der rabbinischen Tradition auf einige Darstellungen in Codex 1164 des Historischen Jüdischen Instituts in Warschau', in id, *Bilder-Pentateuch*, 110-118

– 'Die Illustrationen in der Wiener Genesis im Lichte der rabbinischen Tradition'. *Kairos* 25 (1983) 1-17

– 'Israel im Altertum', in id, *Die Kultur der Juden* 1. Wiesbaden 1977, 223-44

– *Die jüdischen Religionsparteien in neutestamentlicher Zeit*. Stuttgart 1970

– 'Die jüdischen Religionsparteien im Zeitalter Jesu', in id, *Der historische Jesus und der Christus unseres Glaubens*. Vienna 1962, 15-101

– 'Die Miniaturen des Ashburnham Pentateuch im Lichte der rabbinischen Tradition'. *Kairos* 18 (1976) 191-212

– 'Das Problem der Entstehung einer jüdischen Kunst im Lichte der literarischen Quellen des Judentums'. *Kairos* 16 (1974) 1-13

– 'Sacra Sinagoga – zur Heiligkeit der Synagoge in der Spätantike'. *BuL* 54 (1981) 27-34

SCHUBERT, K. (ed) *Der Bilder-Pentateuch von Moses del Castellazzo*. Vienna 1986

SCHUBERT, K. – SCHUBERT, U. 'Marginalien zur "Sinai-Szene" in der Katakombe der Via Latina in Rom'. *Kairos* 17 (1975) 300-2

– 'Die Vertreibung aus dem Paradies in der Katakombe der Via Latina in Rom', in J. Neusner (ed) *Christianity, Judaism and other Greco-Roman Cults (Studies for Morton Smith at Sixty)* 2. Leiden 1975, 173-80

SCHUBERT, U. 'Einleitung', in K. Schubert, *Bilder-Pentateuch*, 7-42

– 'Eine jüdische Darstellungsweise der Wesensgegenwart Gottes auf christlichen Kunstwerken'. *BuL* 56 (1983) 24-28

– 'Eine jüdische Vorlage für die Darstellung der Erschaffung des Menschen in der sogenannten Cotton-Genesis-Rezension'. *Kairos* 17 (1975) 1-10

– *Spätantikes Judentum und frühchristliche Kunst* (Studia Judaica Austriaca 2) Vienna 1974

SCHULZ, S. 'Gottes Vorsehung bei Lukas'. *ZNW* 54 (1963) 104-116

SCHÜRER, E. 'Die archiereis im Neuen Testamente'. *TSK* (1872) 593-657

– *Geschichte des jüdischen Volkes im Zeitalter Jesu Christi* 1-3 (Leipzig 1901-11) repr Hildesheim 1964

SCHWARTZ, S. *Josephus and Judaism from 70 to 100 of the Common Era* (diss Columbia Univ) New York 1985

– 'The Composition and Publication of Josephus's Bellum Judaicum Book 7'. *HTR* 79 (1986) 373-86

SCHWABL, H. 'Notizen über das Volk der Juden und sein Gottesbild bei griechischen und römischen Autoren'. *Wiener Humanistische Blätter* 30 (1988) 1-15

SCHWIER, H. *Tempel und Tempelzerstörung. Untersuchungen zu den theologischen und ideologischen Faktoren im ersten jüdisch-römischen Krieg (66-74 n. Chr.)*. Göttingen 1989

SED RAJNA, G. *Einleitung zur Facsimile Ausgabe der Kaufmann Haggada*. Budapest 1990

SEEL, O. (ed) *C. Julii Caesaris Commentarii rerum gestarum* 1: *Bellum Gallicum*. Leipzig 1961

SEWEL, W. (trans.) *Alle de werken van Flavius Josephus*. Amsterdam 1722

SHUTT, R.J.H. 'The Concept of God in the Works of Flavius Josephus'. *JJS* 31 (1980) 171-89

SIMON, M(arcel), 'Remarques sur la catacombe de la Via Latina', in *JAuC* Suppl 1964 (FS Th. Klauser), 327-35

SIMON, M(arie), 'Entstehung und Inhalt der spätantiken trichotomischen Anthropologie'. *Kairos* 23 (1981) 43-50

SMALLWOOD, M. 'Jews and Romans in the Early Empire'. *History Today* 15 (1965) 232-9, 313-9

Smith, M. 'Palestinian Judaism in the First Century', in M. Davis (ed) *Israel: Its Role in Civilization*. New York 1956, 67-81

– 'The Occult in Josephus', in Feldman-Hata, *Josephus*, 236-56

Sokolová, J. *Le paysage dans la miniature française à l'époque gothique*. Prague 1937

Soltau, W. 'Petrusanekdoten und Petruslegenden in der Apostelgeschichte', in *FS Th. Nöldecke*. Gießen 1906, 805-815

Stanton, G.N. 'Aspects of Early Christian-Jewish Polemic and Apologetic', *NTS* 31 (1985) 377-92

Stechow, W. 'Jacob Blessing the Sons of Joseph – From Early Christian Times to Rembrandt', in Gutmann, *No Graven Images*, 261-76

Stemberger, G. 'Die Bedeutung des Tierkreises auf Mosaikfußböden spätantiker Synagogen'. *Kairos* 17 (1975) 25-56

– 'Hieronymus und die Juden seiner Zeit', in Koch-Lichtenberger, *Begegnung*

– 'Die Patriarchenbilder der Katakombe in der Via Latina im Lichte der jüdischen Tradition'. *Kairos* 16 (1974) 19-78

– *Pharisäer, Sadduzäer, Essener*. Stuttgart 1991

Stern, M. *Greek and Latin Authors on Jews and Judaism* 1-3. Jerusalem 1974-84

– 'Josephus and the Roman Empire as Reflected in the "The Jewish War"', in Feldman-Hata, *Josephus*, 71-80

Stichel, R. 'Außerkanonische Elemente in byzantinischen Illustrationen des Alten Testaments'. *Römische Quartalschrift* (1974) 159-181

– *Die Namen Noes, seines Bruders und seiner Frau. Ein Beitrag zum Nachleben jüdischer Überlieferungen in der außerkanonischen und gnostischen Literatur und in Denkmälern der Kunst* (Abh. Akad. d. Wissensch. Gött., Phil. hist. Kl., 3. Folge, 112) Göttingen 1979

Strack, H.L. – Stemberger, G. *Einleitung in Talmud und Midrasch*. 7th ed Munich 1982

Strauss, H. *Die Kunst der Juden im Wandel der Zeit und Umwelt*. Tübingen 1972

Suevia sacra. Frühe Kunst in Schwaben [Exhibit catalogue]. Augsburg 1973

Sukenik, E. *Ancient Synagogues in Palestine and Greece*. London 1934

Swarzenski, H. *The Berthold Missal* 1-2. New York 1943

Tcherikover, V. *Hellenistic Civilisation and the Jews*. Philadelphia 1959

Thackeray, H.S.J. *et al.* (eds, trans) *Josephus; With an English Translation* 1-9. London/Cambridge (Mass) 1926-65

Thoma, C. 'Die Weltanschauung des Josephus Flavius. Dargestellt anhand seiner Schilderung des jüdischen Aufstandes gegen Rom (66-73 n. Chr.)'. *Kairos* 11 (1969) 39-52

– 'Das jüdische Volk-Gottes-Verständnis zur Zeit Jesu', in *Theologische Berichte* 3. *Judentum und Kirche: Volk Gottes*. Zürich 1974, 93-117

Thomas, M. *Buchmalerei aus der Zeit des Jean de Berry*. München 1979

Tosato, A. 'La teocrazia nell'antico Israele'. *CrSt* 8 (1987) 1-50

Treu, K. 'Die Bedeutung des Griechischen für die Juden im römischen Reich'. *Kairos* 15 (1973) 123-44

Trocmé, E. 'The Beginnings of Christian Historiography and the History of Early Christianity'. *AusBR* 31 (1983) 1-13

Troiani, L. 'I lettori delle Antichità Giudaiche di Giuseppe: prospettive e problemi'. *Athenaeum* 64 (1986) 343-53

Tronzo, W. *The Via Latina Catacomb. Imitation and Discontinuity in Fourth Century Roman Painting*. Pennsylvania St. Univ. Press 1986

Unnik, W.C. van, *Flavius Josephus als historischer Schriftsteller*. Heidelberg 1978

Urbach, E.E. 'The Rabbinical Laws of Idolatry in the Second and Third Centuries in the Light of Archaeological and Historical Facts'. *IEJ* 9 (1959) 149-65; 229-45

– *The Sages: Their Concepts and Beliefs*. Jerusalem 1971 (Hebr); ET, vols 1-2, 2nd ed Jerusalem 1978

Ussani, V. (ed) *Hegesippi qui dicitur historiae libri V* 1-2 (CSEL 66) Vienna 1932-60

Vermes, G. 'The Jesus Notice of Josephus Re-Examined'. *JJS* 38 (1987) 1-10

VILLALBA I VARNEDA, P. *The Historical Method of Flavius Josephus*. Leiden 1986

VINCENT, A. *La religion des judéo-araméens d'Elephantine*. Paris 1937

VITUCCI, G. (ed, trans) *Flavio Giuseppe. La Guerra Giudaica* 1-2. Verona 1974

WALES, Gerald of, *Giruldi Cambrensis opera* 8. London 1891

WALLACE-HADRILL, S.D. 'Eusebius of Caesarea and the Testimonium Flavianum (Josephus' "Antiquities", XVIII, 63f.)'. *JEH* 25 (1974) 353-362

WALTHER, N. *Der Thoraausleger Aristobulos*. Berlin 1964

WATERMAN-ANTONY, E. *Romanesque Frescos*. Westport (Conn) 1951

WEBER, W. *Josephus und Vespasian. Untersuchungen zu dem jüdischen Krieg des Flavius Josephus*. Stuttgart 1921

WEILER, G. *Jewish Theocracy*. Leiden 1988

WEISS, H.-F. 'Pharisäismus und Hellenismus. Zur Darstellung des Judentums im Geschichtswerk des jüdischen Historikers Flavius Josephus'. *OLZ* 74 (1979) 421-433

WEITZMANN, K. 'Die Illustration der Septuaginta', in *Münchener Jahrbuch der bildenden Kunst* 3/4 (1952-3) 96-120

– 'The Illustration of the Septuagint', in Gutmann, *No Graven Images*. New York 1971, 201-31

– *Illustrations in Roll and Codex*. Princeton 1947.

– *The Miniatures of the Sacra Parallela, Parisinus graecus 923*. Princeton 1979

– 'The Question of the Influence of Jewish Pictorial Sources on Old Testament Illustration'. Gutmann, *No Graven Images*, 309-28

WEITZMANN, K. (ed) *Age of Spirituality. Late Antiquity and Early Christian Art, Third to Seventh Century*. New York 1977

WEITZMANN, K. – KESSLER, H. *The Cotton Genesis*. Princeton 1986

– *The Frescos of the Dura Synagogue and Christian Art*. Washington (DC) 1990

WENGST, K. *Pax Romana. Anspruch und Wirklichkeit. Erfahrungen und Wahrnehmungen des Friedens bei Jesus und im Urchristentum*. München 1986

WETSTEIN, J.J. (ed) *Hê Kainê Diathêkê. Novum Testamentum graecum... nec non commentario pleniore ex scriptoribus veteribus Hebraeis, Graecis et Latinis historiam et vim verborum illustrante* 1-2. Amsterdam 1751-52

WEYL, H. *Die jüdischen Strafgesetze bei Flavius Josephus in ihrem Verhältnis zu Schrift und Halacha*. Berlin 1900

WILLIAMS, C.S.C. *A Commentary on the Acts of the Apostles*. London 1957

WILLIAMS, D.S. *Josephus and the Authorship of IV Maccabees: A Critical Investigation* (diss Hebrew Union Coll) Cincinati 1988

WILLIAMSON, P. *An Introduction to Medieval Ivory Carvings*. London 1982

WILMART, A. 'Le couvent et la bibliothèque de Cluny vers le milieu du XIe siècle'. *RM* 11 (1921) 89-124

WILNAI, Z. *Madrikh Erets Yisrael*. Jerusalem 1952

WINDISCH, H. *Die Orakel des Hystaspes*. Amsterdam 1929

– 'Zum Corpus Hellenisticum'. *ZNW* 34 (1935) 124-5

WITTY, F.J. 'Book Terms in the Vivarium Translations'. *CF* 28 (1974) 62-82

WOLFSON, H.A. *Philo. Foundations of Religious Philosophy in Judaism, Christianity, and Islam* 1-2. Cambridge (Mass) 1948

WRIGHT, S.K. *The Vengeance of our Lord: The Destruction of Jerusalem and the Conversion of Rome in Medieval Drama* (diss Indiana Univ) 1984.

WUEST, F. 'La figure de Moïse comme préfiguration du Christ dans l'art paléo-chrétien', in *La Figure de Moïse* (Publ. de la Fac. de Théologie de l'Un. de Genève, 1) Geneva 1978, 109-27

YADIN, Y. *Masada*. London 1966

ZAFREN, H.C. 'Printed Rarities in the Hebrew Union College Library'. *SBB* 5 (1961) 137-156

ZEITLIN, S. 'A Survey of Jewish Historiography: From the Biblical Books to the "Sefer ha-Kabbalah" with Special Emphasis on Josephus'. *JQR* 59 (1969) 171-214; 60 (1969) 37-68; 375-406

– 'Who were the Galileans? New Light on Josephus' Activities in Galilee'. *JQR* 64 (1974) 189-203

Index of Sources

Unspecified references to ancient sources are not listed here but in the index of ancient literary and historical names.

This index does not include references to Josephus in Chapter Two of the Josephus part of the book, nor those to ancient Christian texts where these are thematic (Chapter Three). The same goes for works of art or sites in the second part of the book.

Division of sources:
1. Hebrew Bible.
2. Ancient Jewish Writings.
3. Early Christian Writings.
4. Rabbinic Literature.
5. Other Sources.

Abbreviations:
Names of biblical books, Apocrypha and Pseudepigraha, Josephus and Qumran are abbreviated largely following the JBL system. Philo's works are indicated with the abbreviations of the Loeb edition. For Rabbinic works see following list:

prefixed:

m	Mishna
t	Tosefta
y	Yerushalmi (Palestinian Talmud)
b	Bavli (Babylonian Talmud)

ARN a	Avot de-R. Natan version A (ed Schechter)
AZ	Avoda Zara
BB	Bava Batra
Ber	Berakhot
BM	Bava Metsia
CantR	Canticles Rabba
Er	Eruvin
FrgTg	Fragment Targum
GenR	Genesis Rabba (ed Theodor-Albeck)

Git	Gittin
Hag	Hagiga
Hul	Hullin
LevR	Leviticus Rabba (ed Margulies)
Mak	Makkot
Meg	Megilla
Mekh	Mekhilta de-R. Yishmael (ed Horovitz-Rabin)
MidrGad Gen	Midrash Gadol Genesis (ed Margulies)
MidrPs	Midrash on Psalms (ed Buber)
Ned	Nedarim
PdRE	Pirkei de-R. Eliezer (eds Luria; Friedlander)
PesR	Pesikta Rabbati (ed Friedmann)
RH	Rosh Hashana
San	SanhedrinShevu Shevuot
SifDeut	Sifrei Deuteronomy (ed Finkelstein)
SifNum	Sifrei Numbers (ed Horovitz)
Sot	Sota
Suk	Sukka
Tanh	Tanhuma
TanB	Tanhuma, ed Buber
TgNeoph	Targum Neophyti (ed Díez Macho)
TgY	Targum Pseudo-Yonathan (Yerushalmi)
YalkShim	Yalkut Shimoni (ed Hyman)
Yom	Yoma

1. Hebrew Bible

2. Ancient Jewish Writings

Josephus

3. Early Christian Documents

New Testament

4. Rabbinic Literature

Targum and Midrash

Varia

5. Other Sources

Index of Ancient Literary and Historical Names

This index lists ancient and medieval names of literary or historical relevance, including unspecified references to literary works. Not included are references to Josephus in the Josephus part of the book, nor those to other ancient Jewish and Christian authors, texts or works of art where these are thematic.

Biblical and other ancient names are given in the customary, anglicized greco-latin transliteration (Jacob, Moses); names typically from Rabbinical literature in a simple anglophone transliteration (Akiva, Yose). Talmudic Sages are identified with the traditional R. (Rabbi) for a Palestinian and 'Rav' for a Babylonian.

Index of Modern Authors

The modern period is here taken to begin with the Renaissance.
Not included are references to the authors of this volume in the parts they wrote.

COMPENDIA RERUM IUDAICARUM
AD NOVUM TESTAMENTUM

Published so far:

The Jewish People in the First Century. Historical Geography; Political History; Social, Cultural and Religious Life and Institutions.
Edited by S. Safrai and M. Stern in cooperation with D. Flusser and W.C. van Unnik. In two volumes (Compendia I/1-2)
Assen – Philadelphia 1974-76

Jewish Writings of the Second Temple Period. Apocrypha, Pseudepigrapha, Qumran Sectarian Writings, Philo, Josephus.
Edited by Michael E. Stone. (Compendia II/2)
Assen – Philadelphia 1984

The Literature of the Sages. First Part: Oral Tora, Halakha, Mishna, Tosefta, Talmud, External Tractates.
Edited by S. Safrai. (Compendia II/3a)
Assen – Philadelphia 1987

Mikra. Text, Translation, Reading and Interpretation of the Hebrew Bible in Ancient Judaism and Early Christianity.
Edited by M.J. Mulder. (Compendia II/1)
Assen/Maastricht – Philadelphia 1988

Paul and the Jewish Law: Halakha in the Letters of the Apostle to the Gentiles.
By Peter J. Tomson. (Compendia III/1)
Assen/Maastricht – Minneapolis 1990